Urbanormativity

Studies in Urban–Rural Dynamics

Series Editors

Gregory M. Fulkerson and Alexander R. Thomas, SUNY Oneonta

This series focuses attention on understanding theoretically and historically the development and maintenance of Urban–Rural Systems through a spatial, demographic, and ecological perspective. It seeks a blending or reintegration of the urban, rural, and environmental research literatures under a comprehensive theoretical paradigm. As such, we further specify Urban–Rural Dynamics as analysis of human population distribution on social variables, including politics, economics, and culture.

Recent Titles in Series

Urbanormativity

Reality, Representation, and Everyday Life

Gregory M. Fulkerson and
Alexander R. Thomas

LEXINGTON BOOKS
Lanham • Boulder • New York • London

Published by Lexington Books
An imprint of The Rowman & Littlefield Publishing Group, Inc.
4501 Forbes Boulevard, Suite 200, Lanham, Maryland 20706
www.rowman.com

6 Tinworth Street, London SE11 5AL

British Library Cataloguing in Publication Information Available

Library of Congress Cataloging-in-Publication Data

ISBN 978-1-4985-9702-9 (cloth)
ISBN 978-1-4985-9704-3 (paper)
ISBN 978-1-4985-9703-6 (electronic)

This book is dedicated to the invisible rural workers
from around the world, who labor in service of an urbanizing world.

Contents

Preface

When we (Greg and Alex) started writing this book from our offices in Oneonta (pronounced own-e-onta)—a small micropolitan city located three hours from New York City—we frequently stopped to reflect on and discuss the remarkable history and geography that surrounds us upstate. Our campus at the State University of New York in Oneonta sits atop a plateau overlooking the Susquehanna Valley, offering sweeping vistas of beautiful rolling forested hills. It is hard to imagine that over a century ago these hills would have looked very different—there were far fewer trees, there were fields of crops, and most hills were covered in grass to serve as grazing land for cattle, goats, and sheep. Our small city was established as a strategic railroad stop that housed, at one time, the largest roundhouse in the world. Oneonta was chosen for its central location on the northern edge of the Catskill mountains, in the middle of a highly productive agricultural region. The bounty of upstate farms was loaded on wagons, boats, and trains, consolidated in Oneonta, and sent through the winding hills of the Catskills to the waiting urban population down state. This was the agricultural foundation that made New York City possible. When the Dutch settled it as New Amsterdam in the 1600s, there were self-sufficient farms on rural Manhattan Island—even harder to imagine!

When Westward Expansion provided access to the mega farms and vast grazing ranges of the Midwest, more and more of New York City's lifeline began bypassing its immediate hinterland, demanding less and less of the Catskills and Hudson Valley. Eventually, reliance on upstate gave way to the point of collapse, with regional rail traffic grinding almost to a halt. Oneonta is no longer a rail town. The spot where the world's largest roundhouse once stood is bare, leaving behind the eerie outline of a foundation that can still be detected in satellite images. The one rail line that comes through town is privately owned by the Norfolk Southern Rail Company. The legacy and value of the many small-towns between Oneonta and The City have sunk into obscurity. Remnants of large impressive barns and silos that now stand on the verge of collapse remind us of these painful historical changes. Most of the residents now have no direct tie to the land. Some are living an urbane life in a rural setting, as tourism and second home ownership have replaced farming, creating a rural gentrification that revitalizes as it transforms the character of these once agricultural villages. The afforestation of the post-agrarian region has brought benefits, adding natural beauty while providing habitat for species that were endangered or on the brink of extinction, such as the bobcat, falcon, beaver, and eagle. People are often taken aback by the natural beauty of upstate when visiting from other parts of the country. Many still imagine the region as agricultural, though most of the remaining agricul-tural activity is to our north, closer to the Mohawk valley, and to our west, where the land flattens out onto the Great Lakes plain. We view our local beauty with mixed reaction, as it is simultaneously a symbol of demise for the regional agricultural economy.

Living in Oneonta, reflecting on this history has led us to ask how such a vibrant and active countryside could come full circle, returning to a state of nature that resembles, in more remote locations, the landscape inhabited by the Iroquois prior to European arrival. Amid the natural beauty are villages suffering from poverty, deterioration, and decline. Through all of this, the urban population of New York City has continued to thrive with some not-able ups and downs, but independent of the fate of the surrounding country-side. How can this be? Clearly the urban-rural system centered on New York has gone through a realignment. At first, it plugged into the Midwest; now, it draws on resources imported from the global economy. The hard labor en-dured by more distant rural people has become less visible to the urban consumer in New York, not unlike other cities of varying sizes, including tiny Oneonta. Yet, the reliance on rural people has remained constant, even as their place of origin has shifted. This condition of "urban dependency" is a crucial point we wish to reinforce.

At times our professional lives will take us from our small city to "The City," as New York is often called, to attend conferences or to meet with other scholars. We also visit, occasionally, on leisure to see theatrical perfor-mances, museums, national landmarks, shop, and take in the sights and sounds of the city. There is an excitement that overtakes us when we emerge from the depths of Penn Station to the sidewalks of Manhattan. We enjoy walking, observing, and taking in the blocks of urban wonder that surround us in Times Square. It may come as a surprise that we actually like and enjoy visiting New York and other cities.

Although this book offers a critique of a nearly universal cultural phe-nomenon we call urbanormativity, our motivation for writing this is not to diminish or devalue urban life. Instead we want to bring awareness to urbanormative patterns in order to alter them and thereby revalue rural life. We are critical of the current arrangement of our urban-centric economy, our mistreatment of rural people, the misrepresentation of rural life in various media, our laws and policies that disadvantage rural people, and the general disregard or disdain expressed by many urbanites toward those in the country (including those who move into the country). This does not mean all urban people hold such views or accept the current arrangement as desirable. Yet, the general pattern of urbanormativity is dominant and unjustly devalues rural contributions to humanity.

Our hope is to bring greater awareness to the important place rural people occupy in the urbanizing world—they are the foundation that makes urban life possible as we know it. Behind every city lies a complex trade network. This network begins with resources found in nature, harvested by rural producers, then traded with urban producers and consumers. The terms of trade are generally inadequate, while the sense of obligation to rural producers is mostly absent. The resulting conditions are typically rural poverty and neglect, coupled with urban moral indifference and widely held sentiment that "they should just move to the city." While this may be the answer for some rural people, if every rural person were to follow this directive, who would be left to harvest nature's bounty to feed the global economy and the mouths of hungry urbanites?

We are of the view that major changes should be undertaken that will alter the current state of urban-rural affairs. As we articulate in our chapter on a rural justice ethic, creating a more equitable and just place for rural producers in the world is not a simple act of kindness, it is an act of long-term sustainability for both urban and rural people alike. Our critique of urbanormativity is an attempt to promote the value and worthiness of rural lives and rural livelihoods that we think deserve fair compensation and acknowledgment. Only then can productive rural communities across the planet become the kinds of homes that they should have been all along, as people in cities come to enjoy the fruits of rural labor in gratitude and respect.

Gregory M. Fulkerson
Alexander R. Thomas
15 February 2019
Oneonta, NY

An Introduction to Urbanormativity

It is not often that the creation of a word as awkward or complex as urbanormativity can be justified. From our earliest training as scholars, we received excellent instruction and feedback on what constitutes good and bad writing. One of the central principles of good writing—also echoed in Becker's iconic, *Writing for Social Scientists*—is that most good ideas can be expressed using clear and simple prose. For example, as sociology graduate students, we were both entertained and impressed by C. Wright Mills's *The Sociological Imagination*, where he successfully "translated" the complicated and lengthy prose of Talcott Parsons into a few plainly worded sentences. So why would we betray this excellent training and help create such an awful word as urbanormativity?

Our defense is consistent with the logic offered by Andrew Kaufman's, "Why We Need to Invent Words," where he states (2013):

> Every new word must be crafted. It has to have a purpose, a need. A new word cannot be created with a fisted bash to a keyboard. Like every other word in the language, your new word should be a mashup of pre-existing words. You can steal bits from Latin and German, like everybody else did. Or you can use contemporary English in a new way. But you must capture something that already exists, which for whatever reason has been linguistically mismanaged.

The first criterion is there must be a purpose and a need. In our work with several colleagues on the topic of urbanormativity we have not encountered many possible candidates that capture as precisely what is embedded in this term. We have encountered and used such terms as metro-centric, urban-centric, and metro-normative. These are not bad contenders and they continue to have some application, but none parallel the mashup of urban and

1

normativity quite as precisely. This word is offered only after careful consideration.

To begin with, let's start with urban. The world is growing increasingly urban from a strict demographic perspective—meaning that more people are physically residing in a place with high population density that is contained within a small circumscribed geographic space—a city. The term urban encompasses a mode of spatial demographic organization that spans several millennia, dating back to early agricultural villages and eventually cities (Thomas 2010). The term metropolitan, in contrast, is a more recent invention that tries to incorporate a wider geographic focus than individual urban areas. Metropolitan is a concept that considers the convergence of several large populous agglomerations growing into one another. This is something that one would find only in the latter stages of urbanization when the initially separate urban areas expand and merge together, swallowing up what was once a rural buffer zone. Alternatively, by describing cities and suburbs as distinct places rather than as politically autonomous quarters of the same settlement, metropolitan is only appropriate to modern urban areas. Therefore, in constructing the term urbanormative, we wish to emphasize the longer and more encompassing pattern of urbanization over the more recent pattern of metropolitan growth.

Now let's turn to the normative part of the term. One of the central motivations driving the process of urbanization is the widely held belief that urban life can offer something that the rural cannot, in terms of economic gain, personal or cultural enrichment, education, opportunities for social interaction and engagement, and so on. Whether or not this perception is true is irrelevant—it is the perception that fuels urban migration. According to the Thomas (and Thomas 1928, p. 571–572) Dictum: "If [sic people] define situations as real, they are real in their consequences." This does not mean that rural is summarily viewed as dreadful—in fact most people have a romantic view of rural life. This is something that has been referred to in the past as the "rural idyll" or the "rural mystique." Indeed, this positive view fuels the phenomena of rural tourism and second home ownership. Nevertheless, while rural may elicit positive feelings, the way of life that it entails is something that most people have come to view as archaic and backward. The flip side of this is the notion that urban implies moving forward and making progress. Generally, people like the idea of progress, and may even view it fatalistically as inevitable. By this logic, the unfolding process of urbanization is understood as something that cannot or should not be avoided. Questioning urbanization is like questioning progress itself. The upshot is that the "normal" life has come to imply urban.

Though they did not coin the term urbanormativity, we would like to borrow a line from Ching and Creed (1997, p. 3–4) that captures the definition of urbanormativity, "urban has come to be the assumed reference when terms are used that could in theory refer to both rural and urban subjects." When a journalist writes a newspaper article using the "we" voice, and it is clear that "we" are people who live in an urban setting, then we have an example of urbanormative journalism. When we view a film that portrays rural others as exotic, different, or at times, horrifying, the implication is that this rural other is not normal. This would exemplify an urbanormative film.

In an urban society it is not uncommon for urbanormative messages to reinforce the normality of urban life and the deviant or exotic abnormality of rural life. As the frequency and pervasiveness of urbanormative messaging increases, we might come to define an entire culture as urbanormative. Once urbanormativity captures a culture, it has the effect of rendering urbanites the normal and natural members of society, while rustics are taken as marginal. This creates a cultural hierarchy that comes with a set of privileges for those who can claim an urbane identity, while punishing and depriving the rural rustic. Having outlined our logic for constructing the term urbanormativity, we now turn to a deeper consideration that tries to interpret its origins and current trajectory.

MAKING SENSE OF URBANORMATIVITY

The perception of the superiority of urban life is the tip of the proverbial iceberg. Underneath lies a large foundation of beliefs, images, and ideas that surround life in urban versus rural places. We evaluate places to some extent through a lens of what we consider to be normal. As Hayden (2014) has aptly observed, places go through a process of place-structuration, whereby cultural notions become encoded in the physical character and tradition of communities (see also Moloch, Freudenburg, & Paulsen 2000). Because of this process, rural communities may come to be stigmatized as backward. In her case study of Seabrook, for instance, Hayden noted that the residents acquire a stigmatized reputation simply by virtue of their home address. They were labeled the unflattering term of "brooker." This is synonymous with nearly every negative rural stereotype imaginable, such as redneck, hick, or bumpkin. It is a more localized version of the same set of stigmatized and negative ideas. In other works, Hayden (2016) examines the rural horror genre of film, finding that it embodies the worst of rural stereotypes that portray rustics as inbred, unintelligent, wild, and violent (men) or sexually impulsive (women). The horror genre allows some of the most fantastical ideas to emerge through iconic characters, such as Saw Tooth Hillicker in the *Wrong Turn* film series.

Why does Western culture hold these negative stereotypes of rural people? According to Isenberg (2017), the negative outlook on rural people as "white trash" dates back several centuries in the Western world. She claims that the term "trash" has to do with the notion of people living in an unproductive wasteland. For instance, the residents of the swampy marsh of colonial North Carolina were widely believed to consume mud in order to survive, since farming was nearly impossible. The people of this "wasted" land were seen as sickly, stupid, lazy, and unproductive. Why else would people be content to stay in such a foreboding place? Clearly, the negative views expressed toward the unfortunate settlers of the difficult Carolina countryside reflected a certain amount of classism of the elite class. The wealthy southern aristocracy of South Carolina and Virginia were themselves living in the country, but on highly productive and profitable slave plantations, thereby freed from hard manual rural labor. The negative views aimed toward lower class rural white people, not to mention racial and ethnic minorities, were therefore not just expressed by urbanites, but by people living in the countryside who sought to distinguish, and perhaps, distance themselves. Eventually, with the decline of the plantation system and the rise of industrialization, the notion of white trash would be a stereotype applied at times to refer to all rural people. Today, people who are understood as "white trash" are also generally considered some of the most racist people in society. It is a twist of fate that, historically, the lower working-class white population in the Republican party of Abraham Lincoln, were the most vehemently opposed to slavery. This opposition was born out of a sense of unfair competition: how can you compete with free slave labor if you expect to get paid for the same work? Thus, as Isenberg showed, the basic evolution of the term white trash is an intersection of race (white), class (lower) and what we might call place identity (rural). This may help account for the odd historical evolution of negative images of rural people.

In urban society, rural has come to be devalued and located at the bottom of the cultural hierarchy. Why, then, have rural people not been the subject of intense social scientific investigation? Sociology and anthropology, in particular, are dedicated to studying and redressing social inequality and marginalization, as evidenced by countless studies in the areas of race, ethnicity, nationality, gender, and sexuality, not to mention burgeoning literatures on ability, weight, and other matters of the body. Could it be that the very scholars concerned with such matters of social justice are themselves urbanormative? In their essay, "Recognizing Rusticity," Ching and Creed make this claim. Reviewing several years of scholarship in the critical tradition, they note that rather than coming to the aid of marginalized rustics, intellectual are often quick to join in their demonization. As noted by Ching and Creed, (1997, p. 11), "Thus demonized, rustics seem to merit whatever degradation and neglect they may experience."

Rural demonization is an outcome of overgeneralizations that harm both the intended but also the unintended target. The assumption underlying this demonization is that rural = white, uneducated, lower and middle-class Americans that are racist and sexist. Usually the face is also of a man, as rural and rustic are somehow constructed as masculine terms. Of course, as is the case with any stereotype, it has a grain of truth. The problem is, of course, that the countryside is far more varied, interesting, and diverse than this assumption lets on. The pioneering work on the rural Black Belt South, for instance, by Wimberley, Morris, and Harris (2014), reminds us that there are many rural counties in the United States that are ethnic minority, numerical majority counties. In the Eastern United States, these are typically African American, while in the Western United States, these are often Latinx groups. Scattered around the country are pockets of rural Native Americans. Imagining rural as white, thereby, renders these vulnerable and highly exploited rural populations invisible.

THE ESSENTIAL URBAN AND RURAL

As sociologists seemingly trained in opposite ends of the demographic spectrum, one a rural sociologist and the other an urban sociologist, we have both spent a great deal of time and energy thinking about and comparing the various definitions of rural and urban. The varieties of definitions generally begin with objective conditions that are demographic, political, or economic in nature, and are applied to aggregate areas, such as a "rural county" or a "rural state." The most widely used definitions in research and application are demographic that define urban and rural as a simple matter of population size and density. Rural refers to sparsely populated areas of a small number of individuals, while urban would mean densely settled areas with many individuals. The demographic definition is preferred by many because it offer a clear-cut line of demarcation separating urban from rural, although the actual line is somewhat arbitrary. Using these criteria, the US Department of Agriculture implements something called the urban-rural continuum codes, and then ranks counties on a scale of one to nine, from the most urban (1) to the most rural (9). Such objective definitions are important for administrative purposes, as various policies and programs have been designed to serve urban and rural populations, and implementing these policies and programs requires a definite technique for sorting places into the categories of urban and rural. This is not unlike the much-debated definition of poverty, which has been defined by the government as a low-cost food budget multiplied by three. Critics have rightly pointed to the arbitrary nature of this definition of poverty, but for all its faults, it allows policies and programs the ability to sort people into the category of "poor" and this in turn allows them to deliver services.

Administrative definitions use objective conditions to clearly determine who is eligible for program or policy services, and the need from this level of precision is arguably unavoidable. It would be difficult and untenable to suggest that administrative definitions should be done away with altogether. They should be scrutinized and debated, and adjustments should be made according to the best science available. This process will likely continue indefinitely as a satisfactory definition of urban and rural, or of poverty, will likely always remain elusive. Even recognizing the value and need for administrative definitions, as scholars seeking to understand the deeper meaning of social phenomena, there is no need to be limited by them.

Moving beyond administrative definitions is at once dangerous and freeing. Once we step away from the world of objective definitions, partially or wholly, we open the door to the messy, difficult to grasp, highly subjective world of social constructions. Returning to the concept of poverty, we would now begin to appreciate the evaluation of poverty on the part of agents as being poor. With this logic, scholars such as Walter Runciman (1966) have identified valuable concepts such as "relative deprivation," and distinguish between absolute and relative poverty. With this conceptual toolkit, scholars have been able to compare the objective conditions of actors to their perceptions. In many cases, objective conditions fail to tell the whole story of poverty. That brings us to the construction of urban and rural. While scholars have spent considerable time developing the constructionist version of poverty, the same cannot be said for urban and rural. That is not to say that no work has been done, as will be discussed later. The key point being made here is that increased attention should be devoted to this investigation.

The Definitions of Urban and Rural

It is important when discussing concepts as rich and complex, and urban and rural, to review the various meanings we attach to them. We will not devote a great deal of space to this, as we have outlined the different definitions in previous works (see Thomas et al. 2011). There are three ways to understand urban and rural: the spatial-demographic, the socio-cultural, and the political-economic. To be sure, there is overlap between them, but as we analytically dissect urban and rural it is important to maintain the different types of definitions. The spatial-demographic definition defines urban and rural in terms of the number of people per unit of physical spatial distance within a settlement—the greater the density, the more urban. The actual lines that determine what is urban and what is rural are inescapably arbitrary. The US Census for a long time drew the line at an incorporated place with 2,500 persons or more as urban, while anything less would be considered rural. It now considers the surrounding area, and uses the terms urban cluster and urban area, drawing the line a little higher at 10,000. The spatial-demographic definition is probably the most common one used by rural scholars studying such topics as migration, growth, and population change in urban and rural areas. This is probably due to the availability of administrative data using spatial-demographic definitions.

Definitions of urban and rural that use the political-economic framework note that the mode of organization and production underlying human settlement has decidedly different bases in urban and rural places. Deavers (1992) suggested that rural political economy was uniquely known for its lack of functional diversification and specialized economic activity—urban by implication is diverse and unspecialized. In our own theorization, we offer the terms urban production and rural production to distinguish settlements that derive a living from natural resources that become rural products from those that convert such rural resources into finished urban products—linking urban and rural places together in circuits of production (Thomas et al. 2011). This becomes the foundation of what we call urban-rural systems. These systems are highly uneven, with urban populations extracting more from rural communities than they can ever be repaid.

The socio-cultural definition of urban and rural is based on social constructions—that which we define as urban or rural will be urban or rural in its consequences. In discussions of urban-rural culture and identity this becomes an important way of thinking. This is fundamental to the current project as it is largely devoted to understanding urbanormativity as a cultural phenomenon. We, however, view the socio-cultural aspects of urban and rural to be intertwined and inseparable from the political-economic. In their edited work on rural identity, Ching and Creed (1997), along with their contributors, invoke a socially constructed understanding of urban and rural as part of a cultural hierarchy denoted with the terms of rustic and urbane. We incorporate these terms when discussing the socially constructed versions of urban and rural.

Having reviewed the three types of urban-rural definitions, we would like to again point out that we are not claiming that one is superior to the others. Each offers a unique angle that cannot be subsumed by the others. In our view, demographically urban places can only support their population density because they have a supportive political economy built on urban production. This organization only works because it has become normalized and ingrained socially and culturally. It is the exploitation of rural by urban that receives its cultural justification in an urbanormative society.

POLITICS AND RENEWED
INTEREST IN URBAN-RURAL DYNAMICS

With the 2016 election of Donald Trump as president of the United States, came renewed public interest in urban-rural differences. Trump ran a campaign that was designed to appeal to working class rural white populations.

He promised, for instance, to make traditional rural occupations, like coal mining, a top priority for his administration. After his surprising win, several interpretations began to emerge. A quick look at the electoral college map of the United States revealed a stark pattern: nearly all rural areas of the country chose Trump, while nearly all urban areas opted for Hillary Clinton. From this simple observation came a deluge of scathing critiques, public outcries, outright disgust and disdain for rural voters from the left. Supporters of Clinton argued that Republicans appealed to the racism of rural whites that had been heightened due to the rising success of mostly urban racial and ethnic minority groups, coupled with the relative decline of mostly rural white populations. There is some truth to this, but the view was taken too far as we discuss below.

In his widely popular, *Hillbilly Elegy*, J.D. Vance (2018) points out that the rural white voters of his hometown in the Appalachian part of Ohio and Kentucky had not always voted Republican. In fact, traditionally, they voted Democrat. He offers that the reason for this was the unwavering support of white working-class people for labor unions. As long as Democrats remained the party of labor unions, they would continue to get the rural white vote. However, after the 1980s Reagan-era policies and subsequent weakening of labor unions, their loyalties shifted. Now rural workers felt as though they had to express their loyalty to corporations, and the party that represented them was the Republican party. In a sense, this is a "boot-licking" theory: kiss up to the big wigs or kiss the jobs goodbye because the labor union is no longer there to protect you.

With the decline of labor unions, the outsourcing of rural jobs to other countries, the automation of many traditional rural occupations in agriculture and mining, and the imports of cheap third world rural products, the future of rural people is looking increasingly grim. Trump promised to undo the unfair trade deals that hurt rural jobs, while promoting protections and subsidies to jumpstart the rural economy. Ironically, these are policies that the Far Left also viewed as valuable—they are not traditional Republican policies, since Republicans have tended to favor free trade over protectionism. In fact, left-leaning Bernie Sanders, who lost the Democratic primary election to Clinton, promoted many of the same ideas. For these reasons, it is not terribly surprising that Trump won over rural voters. It had been several decades since politicians even bothered to voice concern about rural issues—not since the time of the Great Depression when winning the presidential election required approval from the rural population by promising to protect farming (Prasad 2012).

After the 2016 election, rural voters felt the wrath of urban disgust—especially from the urban intelligentsia of journalists, pundits, and college professors—through veiled and often public displays. Cynical, and often sarcastic, commentaries would mock rural voters by slipping into the stereo-

typical redneck dialect that gushed ignorance and poor education. In response, the rural people who voted for Trump became angered and hardened
in their conviction. The overall sentiment was that Democrats had forgotten
the rural white working-class voter, and had ignored the declining conditions
in the countryside, where crystal meth and heroin addiction were surging,
while crime rates were rising (while falling for the rest of the country) and
economic opportunities were absent (though plentiful for the rest of the
country). Rural white resentment toward the urban elite has at times morphed
into an outright rejection of intellectualism itself—associated, as it is, with
urban life and the urban elite. Despite common-sense as well as economic
analysis that cited economic frustration as one cause of the election results, a
body of scholarly literature developed that cited social anxieties about race
and gender as the primary issues while minimizing economic anxiety, effectively absolving Democrats of a poorly-run campaign that marginalized
working class, and particularly rural and small city, voters (see Ferguson et
al. 2018, for a review of the literature and discussion).

Hence the 2016 election witnessed some of the worst displays of urbanormativity. In a fairly typical outburst of urban elitist fury, Bill Maher (2017)
summarized New Yorker Donald Trump's seeming unease with Republican
leaders in stark urban-rural terms:

> Trump's disillusion with McConnell and Ryan, it's not really political, it's just
> that for the first seventy years he would never be caught dead with a traveling
> Bible salesman like Paul Ryan or a corny, countrified goober like Mitch
> McConnell. For Christ's sake, the man is from Kentucky! Jeff Sessions is from
> Alabama! When he talks all Trump hears is a tiny little *Ernest* movie. And
> Mike Pence? It must be torture for Trump to be in the White House everyday
> with that homespun, Christian, tightly-wound human hard-on.

At the time, only Attorney General Jeff Sessions lived in a non-metropolitan
area: Selma, Alabama, with a population of less than 45,000 residents in the
city and surrounding county combined in 2017. Vice-President Mike Pence
hailed from a small metropolitan area of 81,162 in 2017, with only 47,143 in
the central city of Columbus, Indiana. House Majority Leader Paul Ryan was
from Janesville, Wisconsin, a city of roughly 63,000 in a metropolitan area of
160,331. Countrified goober Mitch McConnell lived in the suburbs of Louis-
ville, Kentucky's largest city and the center of the Combined Statistical Area
of over 1.5 million people—the thirty-fifth largest urban agglomeration in
the United States. New York or Los Angeles. Rural? Suffice it to say that if
these are the exemplars of Rural America then actual rural people are more
or less invisible. In any case, the accusation of rurality debases these law-
makers for Maher and many others—perhaps more so than their politics.

While there was justifiable anger at the surprise victory of Trump, who at
times seemed to work his rallying crowds into a frenzy of racial hate, the

perception that all rural people were racist and backward was an unwarranted conclusion. Rural white people were right to want a change in the direction of their communities that had experienced both relative and absolute decline during a period of what many view to be a long stretch of urban prosperity under Obama (Vance 2018). Democrats, by rejecting Bernie Sanders, had not even attempted to win the rural vote, and when they lost, became more incredulous with their urbanormative attacks. Rural Americans, in turn, were equally angry and carried this to extremes by rejecting intellectualism.

So what do we take away from this? The cultural gap between urban and rural populations has indeed widened, while the political landscape continues to shift accordingly. The ideology of urbanormativity had backfired and the result was a deeper urban-rural rift. This happens at a time when scholars generally lack a language or foundation for thinking about urban-rural relations or the difficulties that surround them. We hope to inform an understanding of what it means to be urban and rural from all possible angles and at different levels, from individual identity to local communities, national dynamics, and global urbanization. We will now lay out our plan.

OUTLINE OF THE BOOK

The three parts of this book correspond to the ideas of Halfacree (2006), who conceptualizes rural space as having a three-fold architecture of (1) locality/materiality, (2) social representation, and (3) everyday life. The first of these deals with the material reality of the productivist or post-productivist rural landscape. The second, with the formal discourses and narratives surrounding rural spaces. The third is where the first two intersect in the lives of everyday people. We approach these through the lens of urban-rural dynamics, so we have a slightly nuanced focus. Chapters 1–3 will examine the materiality of urban-rural dynamics, emphasizing demographic realities as well as the changing economic and environmental dynamics linking urban and rural places. Chapters 4–6 will examine the cultural dynamics linking urban and rural people, emphasizing the cultural capital involved (chapter 4), the popular imagination of rural (chapter 5), and the development of urbane and rustic identity (chapter 6). The last section addressing the everyday lives will emphasize policy and legal consequences of urban-rural dynamics (chapter 7), focus on life in urbanormative communities (chapter 8), and will end with an attempt to develop a rural justice ethic (chapter 9). The conclusion will link these themes together. Before proceeding, we offer more previews of the chapters contents.

In exploring the concept of urbanormativity, the first section of the book will begin with a review of the three different ways of defining urban and rural. We begin with a look at global trends, using a spatial-demographic definition. As we will see, the world has been urbanizing for some time, but has only recently become predominantly urban. There remain several countries and regions that are primarily rural, carrying out the vitally important work that supplies the global economy with its natural resource base, and without which would cease to function or exist. This discussion will preview global demographic trends and estimates of the future that are currently expected to reach 70 percent urban by 2050. With so few bodies left to collect energy from the countryside, the global urban dependency on rural resources will become increasingly precarious.

Following the demographic review, we examine the relationship between physical space and social interaction. This will allow us to simultaneously consider the spatial-demographic and socio-cultural aspects of urban and rural. From a theoretical standpoint, we want to know how it is that physical separation of urban and rural people translates into various social and cultural outcomes. Key ideas here revolve around the notions of propinquity—the idea that we associate with those physically close to us—and the notion of homophily that means we associate with those who are socially close to us. As urban and rural people, by definition, reside in separate communities, there is low propinquity—the physical basis for association and interaction. Meanwhile, as urbane and rustic have become markers in a cultural hierarchy, the low homophily or, alternatively, high social distance, also undermines the likelihood for interaction and association. With both physical and social space separating urban and rural, the understanding of the other becomes a matter of cultural creation. Since urban is the dominant group in the cultural hierarchy, we are mainly interested in how this translates into rural representations that are rife with stereotypes that may fuel prejudice and discrimination, leading to moral indifference.

The next chapter takes us back to the political-economic concept of urban and rural—central to our theoretical foundations that are outlined elsewhere (Thomas et al. 2011). To discuss this, we draw on the concept of oikos, the Greek term that refers to the home, and is the basis for economy and ecology. This close association is important for the way we theorize the material interconnections of urban-rural systems. Rural settlements engage in activities that are directed toward the extraction and collection of natural resources found in the environment. This includes the harvesting of food, fiber, timber, metal ores, energy supplies, and so forth. Urban settlements trade for these rural products so that they may produce urban items that do not require direct access to environmental resources. This chapter is important as it reminds us that, while the current goal is to explore the cultural meaning of urbanormativity, this cannot be understood without appreciation of the underlying material realities of urban-rural systems. The historical-comparative approach serves to remind us that our current world is but a moment in time, and while similar social dynamics have occurred in the past, our own present circumstances are unique in human history.

In the second section of the book, we take a deeper look at the socio-cultural dynamics of urbanormativity. Central concepts for this discussion will be social and cultural capital. Chapter 4 will pick up on the theme from chapter 2, on epistemic distance, by expanding on the topic of the urban-rural cultural hierarchy. As an illustration, this chapter will focus on language itself—an important marker of socio-cultural status. Bourdieu theorized the relation between economic, cultural, and social capital, and we extend his ideas to consider the urban-rural axis. One's position becomes embodied in the habitus—the way we walk and talk. Language is therefore central to habitus and allows us to understand how rural dialect is interpreted in urbanormative cultures. Perhaps more importantly is how the cultural devaluation of rural closes lines of access to institutional forms of cultural capital, such as being admitted into a prestigious college or working for a valuable company.

In chapter 5 we examine what an urbanormative culture looks like in terms of the popular imagination. This will involve a review of popular media sources that construct, as much as they reveal, about life in rural areas. Rural representations were key subjects in our previous works—*Critical Rural Theory*, *Studies in Urbanormativy*, and *Reimagining Rural*. This chapter will provide highlights from these projects, while adding commentary on how rural representations inform life in an urbanormative culture.

In chapter 6 we tackle the topic of the urban-rural dynamics of identity. While not purporting to review all central ideas or theories of identity, we focus exclusively on how the urbane and rustic are socially constructed. This is a combination of individual and group level processes that sometimes dovetail into an identity fusion. Identity allows us to consider the objective anchors of rural residence and rural work as they pertain to subjective identification as rustic. Through real and hypothetical cases, we explore the problem of essentializing rusticity through a comparison to the analog of sex and gender. While the socially constructed gender identity of masculine and feminine tends to overlap with assigned biological sex, this is far from deterministic. It is a mistake to assume gender from sex. We argue it is equally problematic to assume rusticity or urbanity based on residence and work that is rural or urban.

The third section of the book considers the consequences of living in an urbanormative culture. Chapter 7 will examine the manifestation of urbanormativity in the forms of public policies and laws. The work of Lisa Pruitt and colleagues is exemplary in this expository work. Considering issues based on poverty, social welfare, parenting rights, medical access, abortion rights, and environmental problems, we find ample evidence of spatial inequality being created or reproduced through law.

Chapter 8 will consider how it is that urbanormativity becomes manifest in the physical spaces of communities. The process of place-structuration (Molotch, Freudenberg, & Paulsen 2000) drives this manisfestation. Real places where people live, work, visit, and vacation can incorporate rural simulacra that are icons of urbanormative rural representations. Over time, as these accumulate, the character and tradition of communities may begin to transition away from the traditional authentic rural community it once was to the reinvented community derived from the depths of the urban imaginary. This phenomenon is addressed by considering the place of older residents and the rights they have to shape the direction of their communities, once filled with urbane newcomers. Also considered will be the mechanisms such as property values and taxes, as well as building codes that may serve as the basis of rural gentrification and the pushing out of original residents.

Chapter 9 responds to the spectrum of problems raised throughout the book, by turning to the prospects of rural justice through the creation of a new ethic. After reviewing the dominant frameworks of utilitarian and Rawlsian justice, we arrive at a modified version of the capabilities approach to rural justice, based on the work of Sen (1999). The tyranny of the urban majority cannot be confronted if the prevailing justification rests on the urbanormative principle of the greatest good for the greatest number. We endorse a view that seeks to maximize the opportunities and capabilities of rural people by addressing two broad categories of concern: spatial inequality and devalued rural production. Ultimately, we try to demonstrate how modest changes in the operation of global markets and construction of policies that take physical space into consideration can open the door to a more just rural future in both advanced urban and predominantly rural nations. We further maintain that the value of these efforts will be shared by everyone, as the future success of rural people cannot be separated from the future success of all. The global economy depends, after all, on a sustainable rural future.

Part I

The Reality

Chapter One

The Urbanizing Planet

The world is growing increasingly urban, as is well documented by the United Nations, and it will continue to follow this pattern through at least 2050 (see figure 1.1). The rural population is predicted to level off with a stable population of 3–4 billion. Meanwhile, the urban population is predicted to continue its upward growth trend, in a nearly linear fashion, leveling at around 6–7 billion. The cross over—when the planet shifted from being predominantly rural to urban—occurred sometime in 2008. Though the actual day is hard to pinpoint, it marks the beginning of a new global era.

Urbanization at the planetary level can be analyzed in two ways: (1) the overall global urban population, and (2) the nation-by-nation urban transition. Moreover, these may be examined in terms of raw numbers or as percentages. In the case of the planet, we can observe that the vast majority of rural people live in just two very populous nations: China and India. Each of these nations combines to support a rural population that exceeds 1.4 billion people, constituting roughly 20 percent of the entire world population. These two Asian giants, thus, host the greatest numerical concentration of rural people on Earth. On a nation-by-nation level, we see a more complex and nuanced story, with different nations falling into a different spot on the urban-rural continuum. Most of the world's predominantly rural countries can be found in central Africa and Asia, while the most urbanized nations are in North America and Europe. Latin America and Oceania are in between these extremes, with higher levels of urbanization than most other developing nations, but lower levels than the wealthy Global North.

It is important to distinguish between levels of urbanization and rates of urbanization. This is critical, as those nations that have the highest levels may also boast some of the slowest rates of urbanization. At one extreme are city-states, such as Singapore, where the picture is one of complete urbaniza-

A majority of the
world's population
lives in urban areas

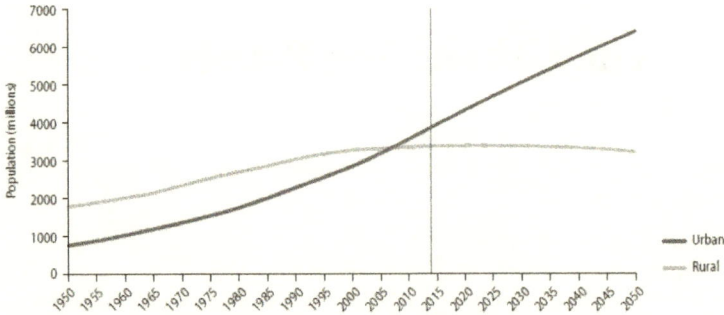

Figure 1.1.   World Rural and Urban Populations
World Urbanization Prospects, United Nations (2014 revision)

tion (100 percent). If a nation is fully urbanized, then the rate of urbanization can become negative, but cannot exceed zero. The world's most developed nations are not quite to the level of full urbanization, striking a different urban-rural balance, yet many will reach 90 percent. Nations with larger land areas tend to retain a sizable rural population employed in rural work, such as mining, agriculture, energy development, and so on. While automation and outsourcing may alter the urban-rural balance among the most urbanized nations over time, the rate of urbanization will be comparatively slow. Alternatively, in the most rural nations, where the majority of people work in rural occupations, we observe the fastest rates of urbanization. In some cases, the conditions of rural life have become highly unsustainable or even intolerable, while in others rural people are being removed from the land involuntarily due to privatization or changes in land tenure policies. The push factors of a difficult rural life combine with the pull factors of a potentially more lucrative urban life to drive rapid urban migration in these nations. Demographers refer to this general process as the "urban transition." Rural nations, such as Uganda (less than 40 percent urban), have urbanization rates that currently hover around 6 percent! At this rate it will not take long to become predominantly urban.

URBAN-RURAL HIERARCHY

The location of nations on the urban-rural continuum tracks closely with location in the economic hierarchy, as shown in figure (1.2) below. Very simply, the highest income countries are the most urban, while rural countries tend to have the lowest incomes. This pattern is more than coincidence. It is evident that the current global economy favors urbanization, perhaps, as we argue, due to overvaluing urban production while undervaluing rural production.

Through commodity markets, the prices for rural products have been allowed to plummet primarily through the manipulation of supply-side economics. This happens by allowing rural producers to maximize their individual production, while disregarding the overall supply that is permitted to grow uncontrollably to enormous levels. Based on the basic laws of supply and demand, when supply outstrips demand this precipitates a fall in prices. If there were global policies that may, for instance, promote partnerships that track supply and protect the value of rural products, as is the case for oil (OPEC), then the undervaluation of rural products may be prevented. The oil producing nations of the world meet in order to determine a reasonable global price. They then apply limits on the amount of oil that each member nation is allowed to produce. If they disregard the limit, everyone knows the prices will fall and everyone will lose if this happens. There is no such corollary to OPEC for the variety of agricultural, mining, or other rural products that circulate the global economy. Increasing production of rural products may be in the best interest of the individual rural producer as that seems the most strategic way to get ahead, but at the collective level it spells disaster. Under the auspices of free trade, policies that are geared toward

Proportion urban by income groups, 1950–2050

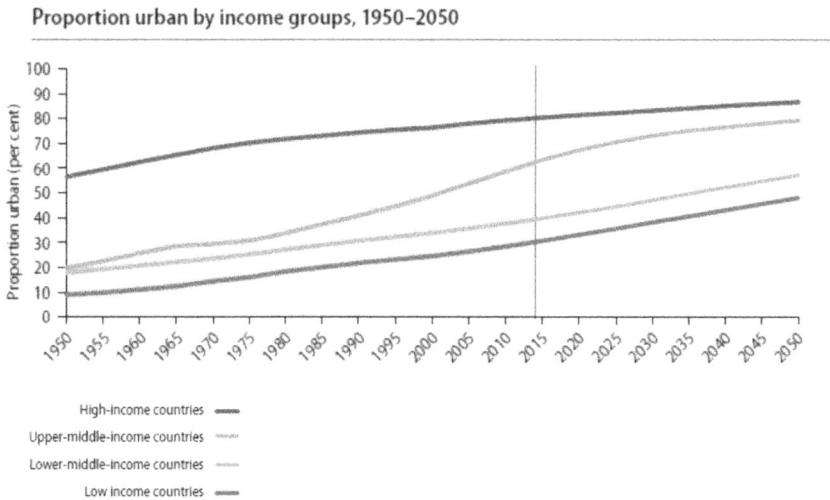

High-Income countries
Upper-middle-income countries
Lower-middle-income countries
Low income countries

Figure 1.2.   Urban Levels and Income Groups
World Urbanization Prospects, United Nations (2014 revision)

curbing overproduction have been avoided as "anti-capitalist" and "protectionist" (for an excellent discussion of how this plays out in the realm of agricultural grains, see Winders 2017). Without some kind of regulation, however, rural products will continue to fall prey to oversupply until natural limits end the cycle.

With rural products in a constant state of overproduction and undervaluation, urban companies have been able to swoop in to purchase all that they need for a miniscule price, allowing them to invest in other parts of the production circuit in such things as the packaging and marketing, while also being assured of high profit margins. The overall cost of an urban product, therefore, has almost nothing to do with the cost of rural resource inputs, even though such urban products would be impossible to produce without them. Without metals, no batteries, without batteries, no smartphones. Yet the cost of a smartphone, fetching as much as a $1000 (US) in value, may encompass only pennies worth of cost in acquiring the essential product materials. The profit margin is therefore enormous, enabling the enrichment of the urban company shareholders, on the backs of the undercompensated rural producers—many of whom live on the brink of starvation.

If the current system remains in place, then, it should not be surprising to find that within the most rural nations on Earth we also find the most rapid rates of urbanization. If the value of rural products were to increase only marginally, the quality-of-life for the global rural producers would increase and lessen the need for urban migration. A set of policies aimed at production controls or price guarantees may achieve these outcomes. The question then becomes one of politics: Who has influence over economic trade policy? The answer points to the world's political centers—universally located in the global cities (Sassen 1992)—and run by urban politicians. The voices of rural people are largely absent from political discourse, and their interests are often underrepresented. Attempts to organize rural workers, by figures like the iconic Chico Mendes, have fallen prey to violent suppression (Rodrigues 2007). International trade agreements, overseen by the World Trade Organization, as well as various regional agreements in NAFTA, ASEAN, and the EU, are dominated by urbanized nations that seek to further their own interests to the exclusion of rural nations. The rights of rural people and the value of their labor is thereby usurped with little resistance or difficulty.

OVERURBANIZATION AND DE-PEASANTIZATION

On the current course, rural products typically wind up undervalued, leaving dismal economic conditions in rural communities. The most logical thing for rural people to do, in the face of these adverse conditions, is to migrate to the city, leaving behind their dwindling rural livelihoods. Unfortunately, the more this happens, the fewer rural producers there will be, and this may lead to a lower rate of rural production that may eventually cause prices of rural products to rise or to create widespread shortages. This becomes an alarming scenario considering that a widespread shortage may translate into food insecurity and famine rippling through the world.

At the same time, as hordes of rural refugees seek new lives in nearby urban centers, they often arrive to find a horrific scene: a city overrun and incapable of supporting the waves of newcomers—a phenomenon that has been aptly described as "overurbanization" (see, for example, Timberlake & Kentor 1983; Shandra & London 2003). What often happens is that along the edges of a city emerge shantytowns (Lomnitz 1977). Here the structures and infrastructure can be described as nothing more than make-shift. Using any available materials, such as scrap metal and wood, temporary shelters are fastened to give shelter from the elements. Clean water is a rare commodity, and the risk of mixing sewage with drinking water is a real and tangible threat. Water-borne illnesses are prevalent, as are illnesses carried by pests, such as mosquitos, which are drawn to the large number of unsheltered bodies living in third world shantytowns. In more economically advantaged nations, overurbanization may lead to similar problems with the rise of edge cities (Garreau 1992) and the associated sprawl that is introduced.

In the context of swelling urban centers found within largely rural nations, are the perfect storm for cheap exploitable labor. Urban producers can employ the rural refugee class at extremely low wages keeping the competition for work fierce. This allows urban producers a second opportunity to benefit from the misfortunes of rural producers (the first based on the exploitation of rural overproduction of natural resources). With the excessive workforce, referred to by Marx as the lumpenproletariat, or underclass, the demands of workers are kept in check, allowing producers to have the upper hand. This process has been described as de-peasantization or proletarianization (Araghi 1995). Within the global economy, urban centers find they can outcompete other urban producers where the conditions are more favorable for labor. While this may lead to some measure of economic development at the national level—the overall response to which is understandably positive—the benefits of such development are far from being shared equitably. Instead, they are concentrated in the hands of the most privileged class of urban elites. The "liberated" rural populations are, in many cases, the source of national growth and development but stand to receive almost none of its rewards. The global economy may be working, but not for them. From an equity and justice standpoint, when it comes to evaluating the benefits of development, we must always ask, *for whom*?

HOW DID WE START DOWN THIS PATH?

In *Strangers in a Strange Land*, Douglas Massey (2005) points out that humans are not evolved and are actually rather ill-equipped to live in cities. Since the dawn of our subspecies, *Homo sapiens sapiens*, between sixty and eighty thousand years ago, we have lived more than half that time in nomadic bands of foragers with at most a few hundred people in our networks, and normally fewer. A fair and seldom asked question is how did we ever start out on this global path toward urbanization, with humans living in settlements with millions of bodies?

The first year-round settlement in the archaeological record is the site of Ohalo II—a collection of twelve huts on the shore of the Sea of Galilee that thrived over twenty-three thousand years ago (Nadel et al. 2004).The inhabitants were, like their nomadic cousins, hunter-gatherers who settled in a location that gave them good access to a number of different ecological niches for food. It is even possible that they cultivated some wheat (Snir et al. 2015). It is likely that similar villages popped up and were abandoned over the next ten thousand years, and the accident of discovery has only yielded a few for archaeologists to excavate. Around twelve thousand years ago the first agrarian villages were established in what is today Israel, Jordan, Lebanon, and Syria—the western Fertile Crescent. These earliest settlements grew crops but continued to hunt for meat for another thousand years (Thomas 2010).

The next major innovation in human settlement was the market town. Unlike the agrarian village, market towns did not rely entirely on local natural resources, though these were likely used to the fullest extent possible. We should stress, however, that what we call a "market town" in a Neolithic context would be unrecognizable as such today. The largest settlements were between five and ten thousand people, were few and far between, and typically served as intermediaries for trade goods between distant sources and smaller affiliated agricultural hamlets. In other words, there was, for the first time in human history, a hierarchy of settlement: an urban-rural system. An urban-rural system is a network of settlements connected through trade, the majority of which are rural settlements that harvest natural resources that are exchanged with a few large urban settlements that base their existence on urban production and trade. The first of these developed in the Euphrates Valley of Iraq around 5500 BCE.

Products harvested from nature, including but not limited to food sources, could be brought to market towns and exchanged for other locally produced items. Market towns could combine and refine resources from multiple locations to create complex forms of production—what we call urban production. It is in the first market towns, therefore, that we see the origins of urbanization. It was a slow and haphazard development that took thousands of years to unfold. Of course, as the extent and complexity of trade increased, the flow of resources flourished, and the size of the population in market towns began to grow far beyond local limits imposed by the natural environment. Self-sufficiency would begin to fade as it was slowly replaced by trade. Indeed, urbanization is significant for freeing at least some of the human population from natural constraints. This, of course, has had some interesting consequences.

As urban centers began to grow and develop, agrarian villages became more interested in trading the fruits of their labor to obtain the unique urban products. This came to replace farming for self-sufficient consumption and altered what was being cultivated. Often, the villages had little choice but to trade with the more powerful cities. We should not understand "trade" to mean "non-coerced." When agrarian villages shifted their focus from self-sufficiency to trade with urban centers, they became, in our view, rural villages. We define a rural settlement as one that exists in relation to urban settlements, playing a supporting role by supplying it with natural resources, but also benefitting from access to new and unique urban products. The first market towns, and all subsequent urban centers, including cities, have relied upon a network of supporting rural villages for their survival and prosperity. If trade were to collapse these urban centers would likely dissolve. If successful, however, they could grow seemingly without limits, as has happened in some cases. Thus, while it is fair to associate urbanization with large and densely settled cities, it is more accurate to consider the underlying processes that make these large settlements possible in the first place: the emergence of urban-rural systems (Thomas 2012).

Writing at the end of the eighteenth century, Sir James Steuart made an insightful distinction between what he called the "cultivators" and the "free-hands." The rural cultivators harvest natural resources, and through trade, support a class of urban freehands, who are then able to devote their energy to pursuits beyond the basics of self-sufficiency. Thus was born the urban-rural division of labor. This distinction remains important as it still forms the foundation of social and economic processes that create cities. It is these processes, not the large resulting populations, which constitute the meaning of urbanization (Thomas 2014). Most importantly, as we think about contemporary examples of urbanization, is that throughout time urban populations have been fully reliant upon rural populations—a condition we term as urban dependency.

COLONIAL AND NEOCOLONIAL URBAN-RURAL SYSTEMS

The global economy has always been organized in a way that privileges advanced urban populations at the expense of poorer rural populations. This was the case under colonialism, beginning with the Spanish and Portuguese Empires in the fifteenth century, and continuing through Dutch and British colonial rule. It remains a facet of the contemporary neocolonial global order. Under colonialism, the domination of rural nations was exacted coercively through military conquest. Rural and indigenous populations were subjugated or summarily removed from the land. The Spanish notoriously enslaved the Inca and consigned them to work in silver mines. Some accounts of this report such an extreme cruelty and desperation that some Inca would maim their own children, amputating their arms, so that work in the mines would become impossible and they would be spared from this awful life (Mann 2012). The Dutch and English, likewise, notoriously enslaved plantation workers throughout the Caribbean, Americas, and Far East, forcing the production of such commodities as sugar. Of course, in addition to enslaving indigenous populations, these European colonial powers also imported African slaves from rural nations to toil in the service of the crowned heads of Europe to harvest agricultural commodities.

Interstate conflicts culminated in two World Wars that eventually led to the ultimate collapse of the colonial system. In its place would emerge the nascent modern world-system, organized primarily around trade (Wallerstein 1987). Markets have replaced militaries, and private corporations have replaced national governments in appropriating resource-rich lands. Despite these changes, the continued maltreatment of the rural poor throughout the world has remained a constant. Stories of rural dispossession and colonialism continue to unfold, and the low value placed on rural lives is reinforced through practices in low-income rural countries of Asia, Africa, and Latin America (Kapoor 2017). Even in high-income countries, rural populations are nearly universally located within the poorest strata (Mactaggart et al. 2016).

In agricultural regions of Africa, the economy tends to be narrowly focused on the export of commodity resources. Beyond agriculture, global corporations have grown increasingly interested in mining precious metals, such as gold, nickel, and silver, along with practical metals such as those used in the construction of batteries, including lithium and cadmium—vital for such modern luxuries as smartphones and hybrid vehicles. The invisible rural bodies involved in the mining of precious and rare metals, or carrying out the labor to cultivate agricultural items such as coffee and produce, are arguably the foundation of the global economy. Without such inputs, the global economy would grind to a halt. Given the importance of rural products, one might think they would be the most valuable of all. This is where the global market has achieved its greatest reversal. They are the cheapest part of the production chain—the harvesting of natural resources. Although cars are mostly made of steel, for instance, the cost of steel is less than the combined costs of transportation, design, manufacturing, marketing, and sales of automobiles—the urban production circuits.

THE SYSTEM DYNAMICS THAT GIVE RISE TO URBANORMATIVITY

In order to fully explain the logic of urban-rural systems, we turn to a brief discussion of the four system dynamics of polity, economy, culture, and environment. It is out of the cultural dynamic that the concept of urbanormativity is derived, but this should be understood as an alternative to the coercive political response to environmental and economic dynamics that create urban dependency.

We will begin our discussion with the environment. The natural world operates through what we call the *energy economy*. Humans are not exempt from the natural cycles that support all life, though we have found unique ways of operating within it—our human *species economy*. All life on earth must find a way to absorb energy, from the simplest plankton to the most complex organisms—it begins with the energy. Solar radiation is consumed by plants through photosynthesis, herbivores consume plants, and carnivores consume herbivores; omnivores like humans consume plants and animals. All living things ultimately derive energy from the sun either directly or indirectly. Without sunlight, there would be no plants on which to base a food system. Of equal importance is water. This liquid chemical comprises much of the surface of the planet as well as comprising the fundamental structure of plant and animal physiology. Without water, all life would cease to exist. These two inputs—water and (solar radiant) energy are the key parameters of the energy economy.

The second dynamic is the human species economy. Humans historically navigated the energy economy the same way most animals do—by moving to the energy source where it naturally occurs in order to consume it. This is nomadic foraging—a successful strategy that supported human populations for many millennia. Though less common, it is important to observe that it still exists today. Historically, it was the Agricultural Revolution that sparked a new trajectory in the human story. Agrarian villages learned to cultivate what they needed without moving and would eventually become rural villages that cultivate in order to trade with market towns and cities full of "freehands." In urban-rural systems, the strategy for navigating the energy economy is to enlist rural people to cultivate energy in various forms (food, clothes, wood, etc.), working within the limits of nature for a given locale. Rural products are then traded with waiting urban populations, who provide access to unusual and hard to find urban products.

The way we have defined urban, rural, and urban-rural systems, is predicated on the economic action of trade. Trade is not necessarily something that involves currency, as is typical in the contemporary world economy. Initially, trade within and among agrarian villages and nomadic peoples involved bartering what might now be considered "luxury" gifts. The gift economy was utilized to establish peaceful relations, and also acted as a source of insurance—if one settlement experienced disaster, another may come to their aid, for instance, if they were on good terms. The gift economy was an important mechanism for creating those good terms. Not only does urban-rural trade predate capitalism, it predates the invention of currency and therefore required direct barter. This economic form also still exists in various forms in the modern world economy—usually as part of what has been referred to as the informal sector.

When the currency-based economy replaced direct barter, the notion of value was altered to incorporate a more socially constructed dimension. If I barter for a pound of coffee, then I must supply perhaps a pound of wheat in return. If we monetize coffee, the amount of money I exchange for the pound of coffee may not be an equivalent, but this will be less obvious or direct. Commodity markets in New York and London now set an arbitrary price for products such as coffee—not based on fairness, but on perceived supply and demand. This element of perception is where the social construction comes in. Unwitting farmers may perceive that the low price they are offered for their goods is the best they can hope for, even when the commodity price is far higher. The construction of value is not totally based on objective criteria, but on a social perception that is limited by the availability of information. The low value may then prompt overproduction and oversupply and create the conditions of a self-fulfilling prophecy of objectively low prices.

Whether economic trade is based on gifts, barter, or currency, the goal is to achieve a condition in which all parties feel fairly compensated so that trade relations can remain stable and sustainable. Of course, history is replete with examples of this breaking down. In some cases, one or all parties feel unfairly treated and withdraws from trade. In other cases, the more ambitious seek to obtain more than a fair share based on equitable exchange. This brings us to the role of polity and power.

Polity is the dynamic that contains two important pieces: how decisions get made and how power is used to enforce those decisions—coercive and persuasive/administrative forms of power, or hegemonic power. Early agrarian settlements appear to have been fairly egalitarian, implying a somewhat democratic decision-making apparatus. Trade was not frequent as these were by definition self-sustaining populations. Generally, with increasing levels of wealth comes greater social stratification that acts to undermine egalitarianism.

The most critical political decisions shaping the survival and prosperity of settlements are those that involve resources—how to go about obtaining them, how to go about distributing them, and how to protect them from threats such as raiding parties or military invasions. The rise of military power can itself be attributed to both the ambitious desire to obtain greater resources and also to the desire to protect them once obtained. In other words, military action is an outgrowth of polity that may be used for offense to obtain resources, or it may be for defense to protect resources. Urban populations deriving their resources from military conquest are not limited by local environmental limits imposed by the energy economy, so populations are permitted to reach very large numbers. This has the effect of creating a greater military capacity for conquest as well as a greater demand for more resources. Thus, unfolds a spiral of military conquest, resource expansion, population growth, need for yet more resources, and further requirement to mobilize additional military actions to both capture more resources and defend what is taken.

The capturing of resources by force is a coercive strategy, and while it may be somewhat effective, it also carries a heavy cost in terms of lives lost and the constant threat of retaliation (Thomas 2010; Mann 1986). More effective than the use of coercive force is the political strategy that relies on administrative power carried out ideologically through persuasion. Through ideological control the transfer of resources appears legitimate and fair, even when it may be quite uneven. The use of ideology to foster administrative power is an act of culture rather than act of military force. This brings us to the fourth dynamic.

The cultural dynamic involves values, beliefs, norms, and practices shared by a collectivity within a particular context of time and space. It provides the knowledge and ability required for individuals to navigate through life, and it allows for adjustments and modifications to evolve and change in response to new conditions. While urban settlements have often dominated rural settlements through military force historically, we are now seeing this coercive strategy replaced by a hegemonic form of cultural domination. The core of this stems from the belief and values that place urban above rural. Deference for the urban begins to set in and urbanormativity is the result. The ability to win favor for urban over rural life, and to coordinate activities that support urban populations even against the needs of rural populations defines the urbanormative dimension of urban-rural systems.

THE CONTEXT OF URBANORMATIVITY

The above discussion of system dynamics is offered to reinforce an important point that should be taken in conjunction with the concept of urbanormativity—that it is a cultural response to a particular set of environmental, economic, and political conditions (Thomas et al. 2011). Therefore, while it may be possible to examine urbanormativity strictly at the cultural level—without simultaneous concern for these underlying conditions—there should at minimum be a realization that these conditions are important for the existence of urbanormativity. We emphasize this point because it places us within a long-standing philosophical debate among social scientists between the materialists and the idealists.

This debate dates to nineteenth-century German philosophy, when Karl Marx, who was considered the first historical materialist, is said to have turned Georg Hegel on his head by insisting that material conditions shape culture. Hegel posited that the development of society was a cultural process in which the collectivity engages in a process of self-realization and that out of this results the material conditions. Marx, thus reversed the causal order, going as far as to claim that culture was merely a superstructure of material conditions—any ideas that were held by people that did not reflect their material conditions were a form of false consciousness. Years later, Max Weber famously debated the "ghost" of Marx, turning Marx on his head. Weber agreed that material conditions were important for understanding culture, but maintained that culture retained the power to shape material conditions, as was his central thesis in explaining the rise of capitalism—as a by-product of the Protestant work ethic.

While we do not wish to mire the reader with greater details of this philosophical debate, it is worth some reflection as we offer our view of the four dynamics of urban-rural systems discussed above: environment, economy, polity, and culture. As may be clear, our position is closer to Weber, as we consider social change to swing in either direction. Furthermore, we view urban-rural systems within the framework of complex adaptive systems (Gell-Mann 1994; Lansing 2003). This means that we do not assume a singular linear direction of change, we do not expect change to entail a purpose (improvement, civilization, development), and we believe that change is multi-causal and multi-directional. Examination of archaeological data supports this view, revealing that the human experiments with settlement, and later urbanization, were haphazard and occurred through trial and error. It is only after thousands of years of experimentation—most of it marked by failure—that the current urban-rural systems could begin to take shape.

TAKEAWAYS

The brief discussion in the beginning of this chapter on the global urban transition paints a picture sufficient to understand the present demographic changes that are afoot and how they connect to global political economic patterns. One important observation from this is that the increasing growth of the urban populations is taking place alongside a stagnant or shrinking global rural population. This means the condition of urban dependency is becoming more entrenched. This demographic profile is a result of how we have organized the structures of the world economy: privileging urban over rural producers, undervaluing rural resources and overvaluing urban products, and creating a hierarchical divide between the urban haves and the rural have-nots.

Perhaps what is most remarkable about this is the widespread inattention urban-rural dynamics receives. In fact, this unfolding urban reality is typically met with moral indifference or enthusiastic approval by national governments, development practitioners, and academics. The prevailing attitude is that the current suffering of rural people is a short-term cost endured to achieve long term goals of urban development. Meanwhile, as nations urbanize, they must reconcile the heavy cost exacted by rural-to-urban migration creating a condition of overurbanization, overwhelming the existing infrastructure of cities. Excessive growth in urban populations creates the conditions for an underclass of urban workers that is easily exploited as cheap labor.

For those rural producers who manage to remain in the countryside, they are forced to contend with reliance on unreliable commodity exports that fetch a low price that fails to support them, leading to outcomes such as famine. The populations cultivating the basic resources of the global economy—responsible for feeding the swelling urban populations—are being starved out of work. Some are, perhaps wisely, reverting to agrarianism in place of commodity production. This may be a successful strategy, provided they are not dispossessed of the land on which they rely for self-sufficiency. A change in land policies, including selling land to foreign interests through land grabs, can make this problematic. Usually, such foreign interests are highly urbanized nations that have almost no capacity for rural production due to foreboding environmental conditions, so they purchase land from abroad to meet their needs. This practice calls into question such basic ideas as national sovereignty.

Since the first urban settlements in the Fertile Crescent, rural communities have played a critical supporting role—though it is not always visible. Without them, urban settlements could not survive. What is often overlooked is the fragility of urban life that remains as much a reality for contemporary urban settlements as it did for the first cities that were built thousands of years ago. Urban dependency is the reason we will never achieve a global urban population of 100 percent. While urban populations can generate some level of self-sufficiency through such practices as urban food production, the overall massive demand for food is rarely addressed in a meaningful way. Huge quantities of crops—mostly grains—are required to feed the millions of city dwellers that live in small, confined, and paved environments. The desire for meat prompts an entire industry based on large feedlots and slaughterhouses that nobody in a city wants to see, even if these facilities could fit within the city limits. In any case, the grains required to feed these animals would still rely on millions of acres of production. If city dwellers were to develop a taste for rodents and insects, a far greater proportion of diet could be met within the city limits, but this cultural preference is not likely to flourish in affluent urban contexts. The upshot is that no matter how we try, we will not be able to create truly self-sufficient cities—rural resources and the communities that produce them will remain as vital in the future as they are today and were over the last several thousand years (Steel 2013).

We suggest that urban life continues to be accepted and promoted as the desired state of affairs the world over, not because it is inherently superior, but because urbanormative values have become pervasive and nearly universal. Apart from small subcultures, such as those who participate in the intentional communities movement that are practicing self-sufficiency, the trend for every nation in the world is to view rural life as archaic, limited, and undesirable, while urban life is hailed as the future, as a sign of progress and prosperity, and as the superior way to live. In the absence of a rallying cry to value and protect rural people, or improve the quality-of-life in rural communities, there is nothing left to challenge urbanormativity or the general trend toward urbanization itself.

Chapter Two

Distance and Interaction

In the last chapter we argued that within the context of the energy economy, urban populations would face certain collapse without the aid and support of a network of rural communities. There are simply not enough resources to feed the millions of hungry mouths living in cities in the absence of imports from the countryside. To avoid disaster, urban populations may (a) use economic mechanisms to ensure that rural products remain undervalued and cheap, they can (b) use political strategies of coercion to forcibly take resources, as under colonialism, but more likely, (c) they can facilitate the unequal transfer of rural resources to urban populations as the end result of cultural domination—urbanormativity is the ideology at the center of this. Later we will argue that the cultural devaluation of rural also shapes the economic devaluation. Urbanormativity instills the view that urban life is superior to rural life and as it permeates culture, rural producers may become more willing to accept the unequal exchange for the fruits of their labor—they may even blame themselves for not finding a way to the city to make a better living. Considering how horrific the conditions have become in many rural communities, it is not surprising to find hordes of rural people trying to enter cities for a better life, exacerbating overurbanization while joining the ranks of an exploited urban underclass.

In this chapter, we focus more closely on how culture interacts with physical and social distance to make urbanormativity a reality. Chapter 1 sought to address the "why" question, and here we approach the "how" question. We begin by drawing on classic works that observed disparate patterns in the way that people interact *within* rural and urban settings. The classic observations remain relevant over a century later. They observed that rural areas tend to have fewer weak ties relative to strong ties and are more likely to promote a close and familiar kind of social interaction. In urban

31

areas, they observe more weak ties relative to strong ties, such that a stranger and more distant form of interaction becomes the norm. While this explains internal dynamics for rural and urban communities, questions remain in terms of what accounts for differences *between* urban and rural areas.

We approach this with emphasis on the role of physical and social distance in the creation of *epistemic distance*. The way we come to know the world—our epistemology—is conditioned at least partly by our social and physical surroundings. As a result, what we come to define as "normal" has an urban-rural dimension. Our explanation can be stated simply: those reared in an urban setting (urbanites) will come to know an urban world, and those reared in a rural setting (rustics) will be most familiar with a rural world. Since urban people are more likely to have exclusive ties with other urbanites, they are less likely to form ties with rustics. The urban imagination of rural—*rural representations*—loses its basis in reality, thanks to epistemic distance, and becomes a product of secondhand accounts. There is precious little opportunity to see how the rustic side lives or to muster compassion and understanding for the challenges facing rural communities. This is expressed through a sense of urban moral indifference for the plight of the rural. Since the global demographic patterns, reviewed in the previous chapter, project populations to continue urbanizing, we expect to see even deeper consequences of urbanormativity and epistemic distance.

INTERNAL PATTERNS OF URBAN-RURAL INTERACTION

As the world shifts more heavily urban, there is a simultaneous shift in cultures taking place. The stimulating and exciting qualitative experiences of urban life can become overwhelming—as reflected upon by Georg Simmel (1971) in nineteenth-century Europe. Simmel thought that individuals needed to protect themselves from the sheer overload of the hustle-and-bustle of city life, leading them to develop what he called a "blasé attitude." This attitude becomes a layer of armor that protects, while it also hardens the exterior of those who carry it. The interactions between individuals with the blasé attitude become cooler, and, as Weber (2002) would note, more rational. The light exchanges of unhurried rural life—sharing a joke or anecdote for the simple sake of sociability—become a distant memory. Transactional exchanges become the norm.

Consider the following vignette. A woman rushes into her favorite café for a quick shot of espresso before hurriedly jumping into a cab that whisks her away to work. The barista in the café and the cab driver both exchange a few polite words as they provide their services to the woman. Once at work, the woman sees the familiar faces of coworkers. They exchange niceties, but everyone is there to work, and extended interaction will be met with impatience. The flow of rational exchanges rages forward. The next day, the woman finds herself behind a customer at the same café who is slowly telling a story to the barista. The woman, now running late, exclaims, "Excuse ME, I have to get to work!" The person telling the story thinks, "How rude!" Next time, however, they will be hardened and think twice about making small talk. And, so, the storyteller becomes a little more callous and less personal in their future exchanges. Thus, forms Simmel's blasé attitude.

Observing the transformation of social interaction from the characteristic warmth and intimacy of small rural settings to the fast, impersonal interaction of urban settings, informed the logic of Tönnies's classic work, *Gemeinschaft und Gesellschaft* (2000). For Tönnies's, growth in urban settlements brought a replacement of small town gemeinschaft with big city gesellschaft. Gemeinschaft is a German word that describes a pattern of interaction based on the "natural will" relations that exist between those who are familiar (kinship-based), while gesellschaft is interaction based on "rational will" and relations between those who are strangers. For Tönnies, the urbanization of society meant declining kinship and increasing strangeness. Along the same lines, Simmel wrote an essay called, "The Stranger," reflecting on similar observations. In his essay Simmel anticipated the concept of social distance, stating (Simmel 1971, p. 143), "the distance within this relation indicates that one who is close by is remote, but his strangeness indicates that one who is remote is near." This is not a reference to spatial, but to social strangeness. We can be in close physical proximity while at the same time feeling distant socially. This is the hallmark of urban interaction.

At this point we should offer a critique: Does the classic view discussed so far not oversimplify matters—romanticizing rural while demonizing urban life? We must be careful not to paint with too broad of brush strokes *all* urban or *all* rural areas, as each urban and rural place has unique elements. To be fair to Tönnies, his writing reveals a level of complexity and nuance that often goes unnoticed in secondary interpretations of his work. Importantly, he claimed that gemeinschaft and gesellschaft rarely exist in pure form and may instead be found in different proportions in a given place. In other words, most rural areas have a certain amount of gesellschaft, while most urban areas have some degree of gemeinschaft. A closer look at Simmel shows that he too understood that, while urban areas could be impersonal and alienating, they can also be freeing and more supportive of individual expression. There is more room to be an individual in the absence of a stifling social control that often colors rural communities. For example, he claims (1971, p. 332):

> The most elementary stage of social organization which is to be found histori-
> cally, as well as in the present, is this: a relatively small circle almost entirely
> closed against neighboring foreign or otherwise antagonistic groups but which

has however within itself such a narrow cohesion that the individual member
has only a very slight area for the development of his own qualities and for
free activity for which he himself is responsible.

The strong bonds of the group leave little room for the individual to
breathe. Thus, the critique that the classic view tends to oversimplify urban-
rural difference is important, but not fully justified. It should be recalled that
we are talking about tendencies that characterize many, but not all urban or
rural places. While exceptions may be found, there is a tendency for rural
areas to be dominated by gemeinschaft and urban areas by gesellschaft patterns of social interaction. As anticipated by Simmel, patterns of interaction
in urban and rural places are based largely on the amount of distance that
exist between individuals. Observations of the effects of urban life are not
limited to those of social scientists. Biologists have documented similar
psychological effects in humans living in cities (e.g., Morris 1996), and have
found parallels among experimental rats living in overcrowded conditions
(Calhoun 1962).

Physical Space and Interaction

Internal patterns of social interaction are not just cultural. The physical environment plays a crucial role in shaping the opportunities for social interaction and the formation of social ties. As we elaborate in the next chapter,
urban and rural areas often developed around alternate forms of economic
activity. Urban production involves manufacturing and the transport of resources from a variety of locales to the city for processing. This allows a high
density of population to form within the compact spaces of cities and towns,
owing to the absence of natural limits to growth. Alternatively, the harvest of
natural resources forms the basis of rural production. It takes place across a
broad physical landscape that is heavily shaped by the natural availability of
resources. For instance, while some forms of agriculture may be carried out
in an urban space—a modest garden could occupy an abandoned lot—it is
only rural areas that offer the vast, sparsely populated spaces required to
achieve the level of production capable of meeting urban demand. A corn
stalk requires a certain amount of space to grow, for example, and although
this can be intensified with technologies such as chemical fertilizer and pesticides, it is still nature and physical space that determines the limits to corn
production. Hence the basis of urban and rural economic activity guides the
development of alternative urban and rural spaces, while creating differing
spatial patterns and opportunities for interaction.

We refer to the environment in which people live as *settlement space*. The
most obvious aspect of which is the built environment that includes housing,

streets, water and sewer infrastructure, and other aspects of the physical layout. As Gottdeiner (1994, p. 16) noted:

> It is built by people who have followed some meaningful plan for the purposes of containing economic, political, and cultural activities. Within it people organize their daily actions according to the meaningful aspects of the constructed space.

Urban and rural communities are designed with urban and rural production strategies in mind, so that even if these strategies shift over time, the initial design of the community remains. This explains why many rural communities continue to offer a settlement space long after the activity of rural production has ceased—as is the case, for instance, in ex-mining towns where homes and local businesses continue to be inhabited.

Settlement space is frequently the site of intergroup conflict, shaped by such forces as political machines (Logan & Molotch 2012), neighborhood associations (Rabrenovic 1996), and social movements (Castells 1977). Conflicts often emerge over competing visions for how a given settlement space should develop. Oftentimes, value difference lies at the base of the conflict with some factions favoring economic development and others favoring, perhaps, cultural developments or environmental conservation.

While settlement space has a visible reality, people do not live their lives in unity with it. Rather, they experience their environment as a circuit of places they visit regularly, irregularly, rarely, or not at all. The spaces individuals experience on a regular basis are part of their *viable space*, the essence of which has been described by Thomas (1998, p. 20):

> Most individuals experience their communities as limited to the space most easily accessible to them. This space is experienced at regular and frequent intervals, and is familiar and comfortable. In contrast, space experienced infrequently or not at all comes to be perceived as outside the realm of everyday life.

As space structures the environment in which social interaction takes place, the relationship between settlement space and viable space determines the level and quality of interaction found in a community.

Because urban production favors higher population densities, the viable space for a given urbanite is likely to include only a small segment of the total urban settlement space. A resident of a city can go about their daily commute and other activities without leaving the settlement space. Residents of a suburban community may travel into a central city for employment, but even as the settlement space spans political boundaries, the act of leaving one municipality for another does not constitute an exit from the settlement space. In large modern cities, there are often large swathes of settlement space that are never experienced. This can lead to a cognitive map in which the individual experiences parts of the settlement space in only cursory ways—such as driving at high speeds and viewing exits off an expressway. The home neighborhood and the work neighborhood are more recognizable venues of interaction than the space between. Though less central, the intermediate areas remain part of the viable space. Areas outside of regular travel are not. This is true in a pedestrian context as well: Gans (1962) noted that residents of Boston's soon-to-be razed West End neighborhood supported healthy streetscapes and occupied storefronts as part of their "world," while ignoring or glossing over abandoned areas in between.

Important to understanding viable space is the underlying network of *attractor points*—sites that pull in large numbers of individuals and serve as focal points of social interaction. The neighborhood school is an example, as are religious buildings, civic centers, sports venues, and shopping districts. One trend of the late twentieth century was the development of large regionally-oriented shopping malls designed to attract shoppers from a metropolitan region, often at the expense of older and smaller neighborhood business districts. A typical city will be overlain with attractor points, with more powerful ones serving the entire metro region (a mall or sports stadium) and others that are more locally oriented (e.g., a neighborhood elementary school or local cafe). In a large metropolitan area, the network of attractor points and resulting viable space is by-and-large contained within the settlement space, even when crossing political boundaries that may divide a suburb from the city proper.

As with urban communities, rural communities are spatially structured by attractor points, but its residents are more likely to leave the settlement space than their urban counterparts. The network of attractor points will often include external settlement space that is urban. For example, some rural communities are food deserts, requiring residents to travel to a nearby city to obtain groceries. In medieval French villages, it was common to live in a small central settlement and leave to work in surrounding fields. The viable space for the individual would include the agricultural area outside the hamlet, as well as attractor points within, such as the village church. In the modern American context, people living in rural communities often reside in one village but work in another; in this case, the viable space extends beyond the settlement space and incorporates significant rural land as well as the other village (Thomas 2003). Indeed, it is quite common for residents of rural communities to incorporate considerable geographic space in their lives—both urban and rural. This will be an important point when we later consider the phenomenon of spatial inequality.

Interaction without Space?

Simmel's reflections on distance, written over a century ago, noted the dual importance of physical and social distance in shaping patterns of social interaction and the formation of social ties. Melvin Webber (1964) would later theorize about the declining importance of physical space in human settlements, maintaining that social distance will become our only concern. Webber proposed that, owing to new communication technology, the distinctions of center and hinterland, or of urban and rural will dissolve. He maintained that the urban place—once the focal point of industrial, cultural, and social activity—was being eclipsed by the non-place urban realm. This argument is the *community without propinquity* hypothesis—community without physical (settlement) space. The main idea here is, as Little (2000, p. 1814) puts it,

> This approach switches the emphasis of urbanity from physical built form to the quality of interaction in cultural life through the exchange of information. This definition implies that suburban and ex-urban dwellers enjoy a measure of urbanity not previously acknowledged.

This is a helpful way to think about the urbanite who resides in a remote exurban community, but commutes (physically or virtually) to work. As cities become intensely populated and unaffordable, we can expect urbanization to continue pushing urbanites out into the country—a widening of viable space.

Scholars such as Little (2000) have taken notice of Webber's (1964) prescient prediction of the coming internet revolution three decades before it happened. Under globalization, communication technologies have indeed altered the ways in which households connect to the outside world. They have become a place of both consumption and production, as more and more people find they can work from home. Little (2000) claims this returns us to a model that characterized preindustrial times, before the separation of work and household created by going to work in factories. Economic success now has less to do with location and more to do with access to technology. For small towns in the nineteenth century, success depended heavily on physical location and this mostly depended on who was able to negotiate the best railroad stops or shipping ports. Now, small towns depend less on physical and more on digital access—something many rural communities still lack. In short, the argument is that physical distance has become less consequential for shaping community. But does this mean the end of physical space?

Indeed, the rural community of the 2000s is not the same as what was observed by the classic thinkers of the nineteenth century. In terms of empirical research on the declining importance of physical space, the evidence is somewhat mixed. Sharp and Adua (2009) conducted a study that supports the community without propinquity hypothesis. They find social distance to be a better predictor of agro-environmental concern than physical distance. Their research found that urban and suburban people may actually hold *more* sympathetic views than other rural people toward farmers, provided they formed social ties with the farmer. Living in proximity does not guarantee the formation of a social tie to a farmer and thus proximity has less power in shaping attitudes. Sharp and Adua find that the effects of physical space (propinquity) vanish entirely when measures of social distance (homophily) are added to the analysis.

A case study of a Southern new urbanist neighborhood, by Hipp and Perrin (2009), arrived at contrary results. They find that the likelihood of forming weak and strong ties in a neighborhood decreases substantially when physical distance increases. As measures of social distance are added, the effects of physical distance remained significant and were of a higher magnitude than the social distance measures. Returning to the above research, this would suggest that rural people living in proximity may be more likely to form a tie with a farmer. The farmer's market serves as an attractor point that creates the opportunity for social interaction and the resulting possible formation of a weak tie between an urban customer and a rural farmer. Hipp and Perrin would expect a higher likelihood that rural residents and the farmer would form ties, due to proximity.

Hipp and Perrin found that social distance—based on categorical differences in socioeconomic status, gender, age, marital status, having children, and length of residency—were weaker and less consistent than physical distance in predicting the establishment of social ties. The one that had the strongest influence was marital status. In short, those who are married have a difficult time forming ties with those who are not, and vice versa. An older study by Marches and Turbeville (1953) found that propinquity was one of the greatest predictors of marriage—you are more likely to marry one who lives nearby. These observations contradict the views of Webber (1964) and Sharp and Adua (2009) that physical distance has become irrelevant to social tie formation and social interaction, while supporting earlier propinquity research that underscores the role of physical distance (Caplow & Forman 1950; Festinger, Schachter, & Back 1950). While new technologies have upset the apple cart, it would be premature to declare the death of physical space.

Internal Urban-Rural Social Ties

What is significant about both physical and social distance are their role in shaping the formation of social ties—weak and strong. The formation of ties is important for several reasons. Neighborhoods with a higher number of social ties tend to report greater satisfaction levels (Sampson 1991), more cohesion (Kasarda & Janowitz 1974; Sampson 1988), lower rates of crime and social disorder (Sampson, Raudensbush, & Earls 1997), and have higher levels of political engagement (Tilly 1974). Wilkinson (1991) claims that both urban and rural areas have their share of strong ties, but that rural areas have comparatively few weak ties. Citing the work of Granovetter (1973), Wilkinson reminds us about the "strength of weak ties" for providing individuals with valuable bridges to the outside world that can translate into crucial opportunities. Having a dearth of weak ties, as is typical of rural communities, therefore translates into diminished opportunities. Strong ties are valuable because they provide the individual with a source of social support. As Wilkinson and Granovetter claim, however, too much emphasis on strong, relative to weak, ties can lead to fragmentation in a community and limited mobility for community members.

The dynamics of social tie formation are different for urban and rural areas. Rural areas tend to promote more strong, relative to weak, ties, thereby achieving the greatest cohesion, while for urban areas there is a wealth of opportunity resulting from weak ties but a heavier burden for individuals who may lack social support. In thinking about strong or weak ties, the classic French sociologist, Emile Durkheim (1984), made a distinction between what he referred to as mechanical solidarity (based on strong ties) and organic solidarity (based on weak ties). Durkheim claimed that strong ties are based on sameness—a shared sense of togetherness and of being a part of a larger aggregate such as a team. Weak ties are based on difference and complementarity.

Two plumbers might have a lot in common through their shared trade and develop a strong tie. This may be strengthened through common membership in the same labor union. A plumber and a banker, however, may not have as much in common. Yet, each sees how the other complements their abilities, and from this may develop a weak tie and a sense of mutual dependence. The notions of sameness and difference, to which Durkheim referred, are related to social distance. Homophily is the social scientific concept that corresponds to low social distance and sameness— homogeneous rural areas tend to have high levels of homophily and thereby often play host to mechanical solidarity. Alternatively, more heterogeneous urban areas tend to offer a space for organic solidarity to flourish. Once again, we must be careful not to overgeneralize as more homogenous cities and more diverse rural communities do exist—but these are the general patterns.

So how exactly do physical and social distance promote or inhibit the formation of social ties? In thinking about physical distance, Zipf (1949) offered the *principle of least effort* hypothesis. He claimed that people will associate with those living closest to them simply because initiating interaction will take the least amount of energy. It is much more convenient to walk next door than it is to walk ten miles to introduce yourself to a stranger. Mayhew and Levinger (1977) formalize this observation as the *Law of Dis-*

tance-Interaction, which states that the probability of interaction or contact between two elements diminishes with increasing levels of physical distance. They go on to generalize this to incorporate social distance as well, claiming that it likewise takes more energy to interact with people who are categorically different—where there is a low level of homophily. In both cases, the argument is that overcoming distance—physical or social—requires energy, and most people try to conserve energy.

EXTERNAL PATTERNS OF INTERACTION
BETWEEN URBAN AND RURAL SETTLEMENTS

It should not be surprising to find that individuals living in urban communities are unlikely to overcome the vast physical distance that separates them from rural communities in order to meet new people. It is possible for urbanites and rustics to meet but the opportunity for day-to-day chance interaction is low to nonexistent. There are exceptions as happens when rural farmers travel to the city to participate in a farmer's market. While there, farmers may form social ties with some of their urban customers. The farmer's market is an attractor point that becomes a catalyst for weak urban-rural tie formation. Another example is the county fair, where urban populations travel in large numbers to a rural location in order to enjoy different festivities, rides, and food. In this case, urban and rural people may occupy the same space thereby enhancing the probability of interaction, but while together the level of social distance between them may inhibit interaction. In any case, as noted by Wilkinson (1991), rustics must adapt to the constraints imposed by "Sparsity of settlement and distance from centers of economic growth" (p. 58). One strategy involves traveling to urban areas for economic opportunity, another is to lure urbanites to the countryside for recreational experiences. In either case, this generates an opportunity for social interaction and subsequent formation of social ties.

Urban-Rural Migration

Beyond the occasional opportunities for social interaction and social tie formation between urban and rural people is the more permanent opportunity afforded to one who migrates. Ravenstein (1889) identified several key characteristics driving migration, noting that it (1) is based on economic motivation, (2) would diminish with physical distance, (3) happens in stages, (4) differs for individuals based on their social location, and (5) was not unilateral—migration patterns could move in bilateral or multilateral directions. These postulates form what is now called *push-pull theory*. It has been extended by Lee (1966) to incorporate noneconomic factors such as political motivations, the impact of natural disasters, lack of amenities, prejudice and discrimination, poor housing or schools, and so forth. Todaro (1976) applied push-pull theory specifically to urban-rural migration. He emphasized the role of economic expectations held by potential migrants who weigh the costs and benefits of moving, but noneconomic push-pull factors should also be considered. Urban to rural migration is often driven by noneconomic factors, such as the desire for a better quality-of-life. Rural to urban migration is typically driven by economic motivation such as finding a job or obtaining an education as a means for finding work. The social distance between rustics and urbanites may be difficult to overcome after migration, and this may fuel return migration.

While not necessarily a cause of migration, one of the most important catalysts for getting established is having social networks and ties in the new destination, and especially those strong ties involving kinship (Massey 1988). The decision to migrate could make perfect sense economically, socially, politically, and culturally, but the difficulty of settling in without the support of family or friends may prevent migration from happening. Having an established support network overcomes this obstacle, which is why chain migration is a common pattern. This means that the volume of rural-urban migration will increase over time as supportive social networks take root.

Of course, migration assumes mobility, and not all individuals are mobile—some individuals may find it very difficult to leave the place where they are born. The decision of Amish youth, for instance, to leave their community in early adulthood is a simultaneous decision to erase all existing ties to that community and become banished. They must trade in all of their strong ties for the possibilities of forming new ties—all of which will initially be weak. This heavy penalty is oftentimes enough to prevent youth out-migration, though not always. One thing that is certain is that the physical location that we start out with in life is the result of decisions made by prior generations. No one chooses where they are born.

Neither can individuals control the social location they occupy at birth, such as their ethnicity, race, gender, sexuality, socioeconomic status, and so forth. New physical and social locations, however, may be sought and achieved later in life. In some ways it is easier to achieve physical mobility than social mobility. Some would argue that there are layers of the social hierarchy that are out of reach. Bourdieu's theory (1984) of social distinction suggests that social class is responsible for producing different tastes and preferences that make interaction across class lines awkward and difficult—supportive of the *Law of Distance-Interaction* that was mentioned earlier. Bourdieu claimed that cultural preferences are shaped by socialization that become embodied as *habitus*—our upbringing becomes imprinted on the very ways we walk and talk. Going a step further, Bourdieu suggested that the social distance created by social class becomes the mechanism responsible for reproducing social class itself. We return to Bourdieu in our chapter on cultural capital.

Of course, not all social distance is based on class. Self-categorization theory (Tajfel & Turner 1986) suggests that social distance can result from any categorical difference. These differences create an inability to form a shared sense of group identity with others—a sense of "us." This harkens back to Durkheim's notion of mechanical solidarity. Two plumbers can self-categorize as being part of the same labor union, for instance, and this will create a bond. A plumber and a college professor, however, may find less common ground. Merton (1968) suggests that different *role expectations* associated with occupying different social locations are responsible for creating distance. Roles are associated with lifestyles, so people performing different roles will find they have less in common and will be less likely to form a tie, compared to those who are performing the same roles.

Individuals who are born and socialized in urban and rural locales are taught to live by different sets of rules or norms. The pace and nature of social interaction are markedly different, and this has consequences for the number and intensity of social ties that form. Someone raised in a rural town might expect to be familiar with individuals encountered in public, while the expectation for deeper and more meaningful interaction may be higher. Someone raised in a city would be surprised to encounter a familiar face in public, and generally expect interactions to be transactional. In fact, urbanites carry an expectation of boundaries—being too personal may cross a line. The beliefs, values, norms, and lifestyles come to be urban-centric or rural-centric, and these create divergent epistemologies, or ways of knowing the world.

URBAN-RURAL EPISTEMOLOGICAL DISTANCE: EXPERIENCE AND REPRESENTATIONS

The term epistemology was coined by Ferrier (1854) as the study of the meaning of knowledge. Ferrier sought to interrogate the question: How do I know what I know? Here we extend the question: How do rural and urban people know what they know? Much of the way that humans construct knowledge and understanding of the world comes from direct personal experience—what we see, hear, feel, touch, and taste. The process of building understanding from experience—socialization—is so subtle that we rarely stop to think about it as it unfolds. As we experience the world, we do not experience it as it is, we experience it through a filter. We interpret and construct meaning as we use our senses (Husserl 1973 [1900]). Understanding how we interpret and construct meaning is the focus of epistemology.

Direct experience is central to the acquisition of knowledge. Anything that is part of our day-to-day lives falls under the realm of direct experience, and this experience is epistemically close and familiar. C. Wright Mills (1959) referred to this space of experience as the social milieu and it corresponds to what we earlier referred to as viable space. Like a bubble surrounding an individual, the social milieu encompasses the extent of our senses. It is generally ignored, and often taken for granted. Mills suggested that the sociological imagination could help us see past the limited bubble of our day-to-day lives.

The finitude of human existence ensures a limit to what and how much we can know through our direct experience. We often wish to understand things about which there can be no direct experience. For example, I may wish to understand what it is like to walk on the moon, but the likelihood of that becoming a direct experience is very low. I am therefore entirely reliant upon representations—models of the world that are assembled to allow others to understand realities that they will not or cannot ever experience. The further we are from the reality, the less we know about it, and the more we rely upon representations. I may read a book or watch a documentary or even interview an astronaut about moonwalking. In each case I am dealing with a secondary account. I can compare the different accounts, but I cannot evaluate whether it squares with my own direct experience. I am therefore in a position of total reliance on representations. Distance—whether physical or social—can create this reliance on representations.

This brings us to the concept of the social representation (Moscovici 1988, 2001)—a basic model that allows us to grasp some part of reality that is otherwise out of reach. The term *social* representation implies that the process is not simply an individual exercise—it is the work of a group or collectivity. Durkheim (2001 [1912]) coined the term collective representations to explain how entire groups of people may share in the same experiences as when practicing religious rituals. When an entire football stadium with thousands of spectators jeers a referee for making a bad call, they are experiencing something akin to a collective representation of good and bad calls. The term collective, however, creates the impression that there is a high level of consensus around the representation. It is possible, as noted by Moscovici, for a social representation to be contested and debated—not all will be shared uniformly.

Rural reality is something that typically lies outside the direct experience of urbanites, and is something that is mainly accessed through social representations of rural life. In an urban society, the work of shaping and defining an understanding of rural reality involves a range of symbolic activities. Central to this is consuming media content—television, radio, internet, film, print, and so forth. In another chapter we examine this in some depth. For now, we may simply appreciate the fact that with increasing epistemic distance comes greater reliance on rural representations that may distort the imagination and potentially perpetuate stereotype and misunderstanding.

Epistemic Distance

Carolan (2006) offers the idea of epistemic distance to refer to those objects and phenomena that are distant and remote to our own lifeworld. He used this concept to explain why it is difficult for conventional farmers to see value in learning newer sustainable farming practices—the methods are unfamiliar and take time to cultivate, while the returns feel less tangible and the benefits must be imagined. Carolan (2016) offers an important insight,

> The distance, one could argue, also has an impact on our ethical orientation toward distant phenomena, as it is makes it easier for us to act with moral indifference toward those faraway people, places, and non-human animals that provide us with what we eat. (p. 150)

If we elaborate on Carolan's discussion, we might note that as fewer people experience rural life or rural people, not only are they further removed physically and socially, but also epistemologically, morally, and ethically. Thus, an air of urban indifference can arise about what is happening in the countryside. Such indifference has important traction when it involves questions surrounding economic activities in rural areas, such as agriculture or natural resource management. More precisely, high risk practices are often disregarded or met with indifference. Urban consumers are more likely to tolerate long wall coal mining or horizontal fracturing for natural gas, if it means having a lower electric bill each month, even if these practices have devastating ecological impacts for host communities. Similarly, the filth and disgust of a giant Contained Animal Feeding Operation (CAFO) may be disregarded, while the benefits of cheap hamburgers are enjoyed. Figure 2.1 illustrates how epistemic distance accompanies a shift from relying on direct experience to social representation, and how this corresponds to the replacement of direct concern with moral indifference. It is easier to ignore the ugly underbelly of cheap food than it is to face it.

The brutal killing of indigenous rural peoples exemplifies moral indifference and is predicated upon urban epistemic distance. For example, in response to objections to mining practices, the government sent in a military force to assassinate five members of a Lumad family in the Philippines, including two minors (Rodriguez 2017). Meanwhile, police in northern Tanzania are believed to have shot and killed ten villagers for intruding on the operations of a local gold mine (Moloo 2017). While rural people are forced to negotiate these harsh and violent realities tied to rural production, they often object and resist. The political forces of distant urban centers are routinely mobilized to quell this resistance—all outside of the view of the typical urbanite who enjoys the benefits without the slightest twinge of guilt—out of sight, out of mind.

Experience and Urbanormative Attitudes

Urbanormativity in many regards implies a normalization of gesellschaft relations, of weak ties, and the abandonment of expressive gemeinschaft relations. The multitude of problems experienced by rural people are not part of the urban lifeworld and are rendered invisible. When one lives in an urban setting, they many enjoy the comforts of urban life—the latest technologies, reliable access to energy, food, and a wide range of consumer goods fastened out of remote rural resources and invisible workers. The social and environmental costs are physically separated and psychologically distant. This leads to a deeper question of rural attitudes. Why would someone care what happens to rural people, especially in the absence of social ties?

Focusing mainly on environmental attitudes, Heberlein (2012) offers a powerful framework for creating stable, consistent, and long-term attitudes. He states that for an attitude to endure through time, it needs, first, a foundation in direct experience. He discusses how Aldo Leopold underwent a 180-degree shift in his attitude toward wolves as the result of a transformative personal encounter he had looking into the green eyes of a wolf. Leopold also observed firsthand the negative ecological consequences that followed the removal of wolves from their ecosystem. These experiences led to a pro-wolf

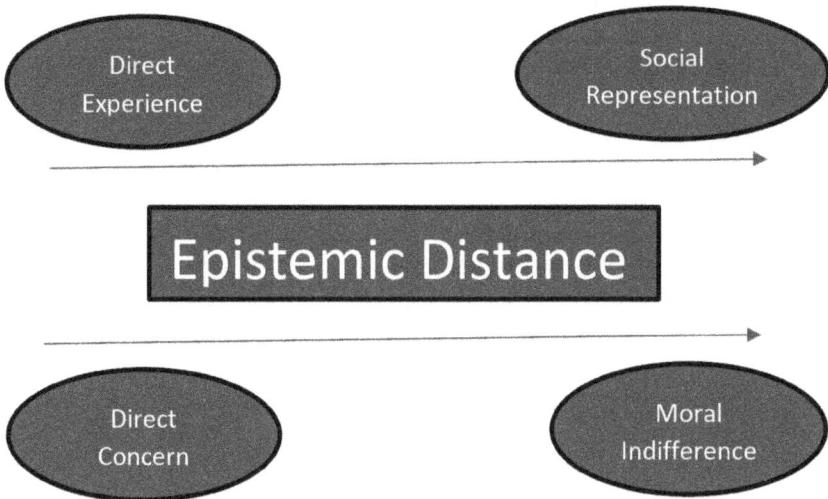

Figure 2.1. Carolan's Model of Epistemic Distance
Created by the author

attitude in Aldo Leopold. Heberlein suggests that Leopold's changing attitude was also due to a second factor, a new identity, since he changed roles from being a forester to becoming a professor. It would be difficult to negotiate a conservationist philosophy if one's occupation was exploitative in nature. New identities come with a package of attitudes giving them a third component, a high level of consistency. The more developed identity becomes, the more consistency forms between attitudes, and then a fourth component arises in the deepening structures of values, beliefs, and attitudes. After years as a professor, Leopold became more committed to his new identity and associated attitudes.

We can extend Heberlein's theory of direct experience, identity, consistency, and value-belief structures to the question of urban-rural attitudes, or ask, who is most likely to be concerned about rural people? By deduction we would expect the answer to be those individuals with (1) extensive direct experience with rural people (perhaps as the result of a social tie), who (2) have an identity that is linked to rural people, (3) hold other values and beliefs that are consistent with rural concern, and (4) develop a deeper structure of pro-rural values, beliefs, and attitudes. With the expansion, physical, social, and epistemic distance in the urbanizing world, there is not much hope of this happening accidentally. More intentional action will be required to facilitate moral concern for rural people and communities.

TAKEAWAYS

In this chapter we attempted to outline the processes and mechanism that account for how urbanormativity comes to be. While classic theories tended to focus on the different patterns of social interaction *within* urban and rural settings, less attention has been devoted to interaction *between* urban and rural settlements. As urban and rural define physically separate settlement spaces, the fact of infrequent urban-rural interaction belies a low rate of urban-rural social interaction and social tie formation. The viable space of most urbanites does not include rural areas, although most rural people routinely traverse urban terrain in their viable space. An exception is when urbanites relocate seasonally or permanently to rural areas, in which case they enter a new settlement space and construct a new viable space that may offer more opportunity for interaction. The result of the physical distance that separates urban from rural realities is a divergent set of urban-rural epistemologies.

While there is some potential for overcoming the physical spatial barrier between urban and rural experience through the use of modern technology, research continues to suggest that physical space continues to stubbornly influences social interaction and social tie formation. We are most likely to meet, befriend, and even marry those who live physically close to us, within the orbit of our viable space. We tend to meet people through community attractor points, such as schools, churches, and other social spaces like bars and restaurants. Urban people often have the ability to go through life creating a viable space that is exclusively urban, as the urban settlement space provides all that they need. Rustics may have some potential to live exclusively in rural settlement space, but are much more likely to be pulled into urban settlement space for a variety of reasons—economic, political, social, cultural, and so forth.

Without personal direct experience of urbanites interacting with rustics and rural places, knowledge of the rural "other" is limited to secondhand rural representations. Rural representations are socially constructed and often perpetuate rural stereotypes and misunderstandings from distorted images that misinform the urban public. Absurd and degrading rural representations help reinforce urbanormative values about the superiority of urban life, while simultaneously allaying moral concern that urban people might maintain for the exploited rural masses who provide the resources they depend on for survival. This leaves urbanites vulnerable to the moral indifference created by epistemic distance that leaves the reality of rural life a distant concern.

Chapter Three

Urban-Rural Oikos

Economy and Ecology

In the last chapter we attempted to uncover the mechanisms that lead to urbanormativity, emphasizing the roles of social, physical, and epistemological distance. All three types impact urban-rural interaction and social tie formation. The absence of interaction and social ties creates conditions for urban reliance on misinformed rural representations, moral indifference, and disregard for the challenges facing rural communities. In this chapter we wish to highlight the political and economic function of urbanormative ideological control. In short, urbanormativity is an ideology that legitimizes unjust urban-rural relations. Developing an understanding of urban dependency requires us to elaborate on economic and ecological dynamics. As we will discuss, both incorporate cycles of energy. The natural ecology of the environment is the source of energy that humans and all living things rely upon for survival. The economy refers to strategies that humans use for tapping into natural energy supplies that can be fashioned into a range of products, from basic food stuffs to complex manufactured goods. While urban centers rely on the manufacture of more complex goods, rural workers are responsible for the harvest of natural energy products that are traded with urban producers. Without rural workers, urban production could not continue—this is the essence of urban dependency, as we will elaborate.

The Greek concept of *oikos* is invoked here as it blurs the line between economy and ecology. At the household level it implies notions of family, home, and property. At a larger scale, the Greeks understood the oikos as a particular kind of urban-rural system: the city and its hinterland. Within the Greek polis, many elites often owned both a city home and a country estate, relying on workers to maintain both. Ideally, the fruits of the countryside

49

would feed the city, and the manufactured and trade goods from the city would be of value to those laboring in the hinterland. Oikos was a unit of citizenship. For instance, a resident of Athens was a citizen of the oikos of Attica (Hall 1998). The Greek model is similar to polities found earlier in the Fertile Crescent and serves as a building block of what would one day become larger territorial states. Our main interest in this chapter is outlining the connection between the economy and ecology of humans, paying close attention to the role of energy that is obtained first by rural workers and transformed and adapted by urban workers. Importantly, the rural economy is where it all starts—without it there could be no urban economy. We therefore begin our discussion with a view toward the rural economy before expounding the broader notion of an energy economy.

RURAL ECONOMY TODAY

Rural populations are overwhelmingly responsible for the labor involved in the continued mining of natural resources that include rare and precious metals, and experience some of the worst forms of exploitation and difficult work conditions along the way. The demand for rural resources is built on a long historical demand for other natural resources that provide energy (including all fossil fuels and most alternative forms of energy), food, and textiles. Rural areas encompass vast tracts of land and natural resources. Utilizing these resources requires labor in the extractive industries, not to mention the supporting activities related to distribution and storage—roads, warehouses, infrastructure.

The rural working class receives little compensation for what they provide, as the economic value of rural natural resources is almost universally lower than the value of finished urban products. This is not something that is objectively determined. Economic value is a social construction, as are markets that purport to determine them. Urban corporations, such as large food companies, mega-energy companies (Big Oil, King Coal), and all industries relying on rural resources, are in a vulnerable position as they cannot provide their goods without rural natural resources, and yet, they are in a position of power when it comes to influencing markets that set the prices for different resources. This influence is used to set the prices low, so that the profitability of the finished items can be maximized. The consequences of this is a callous disregard for the needs of rural working-class people and communities dependent on the sale of rural natural resources for their livelihood. While urban corporations record profits, the bounty does not "trickle down" into the hands of the rural communities.

The physical separation of urbanites from the natural systems that support them has both diminished the possibility of experiencing nature directly and increased reliance on representations. The extractive industries of agriculture and mining are among the worst environmental offenders. That is not to say that urban industries are universally cleaner—indeed, they are responsible for a world of toxic and hazardous waste. Much of this hazardous/toxic waste is collected and stored at facilities found in rural areas. Therefore, even the worst environmental consequences of urban production are often pushed down on rural communities. Rural industries, however, are often some of the most egregious creators of environmental destruction. The field of energy extraction may be the worst. The range of risky practices includes natural gas hydraulic fracturing, long wall coal mining, mountain top removal, and deep water and traditional oil drilling. In agriculture, the over-farming of marginal soil has historically led to desertification and dustbowls; the widespread application of toxic pesticides like DDT has poisoned wildlife and threatened human health; the airborne bacteria of confined animal feeding operations (CAFOs) are associated with a range of ailments in workers, such as respiratory disease. Meanwhile, hydraulic fracturing threatens the safety of underground water resources and has been linked to earthquakes, while mountain top removal to access coal seams has devastated mountains, while filling local waterways with debris, and exposing those nearby to dangerously radioactive metals that are usually found deep underground.

Beyond production, the transport of these extracted rural materials exacts a heavy toll on the climate, as most of it is transported through fossil-fuel driven transportation—mainly vehicles, ships, and trains. The infrastructure that supports this distribution requires massive outlays to maintain roads and railway infrastructure. A great deal of this has been privatized, as governments seek ways to be absolved of the burden of upkeep, but consequently, has given up oversight and the ability to enforce safety standards and regulations. Without oversight, roads, bridges, and railroads may deteriorate and become dangerous.

Next we will elaborate on how the logic of economies operates to disadvantage rural people and landscapes.

What is an Economy?

In a modern society, it is easy to believe that economies operate solely through the exchange of money. The problem with this view is that money has only existed for about two thousand six hundred years, while systems for organizing the provision and distribution of resources (Graeber 2012)—the goal of economies—have existed since the beginning of time (for modern humans that is at least two hundred thousand years). The most basic economic system is found in a society of hunter-gatherers, organized around a nomadic or semi-nomadic lifestyle. The foraging economy relies on finding energy resources wherever they may occur in nature. The goal is to provide each person with two thousand calories of food-based energy per day. Though basic, it is notable that the foraging economic system proved more sustainable and reliable than anything since (about one hundred ninety thousand years). It is only in the last ten thousand years that we find variations, beginning with the agrarian economy, followed by the economy of urban-rural systems that eventually morphed into what we now think of as a modern capitalist economy. We return to this point later.

Defining the activities of hunter-gatherers as economic, however, requires a broader definition—we refer here to the *energy economy*. The energy economy spans the globe, while integrating the needs of all life. The basic starting point is energy sourced from the sun. It circulates in various ways throughout the environment—plants utilize solar energy most directly, while animals that eat plants receive energy indirectly. A wolf that consumes rabbits is two steps removed, the rabbit is one step removed, and the carrot is fed directly by the sun. Energy is not simply manifest as food. Fossil fuels that are used for electricity and transportation also tap into the energy economy. Coal and oil are ancient forms of solar energy that were deposited millions of years ago as decaying plant matter.

The *species economy* refers to the networked strategies of a given species for obtaining required energy—by ingesting the calories necessary to sustain life, for instance. While this is required for any species, our main interest is with one particular kind: the *human economy*. The human economy does not exist independent of other species but is interlaced—hence our use of the term *networked*. All species occupy a niche within which they seek out their energy requirements, ideally in ways that do not require competition with other species. The human economy should be understood in relation to other species, including those we may eat, those we may adopt as pets, and those we may impact through our pursuit of seemingly unrelated activities. For example, domesticated cattle are largely incapable of survival without human intervention, and in return we utilize their milk and their meat for sustenance. Our relationship with dogs—a subspecies of wolf (*Canis lupus familiaris*) (Serpell 2017)—stretches back tens of thousands of years. Historically, dogs were useful for such things as hunting, providing a look out for unwelcome intruders, and companionship—a somewhat symbiotic cooperative relationship.

Another relevant animal to human history is the Oriental Black Rat, not because it is a loyal companion, but as an unwelcomed stowaway that joined humans amid their travels along various trade routes. Much to our chagrin, this rat not only consumed countless measures of grain from under our noses, but also spread Bubonic Plague, killing nearly half the population of the Roman Empire during the reign of Claudius (Harper 2017). Our own subsistence strategies are, therefore, networked with other species in sometimes beneficial and sometimes harmful ways.

Our ability to leverage resources impacts our chances of survival, since our bodies have evolved to interact with the energy economy by metabolically storing or releasing calories. If we expend more energy than we ingest we lose weight, and this can impact our ability to resist disease. If we ingest more than we expend we gain fat—a system for storing excess energy for use in lean times. As we age, we have evolved to retain calories as a hedge against disease and prolonged famine. Beyond the dynamics of individual energy metabolism, are those associated with the environment.

The Caloric Plain

In an ideal world there would be enough food for everyone. We can imagine a fertile plain where exactly two thousand calories of food grows per human per day. Let's say that such magnificent fertility comes with a cost: the plain is fertile, but is also rather flexible. When humans are spread evenly across the plain, eating their daily requirement of calories, the plain is perfectly flat. Humans, however, tend to collect near one another, creating added weight that causes indentation in the plain, like persons gathering in the center of a taut trampoline. The more bodies that are added, the greater the weight on the plain, the deeper the indentation, until ultimately, the borders collapse inward.

In a hunting-gathering economy, the number of people in one location will exhaust local resources, forcing people to spread out by moving to other locations where calories are more abundant. Over time our indentation will travel across the plain as resources are exhausted and replenished in each location. As long as the number of calories consumed and produced stays the same the system remains stable (see 1a of figure 3.1). Eventually, as the number of births exceeds the number of deaths in a population, our plain fills with too many people to sustain nomadism, and a new strategy begins when people start to settle down.

A sedentary population is one that lives in a single location year-round. In this circumstance, the indentation is permanent, and when resources are depleted they must be brought in from areas adjacent to the population center. Imagine the edges of a trampoline being pulled outward to remove the indentation formed by the weight of population in the center. There is a deep well in the middle, but it shallows as one goes further toward the edge. We refer to the indentation from which calories are derived as the *caloric well*. As the well deepens, the border area from which calories are gathered broadens— this is called the resource horizon (see 1b of figure 3.1). As caloric wells deepen, the resource horizons are pushed farther afield (see 1c of figure 3.1).

This model assumes a population moving from the central settlement space into the surrounding hinterland to gather resources, resulting in a wider resource horizon. At higher population levels, however, it is possible that the

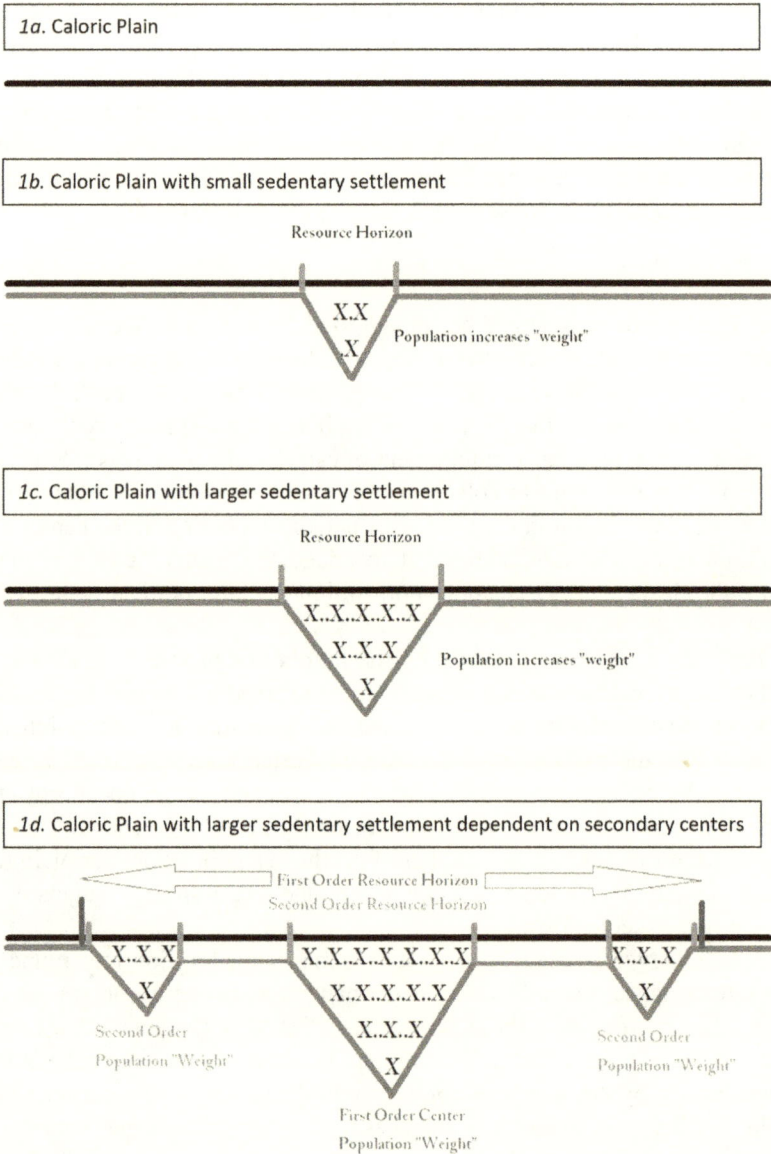

1a. Caloric Plain

1b. Caloric Plain with small sedentary settlement

Resource Horizon

X.X
.X   Population increases "weight"

1c. Caloric Plain with larger sedentary settlement

Resource Horizon

X..X..X..X..X
X...X..X   Population increases "weight"
X

1d. Caloric Plain with larger sedentary settlement dependent on secondary centers

First Order Resource Horizon
Second Order Resource Horizon

X..X..X   X..X..X..X..X..X   X..X..X
X   X..X..X..X..X   X
Second Order   X..X..X   Second Order
Population "Weight"   X   Population "Weight"
                 First Order Center
                 Population "Weight"

Figure 3.1.   Caloric wells. At top, a nomadic hunter-gatherer population moves around the environment (1a). Sedentary villages utilize resources nearer the village, and the larger the population the wider the resource horizon from which food is gathered or farmed (1b-c). Larger towns and cities require secondary centers to expand the resource horizon and support the center, which exhibits urban dependency on the smaller centers (1d).
Created by the author

resource horizon becomes so broad that the gathering operation becomes inefficient. In the case of a very wide resource horizon, smaller operations emerge as secondary centers that, in turn, transport resources to the primary population center. When this takes place, the secondary centers produce their own caloric wells shallower than that for the primary center, thereby extending the resource horizon of the entire system.

At higher populations, efficiencies of resource gathering and distribution creates a deeper and more complex network of secondary centers. They may generate their own outposts—third order centers. As this pattern continues, we find many "orders" of centers: the primary city remains the first order settlement, with additional orders (second, third, fourth, etc.) contributing to the functioning of the system overall (see 1d of figure 3.1).

As noted in chapter 1, the full system responsible for bringing rural resources into the primary urban center, including all secondary centers intermediate in the process, is referred to as an *urban-rural system*. An urban-rural system contains a primary settlement space that is dependent upon other communities, the secondary (and lower order) centers in the system. This network of settlements harvests and transports energy resources (raw materials) to the first order (primate) center to the point that the center eventually withdraws entirely from the work of gathering energy resources. Instead, it relies entirely on the lower order centers to coordinate the flow of energy products, so that it can transform them into more complex products that are traded downward. This relationship is the basis of urban dependency. Higher order settlements that have a network of supportive lower order settlements are cut off from direct participation in the energy economy, though they still require energy. Of course, the world of the calorie-rich plain described above remains in a world of theory; how does our model fare in the actual world in which we live?

Population and Resources

Like other omnivore species, humans evolved as hunters and gatherers, and the largest length of time since the evolution of our subspecies, *Homo sapiens sapiens* lived eighty thousand years in such nomadic foraging societies (Tattersall 2013). For most of human existence there was neither urban nor rural, as one cannot exist without the other: there was only nature and direct participation in the energy economy. In fact, the transition away from such a lifestyle revolved around access to resources.

The Broad Spectrum Revolution

For much of the Paleolithic, or Old Stone Age, that ended around twelve thousand years ago, humans hunted and foraged for a relatively narrow array of foods. The advantage of hunting a narrow range of animals, however, provided the advantage of allowing for a degree of specialization that ensures success. This specialization (our niche) is effective when population levels are low enough that the desired resource is abundant in the caloric plain. Given that hunting requires an expenditure of energy, it is not surprising that for much of prehistory, humans had a preference for high-return kills: a mammoth, reindeer, or wild cattle might have required considerable energy, but the return certainly justified the expense and risk of injury.

As population densities approached the carrying capacity of the environment, such specialization was no longer viable. Over-hunting would diminish prey, and there is evidence that in some regions humans hunted such animals as wooly mammoths to extinction (Lewis et al. 2015). To survive, humans had to exploit a greater spectrum of plants and animals—thus emerged the *broad spectrum revolution*. It began in the Fertile Crescent of southwest Asia, a boomerang-shaped arch stretching north from modern Israel and Jordan along the rift valley to southern Turkey, then turning down the Tigris and Euphrates Valleys into modern Turkey. The broad spectrum revolution was in full force by 15,000 BCE, but reached Europe and East Asia much later. It was aided by the end of the Ice Age as warmer waters became home to more edible sea life, as well as greater numbers of birds (Flannery 1969). Humans in marginal regions turned to small game, fish, and birds in order to ensure survival. The broad spectrum revolution created a caloric plain that was far more abundant and capable of supporting sizable populations year-round.

Agrarian Villages

The cultivation of plants should be understood in tandem with the broad spectrum revolution. Cultivation involves purposeful planting, and in a hunting and gathering culture could take the form of spreading seeds in a place before leaving in order to reap the harvest upon return. Over time, cultivation can lead to domestication, a consequence of selecting for specific characteristics so that the genetic composition of a population of plants is altered (Cauvin 2000).

There have been multiple domestication events throughout prehistory, and the best (though scattered) evidence we have is from wheat in the Fertile Crescent. At the first known year-round village in prehistory, the 23,500-year-old site of Ohalo II, on the Sea of Galilee in modern Israel, there is tentative evidence of domesticated wheat. When the site was abandoned, the population of local crops of wheat reverted back to a wild form, since those variants were more likely to survive without human intervention (Nadel 2002). A similar event occurred at Abu Hureyra, on the Euphrates in modern Syria, ten thousand years later. Like the settlers of Ohalo II, Abu Hureyra was occupied by hunter-gatherers who located at an ecologically rich site that afforded them access to a variety of food sources year-round. The cultivation and subsequent domestication of wheat and rye was one of a variety of emerging survival strategies. Once again, the crops reverted to wild varieties when abandoned (Moore, Hillman, & Legge 2000).

Between 10,000 and 9500 BCE, twelve thousand years ago, more substantial villages arose in the region that exploited a greater variety of plants, including domesticated figs. The largest of these, such as Jericho in Israel and Mureybet in Syria, grew to as many as eight hundred residents. But these were not truly agrarian villages just yet: cultivation was still a survival strategy that relied on hunting for meat—and therefore, remained semi-nomadic. By 8500 BCE, however, the first livestock—sheep and goats—had been domesticated in the mountains of western Iran and spread rapidly throughout the Fertile Crescent. (Dogs had been domesticated as hunting companions thousands of years earlier, as noted earlier.) Agrarian villages would dominate the landscape for the next four thousand years, some larger and some smaller, frequently in close contact with hunter-gatherers and pastoral nomads with their herds (Thomas 2010). As population densities in the Fertile Crescent grew to the capacity of the environment to support them, the populations spread in every direction. Genetic evidence traces their course from Turkey into southeastern Europe between 7000 and 3000 BCE. As others spread to the south, down the Tigris and Euphrates Valleys into what is now Iraq, the agrarian village encountered desert environments that required change.

From Village to City

Around 6000 BCE, bowing to population pressure, the Samarra Culture began its long trek southward along the Tigris and Euphrates rivers toward what would one day be known as Sumer in southern Mesopotamia (Maisels 1999). As today, traversing from north to south in Iraq brings one into evermore marginal land. This is relieved only by the rivers themselves until one reaches the marshes near the Persian Gulf. Southern Iraq was a desert in climate but home to alluvial soils lain by yearly floods—the mountain snows of Turkey fed the deluge. For the Samarra Culture, the adaptation to these increasingly marginal environments was the earliest experiments in irrigation, beginning as simple trenches but evolving over the years into the elaborate Mesopotamian canal system. In order for irrigation to work, however, more and more sophisticated technical and administrative practices were necessary. As the population spread south it "became" the Ubaid culture, an advanced pre-urban society built around a temple establishment for accumulating knowledge and managing the society. After 5000 BCE the Ubaid itself spread back across Mesopotamia.

Ubaid society was perhaps the earliest to experience a division of labor, being organized into social classes formulated and based on differing economic functions, skill levels, and rewards. The temple establishment developed a knowledge of astronomy that enabled them to know when to plant, when to fix the canals, and when to harvest (Maisels 1999). As our caloric plain model predicts, we find here, for the first time, a two-tier village system wherein the larger settlement contains the temple and conducted much regional trade, while the smaller was primarily dedicated to agriculture (the energy economy). The vast majority of people worked the fields, but the small elite in the temple and some private traders were relieved of such duties. The system worked well enough that it spread throughout the region, and very likely resulted in internecine fighting necessitating defensive walls. In time, a migration of people into larger and better protected settlements occurred. By 3500 BCE, some settlements had grown to twenty-five thousand, and the city of Uruk contained a staggering fifty thousand residents. If the Ubaid villages demanded social complexity to manage it all, the Uruk and Sumerian cultures of the fourth and third millennia are identifiably urban.

The archaeologist V. Gordon Childe (1950) developed a list of features that distinguished early cities from Neolithic agrarian villages and hunting-gathering societies. For those that have stood the test of time, they are identifiable not only by features of early cities but of cities today. As Smith (2009, pp. 9–13) notes, five of these are widely recognized traits that scientists continue to discuss and analyze today (paraphrased):

1. Early cities are more dense and populous than surrounding villages and farmsteads;
2. There is a complex division of labor, and as Durkheim theorized—a complex division of labor involves considerable interdependency of individuals;
3. There is a production of surplus goods utilized to pay for the operation of the state;
4. There are discernible social classes, with differentials in lifestyles and life chances;
5. There is a concentration of power in the upper classes.

Childe also noted the presence of monumental buildings as well as developed writing systems. Smith notes that writing is not always found in urban centers, as with the Inka and their predecessors, though there was recordkeeping for trade purposes. Perhaps the conceptualization of a writing system should be expanded to include such systems of records.

We have seen already that before the rise of the earliest cities in the mid-fourth millennium BCE there were elements of the above traits. Cities such as Uruk, Eridu, and Ur present a full culmination of these traits. In terms of population density (trait 1), the number of settlements in southern Mesopotamia declined as cities grew (Adams 1966). This likely represents an increase in warfare caused by a regionalized urban dependency since the entire region was approaching the carrying capacity. Indeed, at the Syrian site of Hamoukar, dating to the mid-fourth millennium BCE, the archaeological record indicates a stable northern Mesopotamian town was attacked, destroyed, and resettled by southern Mesopotamians likely looking for new land (Ur 2002). People flocked to larger protected settlements that grew denser.

The division of labor (trait 2) similarly grew more complex and culminated in the highly stratified urban settlements of the ancient world. Ubaid towns that held temples released their priests and priestesses from agricultural labor, and once this dynamic began the division of labor continued to expand. As social class (trait 4) is a function of the division of labor, the increasingly stratified societies that resulted in cities is expected. Indeed, neither is the concentration of power at the "top" of the social hierarchy (trait 5). Such societies were based on gleaning a surplus of agricultural production from rural areas to support the city, a trait that also increased over time.

Childe's mention of a production of surplus (trait 3) to pay for the state is an accurate description of the earliest cities, and it is worth noting that this surplus aligns well with our caloric plain model. Once a settlement has achieved a population that outstrips the capacity of its local environment to support it, it relies on the surplus of adjoining environments to support itself. As a village or town or city grows, it is dependent upon the surplus of other environments that must produce resources for their own populations as well as the urban center.

Urbanization is thus related to several features that we often (mis)attribute to capitalism. Though we find these features in modern capitalist society, they existed in advanced forms long before capitalism was invented. Cities are typically dense, although population densities can fluctuate between various urban environments. Cities in Southeast Asia, such as Angkor Wat, had high populations but were typically interspersed with agricultural fields. The resulting pattern was one of higher density than an agricultural society, but certainly not equivalent to the highly built-up patterns found in European cities. Even today, the patterns found in many American metropolitan areas are quite dense in the center of cities, but the expanding rings of suburbs and exurbs are considerably less dense than the city. For example, the outer exurbs of New York City, located about one hundred miles away or more in places such as Ulster County, have a sparse housing pattern. The town of Woodstock, for example, has minimum lot sizes of five acres—established to retain a rural character—that spreads development widely across the landscape. Thus, it is reminiscent of Angkor Wat's outer precincts more than of the density found in Midtown Manhattan.

Several of Childe's early city traits have to do with increasing social stratification. In order to organize and provide for a large population, a level of bureaucratization is necessary, and this follows from an expanding division of labor. Some institutions and individuals are more central than others, and to them both authority and power flow. As power flows to those near the "top" of societal hierarchies so does wealth, which in turn can be utilized to further solidify power (trait 5).

The basis of the whole system on the production and distribution of surplus (trait 3) enabled early cities to grow and thrive, and within cities enabled elites to control other forms of wealth as well as the lower classes. Once social stratification emerged, the control of surplus not only became an important feature of urban institutions but also an end in itself. As elites strove to distinguish themselves from the lower classes, the social pressure for ever more exotic goods pushed them to expand their trade relations. Early Mesopotamian elites traded manufactured goods for Afghan lapis lazuli, pearls from the Persian Gulf, and Egyptian wares. By the height of the Roman Empire, three thousand years later, Rome and the Chinese Han Dynasty extended their reach to one another in the mountains of central Asia. Today, elite preoccupations with exoticism drives much of the global economy. The world trading system emerging as a global world-system after AD 1500. With the emergence of the modern world-system, the framework of our own society, grounded on capitalistic accumulation and extensive global trade, became possible. Not surprisingly, capitalism is built upon earlier frameworks that emerged with urban-rural systems.

Money and Urban-Rural Dynamics

In western Turkey in the seventh century BCE, the Lydian Empire became the first kingdom on Earth to mint coins from a naturally occurring mixture of gold and silver known as *electrum*. The oblong coins were minted according to regular gradations, making coins of the same gradation interchangeable with others of the same value. With this invention the foundation of modern capitalism was laid, awaiting the further refinements of credit systems and joint-stock corporations that today dominate economic markets. The coins took the place of earlier (and irregular) media of exchange, including cowrie shells, grains, and various domesticated animals (Graeber 2012).

It is a common misperception that the value of money is derived from its inherent value as a commodity, such as a coin's weight in gold. The relationship between money and value has, since the Bronze Age, been related to the value of commodities. Ancient Mesopotamian and Egyptian valuation of products is related to a standardized weight in silver, called a *shekel*. Such a system of exchange worked only so long as two products, such as food and silver, were in more or less regular demand. If one item became scarcer, however, the balance would be thrown off: a measure of silver, no matter the utility of metal objects, is always less desirable than food in the energy economy. In a sense, a trading system based on money is reliant on some level of stability over time that allows a money system to develop. A series of prices from ancient Babylon during the first millennium BCE, for example, showed a working market in terms of relative price stability over several hundred years, but dramatic spikes during the conquest of the region by Alexander the Great made food more of a concern than silver (Temin 2017). Of course, food is *always* more important than silver in the energy economy, but in a society in which access to food seems to be a given, a higher order market in silver can exist. Given a cultural assumption about the availability of food, traders are able to conceptualize themselves as trading for silver or other commodities. This enabled a distortion to occur between actual food prices—or, put another way, the cost of human energy—and the price of money. As money itself has evolved over time, from early coinage stamped with a particular value, to paper money, to the blips on a computer screen today, the value of a unit of money in relation to a unit of food (dollars per calorie, for instance) may roam widely, detached from the essential purpose of the human economy: to provide for human sustenance.

There is now alienation between the value of money in relation to caloric value. Indeed, in a capitalist society, it is common to assume that economics centers on money rather than energy, but this condition is not necessarily unique to capitalism. Any complex society generates a particular circuitry of production, and the more complex the circuitry becomes, the more alienated the consumer is from the source of energy consumption. The two basic circuits can be understood as *rural production* and *urban production*.

Urban and Rural Production Circuits

Within the energy economy, nature itself (starting with the sun) provides for the production of energy resources. Plants grow at their own pace according to their own physiology and environmental conditions. Humans can help or hinder these conditions by, for example, manipulating the fertility of the soil or amount of water present. In the end it is the plant that grows itself. Humans might be able to influence the process, but ultimately it is the plant's needs to which the human must cater. Similarly, certain types of fuel, wheth-er wood, coal, or petroleum, develop according to nature's mechanisms. In each case, humans must harvest these ores and resources at their point of origin. The harvest of natural energy is *rural production*, and due to its characteristics tends to take place in rural contexts. That said, urban settle-ments can and have grown up around rural production, such as those found in mining regions like Scranton, Pennsylvania.

With the harvest of raw materials, the processing of such materials into finished products constitutes a second circuit: *urban production*. Technically, the processing of a twig into a tool for harvesting termites by a chimpanzee is a rudimentary version of this second circuit. When two or more resources from differing areas are brought together for processing, however, a qualitatively different process emerges. Urban production requires the producer to plan ahead for acquisition of resources, and often involves gathering the resources in one place. As Thomas et al. (2011, 45–46) noted:

> true urban production involves a multiplicity of circuits of production: it is the collection of multiple resources from differentiated environments in a specific site for the purpose of transforming them into a finished product.

Urban production typically requires minimal space for processing, and the massive scale of such production is often an attempt to produce large amounts of products. For example, once the materials are in place, an individual can, in principal, build a car in their garage. The simple assembly requires that the harvest of raw materials from the environment (the rural circuit) has taken place elsewhere, as well as intermediary urban production circuits (e.g., fashioning of steel into doors, manufacture of a radio). The massive scale of an automobile factory comes not from the space needed to assemble an individual automobile, but from the (1) desire to produce as many as needed in an efficient manner, and (2) the collection of multiple circuits of the manufacturing process under one roof. In the first instance the answer will be an assembly line, and in the second, as collection of particular micro-manufacture facilities (one for stamping doors, one for building dashboards, etc.) in the same complex. As urban production involves multiple and complex circuits of production and trade, particularly in today's global economy, it tends to be concentrated in spatially small but demographically large locations. In other words, cities.

Consider the model of urban-rural dynamics at the beginning of this chapter. As a settlement grows it outstrips the capacity of the local environment to provide food resources, and as the resource horizon expands, secondary centers develop to more efficiently harvest and transport resources to the primary center. This is a simple urban-rural system, and as such systems become more populous it forces the resource horizon further afield, thereby generating tertiary centers, and so on. Each secondary settlement conducts resources through the system on the way to a primary center, but what is directed back to the rural communities? As early as the Ubaid period, the larger towns traded manufactured goods for rural products, sometimes for food but often for raw materials out of which manufactured goods could be made, such as pearls from the Persian Gulf region. In such a network of trade, each settlement functions as a site of transit between the other settlements in the network. In addition to rural production activities (e.g., farming) and urban production activities (e.g., pottery production), the settlement will accumulate transit functions. Transit functions are activities related to trade, including local markets, accommodations for visitors, and communications. In a highly frequented settlement, transit functions might become a significant proportion of the economy, enough so that they attract additional population in order to staff them.

The more urban dependent a settlement, the more complex the networks involved in the provision of resources, the more transit functions each settlement accumulates, and the higher the population is likely to climb—thus producing a deeper caloric well and more urban dependency. When an entire region is urban dependent, such as southern Mesopotamia was dependent upon resources from northern Mesopotamia and western Iran during the third millennium BCE, it is understood as *regionalized* urban dependency. As with a more localized version, the urban-rural system is forced to look further afield for resources, likely coming into conflict with neighbors as they do the same. As resources, whether basic foodstuffs or luxury materials for manufacturing, come from farther distances, the original source of such rural products and the rural labor that produced them are obscured. The introduction of money aggravated these alienating processes.

Capitalism, Alienation, and Modern Urban-Rural Dynamics

Urban-rural systems evolve over long spans of time, becoming more complex at certain moments in history and sometimes losing complexity as such dynamics interact with the environment. An invasion by distant armies, a period of volcanism, climate change, or an epidemic can dramatically alter the fate of an urban-rural system. Even a level of social complexity that becomes inefficient or too extensive to be managed effectively can lead to a collapse of one power and subsequent rise of another. World history is rich with such cases of collapse, with significant events surrounding the end of the Bronze Age around 1200 BCE and, of course, the fall of the Western Roman Empire at the end of the fifth century. Major power centers in one century may be reduced to ruin a century later. There are numerous minor events that are not always even recorded historically. Such booms and busts are found throughout history at all levels of society. The decoupling of caloric value from monetary value may agitate such conditions further. In our own time, capitalism has been the dominant economic system, a system dependent upon the alienation of labor—expended energy—from capital, or the resources available to aid in the production of industry, finances, knowledge, raw materials, and so forth.

It is important to first recall that the alienation of rural labor and resources is not specific to capitalism. It arose with the rise of the first urban-rural systems, and with the ability of some portion of the society to live independent of the energy economy, relying on distant rural labor for sustenance. An early step toward alienated rural labor was taken during the Ubaid period of the fifth millennium BCE in the Fertile Crescent, with its rudimentary temples and associated priests responsible for administering production. The trade circuitry required for urban production evident in the earliest cities in the region after 3500 BCE further alienated rural production from urban. It is unlikely that many artisans in ancient Uruk or Eridu had much sense of the labor of Afghans producing lapis lazuli. By the turn of the Common Era, Rome was dependent upon the labor of peasants in North Africa, and Roman elites stressed the need to retain military and political control of the region rather than perceiving the situation as it was: a state of regionalized urban dependency that was supported by African grains. Empire building was a consequence of urban dependency. The loss of North Africa was arguably the final blow against the ailing Western Roman Empire, a condition that led to a violent and virulent depopulation of the city and its immediate countryside. As such, it is more accurate to say that capitalism aggravates existing dynamics of oppression and alienated labor that initially took form thousands of years earlier in urban, but not capitalist societies.

For Marx (1990 [1867]), the alienation of labor refers to the alienation of a producer from the final project, and associated profit, resulting from urban production. A cobbler produces shoes, and enjoys the wages from such labor, but in a capitalist economy is replaced by a machine. The causes and effects of such alienated labor, including the mechanization of labor, the deskilling of production, and the appropriation of surplus value from the worker to the owner of the means of production are standards of Marxist analysis. However, from where did the cobbler acquire the leather, itself a processed rural good in the form of cattle, which may have served as a source of dairy products before finding its way to the craftsman's shop? Or from what mines were the tin and copper harvested, which in turn were further processed into the brass tacks used to secure the sole to the top of the shoe? Or the wool for the shoelaces? Or, for that matter, the food that the cobbler will buy with the proceeds of production, whether as a price garnered by an independent producer or as a wage laborer? In each case, the assumption of rural labor involved in rural production is made but not placed at the center of the analysis. Even when raw materials are acquired, they are paid for with money or by barter with manufactured goods, both of which presuppose the existence of an urban economy to produce such value.

It is in the interest of a capitalist class to limit the costs of rural products, whether raw materials for urban production or the food on which the urban working class must subsist. Prior to capitalism, an urban-rural system is engaged in a (often fruitless) struggle to find a balance between the needs of urban consumers and the rural producers; the profit motive is present, but the alienation between urban consumer and rural producer is less evident. In modern capitalism, however, this dynamic is enhanced by the fact that not only must the system provide for the sustenance of urban consumers but must do so in such a way that maximizes the profits of the capitalist class. This, of course, turns rural producers into proletarians in the same way that mechanizing shoe production turns skilled labor into proletarians. With rural producers, however, capitalism and urban dependency operate to create additional dynamics.

In the event that there is a balance between the food produced in an urban-rural system and the number of people to be supported, prices for agricultural products will remain stable over time. This worked in pre-capitalist systems where the bulk of profits could be gleaned from urban production, but in capitalism the drive to lower wages for the working classes creates additional incentives to lower the costs of agricultural production as well. One way of doing this is to expand the sphere of influence well beyond the carrying capacity of the system to ensure an oversupply of agricultural goods, thereby driving prices lower. As the Industrial Revolution took hold, however, an additional mechanism became possible: the mechanization of production. This also generated an oversupply of agricultural products while also bringing more rural laborers into the money system, a condition that allows for selling them urban goods. As Thomas (2005) noted:

> In both cases, prices of agricultural products are lowered and with them the "fixed" costs associated with the reproduction of labor. Capitalist producers are thus able to lower wages and in so doing the surplus labor of not only the worker but the farmer as well is transferred to the capitalist. (p. 9)

The integration of rural production into the capitalist economy through the corporatization of agriculture further increases profits by the ability to control both rural labor and the means of production, both in terms of required land and the machines necessary for production.

Capitalism further exacerbates urban-rural dynamics by favoring urban producers in larger cities over those in smaller cities and towns. Cities are, in effect, demographic machines that capitalize on the scale of production that enable costs to be lowered. The larger local markets available in large cities enable their firms to grow larger due to the presumption of market sales, an advantage that similar producers in smaller cities have a correspondingly smaller amount. As similar firms in a particular region grow and merge, it is the larger firms found in larger cities that typically have the advantage when acquiring other firms. Corporate concentration typically has a spatial component: over time larger cities grow still larger and wealthier, whereas smaller cities and towns are stripped of their once-local firms. Firms in larger cities may also be aided by economies of agglomeration, and as such, particular industries tend to consolidate into a handful of very large firms, and this in turn favors urban centers for even greater investment over time. As Thomas (2005) observed:

> It is thus important to recognize that global cities are the beneficiaries of the increased concentration of the world economy precisely because they are in fact so large—their corporations have used their city's size and location as a vehicle for growth that eventually allows them to take over the corporations of smaller communities (see also Sassen, 1991). Not surprisingly, the relationship of the near hinterland thus changes over time as its own institutions and pro-ductive capacity is first absorbed into the city and gradually surpassed by the lower labor costs found in more distant locales. (10)

When one considers how urban-rural dynamics underlie and interact with capitalist forces, the increasing concentration of capital in ever larger cities, both within the United States and globally, is understandable. For example, when, in 2018, Amazon was considering options for a second headquarters, it ultimately split between New York City and the Washington, DC area—two metropolitan areas that hardly needed economic investment. Amazon cited existing infrastructure and educated workforces for the decision, but likely could have saved millions of dollars in wages by choosing a smaller metro-politan area. As is often the case, like other firms, Amazon chose to pay higher labor costs in cities with existing urban resources and amenities over less urbanized regions where such infrastructure and housing would need to be augmented if not created entirely anew.

TAKEAWAYS

Many people think of rural and urban economies as separate and discon-nected and might indulge the urbanormative fantasy that urban economies are more advanced, superior, and complete than rural economies—perhaps even capable of self-sufficiency. Part of what feeds this fantasy is a lack of understanding for how the energy economy works for urban-rural systems that create urban dependency. The money economy tends to obscure the fragility of urban dependency, reinforcing urbanormative beliefs. While rural production is essential from an energy perspective, the decoupled money economy tends to devalue rural inputs. The vast supply of rural resources flowing into urban areas may even go unnoticed, from basic food stuffs grown on distant farms to feed hungry mouths, to the coal mined in distant places to feed the electric grid, to the oil and gas that was mined thousands of miles away to power transportation. The urbanormative fantasy takes these rural inputs for granted. The reality of urban-rural systems is that there is no truly "urban" economy without a "rural" economy that undergirds it. Urban settlements are not plugged into the energy economy, yet the inhabitants have a very intense demand to consume energy in all of its forms—they are truly dependent.

For their part, rural economies are plugged directly into the energy economy, but are also defined by trade with urban populations. When the terms of trade are forced upon them, the rural surplus is appropriated forcefully by urban authorities and elites. Fortunately, since the end of colonialism, this coercive appropriation has become less common. Through modern capitalist markets the surplus is not appropriated, but the fruits of rural production can be so poorly compensated that the end result is very nearly the same. The rural surplus benefits urban markets, while rural communities languish, often unable to buy the products produced in those urban markets. Though trade is central to rural economics, the notion of rural dependency is not equivalent to urban dependency. This is because rural settlements maintain, at least in theory, the ability to revert to self-sufficient agrarianism. The miles and miles with row after row of cornfields in the American Midwest are grown for trade, not local consumption. Rare is the Iowan farmer who dreams of a return to agrarian existence with no strings at all tied to the larger urban world. Yet, the Ethiopian coffee farmer, who finds his harvest incapable of feeding his family may entertain this idea in a very visceral way.

Urban-rural systems are not based on equitable trade. Even when obscured by urbanormative cultural assumptions, the underlying structural dynamics of urban dependency, urban domination of the hinterland, and alienated rural labor may be invisible but remain ever-present. The line between the economy of humans and the ecology of the energy in our environment should be erased, and the oikos should be embraced. Urbanormativity is the ideology that hides these realities. We now turn, in the following chapters, to a deeper investigation into the how and why of urbanormativity.

Part II

The Representation

Chapter Four

Cultural Capital and Urbanormativity

Cultural capital is at once an interesting and difficult concept to grasp. The French sociologists, Pierre Bourdieu (1983) coined this concept and used it to understand how social class and privilege were being reproduced in society. Cultural capital is multifaceted, encompassing such things as the way we walk and talk, our modes of dress, and the types of knowledge we possess, the objects we own, and the institutions to which we have access—all indicate differing levels of status and prestige. The primary mechanisms he identified were informal socialization along with formal education.

One of the core theses that we wish to make is that, in urban society, cultural capital is closely linked to urbanormative standards within a place-based cultural hierarchy (Ching and Creed 1997) that locates rustic people in the lowest stratum and urbane people at the top. Markers of rustic identity limit institutional rewards that one needs to achieve upward social mobility. Expressions of urbanity, in contrast, bestow upon the holder certain assumptions of superior intellect, capability, and overall value. Urbanites are understood as cultural assets, while rustics, stereotypically, are viewed as inferior, unintelligent, and backward. There is a paradoxical possibility rural people will be viewed simultaneously in a positive light—rustics may be granted such attributes as having moral clarity or idyllic country charm. Indeed, there is strong evidence of a "rural mystique," "rural idyll," or a "rural myth" in American culture (Willits, Theodori, & Fortunato 2016), as well as in the European context (Mingay 1989; Bunce 1994; Bell 2006). These ideal traits can translate into lofty expectations of rustics held by urbanites that, for many rural people, will be difficult to meet. Even if they are matched, these expectations carry an inherently limiting quality—reducing rural people to an idealized notion of rurality and not leaving room for more holistic expressions of identity or individuality. For example, rural Native Americans are often held to the standard of the "noble savage," which is a picture of identity that tends to trap individuals in the costumes and lifestyles of the nineteenth century. The idealized imagination of Native American identity does not allow room for expressions that are more modern, pragmatic, or realistic.

In this chapter we wish to consider the meaning of cultural capital, explore how it applies to individuals, explain how cultural capital fits within a broader community through the "capitals" framework, and focus on how it is transmitted through a discussion of legacy, family, and formal education and schooling. The emphasis will be on the cultural hierarchy that is created and maintained by urbanormative hegemony.

FORMS OF CULTURAL CAPITAL

In defining cultural capital, Bourdieu (1977) delineated three types—embodied, objectified, and institutionalized. Embodied cultural capital is most closely related to socialization of the individual. If one is socialized into a rustic identity, they learn to walk and talk as a rural person, and to demonstrate values and ideals consistent with this upbringing. What it means to be rustic varies substantially from culture to culture, and from place to place, yet the indication of rusticity is almost universally taken as a measure of low cultural capital in urban society. One important dimension of this is linguistic capital. Language signals both social location and identity. Perhaps more than anything else, what separates rustic from urbane identity is language or dialect difference. An entire volume, by Seale and Mallinson (2018), entitled *Rural Voices*, explores this in depth. The editors note that, while no language or dialect is inherently better than another, rural-identified language markers often come to be viewed as inferior. The notion of embodied cultural capital, therefore, elevates culture from the ideal to the material world. It is the physical embodiment of culture, evident in the form of the being who carries it.

Objectified cultural capital exists outside of individuals and is found in the different things that one may possess. Bourdieu observed that possessing an abstract work of art conveys high cultural capital in Western cultures. He further argued that it was not enough to simply own the art. One also needed to have the ability to interpret the value of the work by displaying their abstract knowledge of high art—thus drawing on embodied cultural capital. This display of high cultural knowledge allows a privileged background to become known. Not coincidentally, major art institutes and art schools are located almost universally in elite urban settings. In contrast, artwork associated with rustics is often regarded as quaint "folk" art. While it may be valued as charming, is not held to the same level of esteem and prestige—it is low in cultural capital.

When we investigate objectified cultural capital, we search for items that signal rusticity or urbanity. In the United States, stereotypical rustic objects include such things as pickup trucks, shotguns, rifles, plaid shirts, farming implements, hunting gear, forestry tools, along with country music, television, and film media, and lifestyle objects such as chewing tobacco and alcohol. These items signal rustic identity in the United States and locate one within a broader cultural hierarchy. Interestingly, it is not as easy to identify objects associated with urbanity—perhaps because it is not marked as the marginal "other." Rather, urbane is the default or baseline referential category in the context of urbanormativity, and therefore, all cultural objects that are not identified with rusticity may be considered urbane. Urbane objects are taken to be the "normal" objects of life, while rustic objects are unusual, exotic, or disgusting and inferior. Whether the assessment is positive or negative, in either case, rustic is marked.

Institutional cultural capital refers to various rewards, such as credentials from a university or employment with a prestigious firm, that allows for upward mobility. In a place-based cultural hierarchy, it is institutional cultural capital that decides who moves up in the world. In order to access institutional rewards, individuals must display their embodied and objectified cultural capital. For example, a prospective college student applying to an elite urban university may try to convey that they have the appropriate background and upbringing to make them a good fit. A careful display or urbane language, dress, and interaction will be offered. Rustic students may try to bolster their linguistic capital by concealing a marked dialect, or hide the objects that mark them as rustic, dressing in more generic urbane attire, for instance. These acts of presenting an urbane self are also something that happens in job interviews, where candidates create an impression by managing the display of embodied and objectified cultural capital.

Were it not for institutions, cultural capital would have little consequence beyond interpersonal reputation and esteem. Institutional cultural capital allows individuals to achieve financial or human capital gains. A rustic may be denied access to institutional rewards. Belonging to a group that is marked as "other" bears institutional costs, and oftentimes, individuals seek ways to overcome or hide their identity. For our present purpose, we are interested in how urbanity functions as a source of cultural capital that grants individuals access to institutional rewards, and correspondingly, how rusticity functions to deny access. Cultural capital, however, is not the exclusive property of individuals—it is also an asset possessed by entire communities. This was not something that was considered in Bourdieu's theorization.

Community Cultural Capital

As we consider urbanormativity and cultural capital, we need to look beyond individuals and institutions and toward entire communities. While not considered by Bourdieu, we claim that community cultural capital is another important form. The community capitals' framework (Emery & Flora 2006; Flora & Flora 2015) situates it within a wider matrix that also includes political, economic, natural, built, human, and social capital. Rural communities vary in the kinds of strengths or assets that they possess. Some offer wonderful natural capital—beautiful parks, lakes, vistas. Others have high political capital by virtue of being a county seat, for instance. Other communities offer supportive social networks to members (social capital). Some provide superior opportunities for gainful employment (financial capital). The holistic community capitals' framework was developed as a tool for comprehensively evaluating and measuring community progress and development. It also provides a means for assessing the variety of community rewards that members may enjoy. In this regard, community cultural capital runs parallel to institutional cultural capital. Just as institutions grant rewards, so too do communities.

If we apply Bourdieu's ideas of cultural capital to the community, we must adjust our focus to a more macro level. Cultural capital at the community level winds up referring to collective expressions of norms, values, customs, language, patterns of social interaction, modes of dress, and acceptable types of behavior. When individuals conform to local norms in a rural community, they may be granted membership or insider status, and with that, all of the benefits the community has to offer. In an urban community context, the very same individual may be marked as a marginal outsider, thereby closing access to community rewards. As urban communities often have more employment and educational opportunities, being denied this access will have substantial consequences for individuals.

As rustics negotiate their identity and associated expressions of cultural capital, they must consider the trade-off between maintaining local rural ties and accessing extra-local urban community rewards. Accepting a rustic identity may therefore be limiting. Urban communities generally offer more opportunities for human, social, and economic growth. Rejecting rusticity diminishes local ties but opens doors to these rewards. Contending with an urbane identity does not typically present this dilemma. The urbane may enjoy access to urban rewards without losing local ties.

At the community level, objectified cultural capital is inscribed in the built environment. As one walks down the streets of a rustic community, the sight of animals, trees, and other forms of nature may be featured prominently. A business, such as a restaurant, may display rusticity through architecture and a variety of rustic objects—taxidermed animals, log cabin exteriors, signs with names like "Country Kitchen," furniture that has the appearance of unrefined wood, artwork that displays bucolic country settings, and so forth. These objects are strategically placed to signal rusticity that also help to define acceptable local norms. We return to these ideas in a later chapter on community and rural simulacra. We next turn the discussion toward a deeper understanding of cultural transmission, along with a reflection on urbanormative hegemony.

TRANSMISSION AND HEGEMONY

Drawing on Swidler (1986, p. 273), Flora and Flora (2015) note that culture provides a "toolkit of symbols, stories, rituals, and worldviews" (Flora & Flora 2015, p. 56). Culture has a material basis manifested in such objects as food, clothing, machines, and gadgets, and in back of these are immaterial components such as music, language, and customs. Flora and Flora (2015, p. 55) define cultural capital by, "what constitutes knowledge, how knowledge is to be achieved, and how knowledge is validated." The dominant groups in society have the ability to elevate their own values over competing groups, while building narratives around their experiences as the focal point of historical change. This is one of the defining features of cultural hegemony. One of the central questions in studying culture capital is understanding how hegemony is transmitted and socially reproduced.

The notion of legacy offered by Flora and Flora (2015) is helpful, as it reminds us that the culture we are born into is not a culture of our own making—it is inherited from previous generations. The material and immaterial components of culture were designed through trial and error, as generations of people learned to live and adapt to different conditions. Flora and Flora (2015) draw our attention to the legacy inherited by the youngest generation of the Owens Valley Paiute People of California, observing a generational rift. The younger generation was becoming less interested in their legacy, instead drawn to life in mainstream urban society. With the abandonment of legacy comes the associated loss of language, identity, knowledge of how to live and survive in a particular place, the benefits that come from traditional spiritual practices and rituals, and the strength of connection this forms to a wider community. In this example, the dominant urban culture has furthered its hegemonic reach.

This disruption of Paiute cultural transmission is not accidental—it was orchestrated through larger policies, such as the Dawes Act of 1887, that forced Native Americans to abandon traditions, to speak English, to attend public boarding schools, to worship in Christian churches, and to dress in European garments. Beyond cultural damage, land policies effectively removed Native American public land use rights that were crucial to maintaining independence through self-sufficient foraging—this forced them to become dependent private farmers. A resistance movement led by a Paiute man named Wakova (aka. Jack Wilson) offered a desperate attempt to reassert control of culture but was put down violently by the now infamous massacre of the Lakota at Wounded Knee.

What this lesson teaches is that a dominant culture will retain its hegemonic control by any means necessary—perhaps beginning peacefully, through influencing education and socialization, but when needed, falling back on violence to overcome resistance. In the United States, middle- and upper-class white hegemony has operated this way for centuries. Minority groups have resisted, clinging to alternative legacies with desperate determination, only to face backlash and various forms of repression. While racial and class-based forms of hegemony have received a fair share of scholarly attention, there has been comparatively little focus on the urban-rural dimension. There is a need for a deeper understanding of how hegemonic urbanormative ideology—the widespread belief in the superiority of urban over rural culture(s)—is transmitted across generations.

Family and Legacy

While formal education is centrally important to the process of cultural transmission (discussed in the next section), the process of informal socialization begins at home with family. Families provide the next generation with a "toolkit" that helps them navigate their world, develop a sense of meaning and purpose, and build a connection to community. Families that work in traditional rural occupations—farming, mining, forestry, fishing, and so forth—generally develop the view that work does not require a great deal of formal education. It does require, however, a great deal of knowledge, passed down informally through legacy and socialization. In contrast, urbane youth are taught to prepare for a life that depends on formal education. They are often expected to leave their home community to receive education and develop a career.

Rustic youth are deeply affected by urbanormative hegemony, saddled with the tradeoff between maintaining local ties versus developing new prospects for personal growth. They must leave traditional rural occupations and communities behind in order to secure access to urban rewards of advanced education and gainful employment. In order to experience mobility, they may feel a need to reinvent themselves with an urbane identity.

Thorburn's (2018) analysis of a remote rural community in Nain, Nunatsiavut offers an illustration. She writes of disruptions in the transmission of culture across generations of Canadian Inuit living in Labrador, emphasizing the crisis of losing Inuttitut/Inuktitut language. Historically, Nain was founded by Moravian Christian missionaries seeking to proselytize the local

Inuit populations—a form of religious hegemonic control. Shortly after the missionary work took hold, many of the Labrador Inuit began to abandon foraging, opting for a more settled life, though still largely relying on self-sufficiency. The loss of language began in the 1950s as Provincial mandates required English to be the primary language of education, coupled with policies forcing participation in the formal education system. These policies resemble those of the Dawes Act in the United States. Thorburn suggests that the language shift was partly forced but adds that family members would often volunteer to speak English in the home to help the younger generation find success in school. This inadvertently accelerates language shift and loss and the demise of local culture. While the older generation is pained to see their culture abandoned, they recognize the sacrifice the younger generation must make in order to remain local—lost opportunities for personal growth and upward mobility.

As Thorburn's example demonstrates, through legacy, family plays a central role in preparing the next generation for success in life. If a legacy is viewed as a liability rather than an asset, the family may abandon cultural transmission. While this may prepare youth for a more successful urbane life, it does not bode well for the future of tiny but unique rural cultures and languages.

URBANORMATIVE EDUCATION AND SCHOOLING

After family, the most powerful agent of socialization—the core mechanism for transmitting cultural legacy—is formal education and schooling. Formal education can serve to disrupt cultural legacy handed down by families, as noted in the above examples. Curricula tend to reflect the dominant urbanormative culture, acting to expand its hegemonic reach (Sipple & Brent 2015) by creating an experience that denies the value of rural community while affirming the importance of urban social change, development, and history. As rustic youth are educated in such curricula, they are prepared for a future in an urban settlement, with an implied assumption that the student will eventually feel the need and desire to leave their home communities. Unfortunately, if this comes to fruition, they leave behind their social networks of support (bonding social capital). As success in education (and beyond) often depends on such support, this disadvantage may be setting youth up for failure. This may explain why rural students, who outperform their urban counterparts on the National Assessment of Education Progress in the United States, are still less likely to attend college (Schafft & Jackson 2011).

The social theorist, James Coleman (1988), once wrote an influential article that explained how social capital was important to the development of human capital. His study found that high school students who were most likely to succeed lived in supportive communities with high levels of surveillance and social control, widely shared expectations, open information channels, and high levels of trust. In other words, the kinds of characteristics one might expect to find in a rural community (Wilkinson 1991). Students living in the absence of these conditions were found to have a higher probability of dropping out (Schafft & Jackson 2011). The prospects for rural youth success after leaving home for urban educations are thus daunting from the outset.

Rather than argue that educational success results from social capital within the community, Bourdieu was more interested in how the cultural hierarchy was reproduced through education. Bourdieu (1983) considered multiple capitals—economic, social, symbolic, human, and cultural—that he claimed were convertible. He asserted that one could trade in their cultural capital for economic gains or use it to build their human capital. An individual could leverage their privileged cultural position to obtain institutional rewards (institutional cultural capital). Coleman's argument that social capital creates human capital, is consistent with Bourdieu's notion of convertibility. What Coleman failed to consider was the role of cultural capital and legacy. Urban students with a high level of cultural capital might be able to overcome the deficit of a weak social network (a deficit in bonding social capital) and still find success. Rural students living in an urban setting will lack both cultural capital and supportive bonding social capital, creating a double disadvantage. The low cultural capital also finds expression through lowered expectations of rural students that can turn into a self-fulfilling prophecy (Avery & Sipple 2016).

Unfortunately, neither Bourdieu nor Coleman were concerned with urban-rural differences in cultural, human, or social capital. We build on their ideas by asserting that in urbanormative culture, the value of rural is diminished with far reaching consequences for the transmission of culture. This is especially the case when urbanormative standards shape education policy (Sipple & Brent 2015). The view that rural is backward and deviant—the hallmark of urbanormativity—helps legitimate an educational curriculum that is urban-centric. It justifies the closure of rural schools creating a dependency on city school boards. It promotes the rural brain drain that facilitates the export of talented rural youth away from their communities (Carr and Kefalas 2009), while enhancing the human capital of urban centers.

Formal education plays a crucial role in developing cultural capital early in life. Rural students are often taught a hidden lesson when entering into the formal education system: that their community has little to no value for their education. They are presented with history lessons that emphasize urban-centric narratives of social change and development, while emphasizing the important role played by characters who reside outside of their local community. They are taught math, science, and literature in a way that could easily be transplanted to any community—implying that knowledge is universal and that local experience is irrelevant (Avery & Kasam 2011).

Generally, the goal of education policy is to provide a uniform and homogeneous experience (Sipple & Brent 2015). While there are certainly benefits to making sure children are reaching basic milestones in learning, the creation of a singular learning experience inadvertently privileges dominant identities and cultures. Urbanormativity is embedded in this uniform curriculum, in which the importance and value of local rural communities is seldom celebrated or even mentioned, and is never part of the expected learning outcomes (Schafft & Jackson 2011). A rural student might be able to identify when the Declaration of Independence was signed, but not the year when their own village was incorporated. They may be able to identify the president of the United States, but not their own community's mayor. They may learn about the Industrial Revolution, but not the economic factors that led to the settlement of their hometown. If it is not on the test, it is probably not going to be taught.

In response to this homogenizing tendency in education, scholarly attention has been moving toward alternatives such as Place Based Learning (PBL) (Avery & Sipple 2016). The goal of PBL is to reverse the homogenizing trend by emphasizing and celebrating the uniqueness of local community. The same subjects and learning outcomes can be achieved, but the methods by which they are taught frame them in a locally-relevant manner. Avery and Kassam (2011) note that many rural students already possess impressive STEM knowledge that they develop outside of the classroom, and if connections are made for them by teachers, they may actually achieve more. The implementation of paradigms like PBL, however, will be hindered by a policy that does not allow teachers the freedom to explore locally relevant issues, instead teaching to the urban-centric standardized tests such as what is contained in the Common Core in the United States.

School Closure and Consolidation

In addition to promoting standardization and urban-centric curricula, education policy over the last century has privileged the goals of efficiency and austerity over community well-being and rural student performance. This has justified the widespread consolidation of schools and associated rash of school closures. In 1930, the United States hosted 128,000 school districts containing over 238,000 schools. By 1980, this was reduced to just 16,000 school districts and 61,000 schools—the bulk of this loss was in rural communities where 90 percent of one or two teacher classrooms were lost between 1910 and 1960 (DeYoung & Howley 2009). Of course, the true political economic reasons for school closures are often obscured by a rhetoric that emphasizes the enhancement of quality schooling, but the veracity of this claim is thin. We would maintain that behind the push toward school consolidation is urbanormative bias that imagines rural schools to be inferior, backward, and incapable of producing talented graduates. Research on rural school performance often shows the reverse. While rural schools do tend to lag behind privileged suburban schools, they also outperform inner city schools (Brown & Schafft 2019; Schafft & Jackson 2011). Rural student success can be credited to a lower teacher to student ratio that allows more individualized attention. In large overcrowded schools that are typical of urban settings, it is easier to go unnoticed and slip through the cracks.

With so few rural schools to choose from, school-aged children in rural communities are now saddled with the detrimental consequences of vast physical space. The consequences of space (and time) that must be negotiated to attend school is something that has not received a great deal of scholarly attention. An exploratory study by Talen (2001) found that spatial distance accounted for a statistically significant reduction in third grade test scores in a West Virginia school district. This case study, while exploratory, provides evidence against policies that promote busing as a replacement for preserving rural schools. While further research is needed, the evidence suggests that rural students are disadvantaged by space and time that could have been better spent on studying (Talen 2001).

The closure of schools in rural communities can also result in a stigma for students now being bussed to a new school in a neighboring community. In his discussion of the closing of Hartwick Elementary School in 1978, Thomas (2003) notes that students bussed to neighboring Cooperstown often felt stigmatized by their peers, simply because they were from a rural community. In addition to the impact on students, the loss of the school as an important attractor point in Hartwick, was accompanied by a collapse of the local economy. The local supermarket, hardware store, and several other businesses closed as both school employment and customers frequenting the village, due to the school, were now being drawn to the village next door instead.

Thus, beyond the individual student, is the community impact of school closure. An early and prescient article on this topic was published by Sanderson (1938), who warned of the central place of schools in the process of rural community formation. Rejecting the logic of closing schools for the sake of efficiency—something that was already underway by the 1930s—Sanderson (1938, p. 379) claims, "placing the school outside of the community alienates community interest and control." Emphasizing the value of autonomous rural communities, Sanderson derides the movement toward mass education in cities, which he views as more vulnerable to demagoguery and "uncontrolled individualism." Sanderson appears to have anticipated urbanormative policies and standards, while advocating against them.

School consolidation may also be taken as evidence that rural communities are lacking in political capital—if it was higher, the ability to resist consolidation might be stronger and the rate of closure would be lower. The story of school consolidation has been one of long-standing decline, fostering reliance on urban schools that disadvantage rural students, while undermining the organization, autonomy, and control of rural communities. The net result of this is enhanced urban advantage over diminished rural communities.

TAKEAWAYS

As we reflect on the concept of cultural capital in the context of urban-rural dynamics, our focus turns to the creation and maintenance of urbanormative hegemony and hierarchy. The way a society comes to value individuals and communities is at the heart of this discussion. Through the passing down of legacy and other forms of cultural transmission, urban society prepares the next generation of urbanites to rise to the upper echelon, while standing on the backs of rustics who are consigned to the lowest rung of place-based stratification. Indeed, as urban dependency grows deeper, the need to control and dominate rural populations grows more intense, as discussed earlier.

A range of tactics has been employed to corner the market on cultural capital, including attempts to disrupt legacy and transmission of culture across generations within the family. This is most pronounced in cases where linguistic cleavages form across generations, as is often the case with such indigenous rural groups as the Labrador Inuit of Canada. Other attempts to disrupt cultural transmission include those that shape the content and structure of education and schooling. Not only are mainstream educational curricula designed to reinforce an urban-centric and urbanormative worldview, the physical closing and consolidating of rural schools presents spatial hurdles and challenges that disadvantage rural youth, who, if successful, are more likely to leave their home community through the brain drain. Over time, rural communities are devalued, and gradually disassembled through youth out-migration.

The cultural hierarchy that we have discussed appears at the individual level through embodied, objectified, and institutional forms. Institutional rewards—central to maintaining hierarchy—are reserved for those demonstrating urbane qualities through the way they carry themselves in talk and posture (embodied cultural capital) and through the possession of objects that mark them as urbane (objectified cultural capital). In contrast, the embodiment of rustic identity—such as being from a rural town like Hartwick, New York—and the possession of rustic objects marks an individual as unworthy of institutional rewards.

At the community level, cultural hierarchy assumes a more aggregated form. The physical expression of a rural community, as is often seen in the built environment through roads, buildings, and overall character, while it may be regarded in quaint or idyllic terms, is generally understood to be abnormal against the backdrop of an urban referent. The identity of a community can be marked as the embodiment and objectification of rusticity (a theme to which we return in a later chapter).

A central tool for preserving, creating, or disrupting cultural capital is formal schooling. As noted, rural communities are up against a multi-pronged threat when it comes to preserving schools. The number is already but a small fraction of what it was at the peak around 1930—the saga of consolidation continues to unfold. The devastation of losing a local school is felt by students, who now face long bus rides, stigma, diminished time for study, or resources for success. The communities that lose schools often lose their identity and viability as a by-product of losing a primary or sole attractor point. For those schools that remain open in rural communities, they face challenges of an increasingly urban-centric curriculum, not to mention the pressure to close within an austere policy context that will provide meager resources.

In sum, cultural capital is a reflection of the value placed on people, ideas, language, objects, and institutions. Those who have a high level of cultural capital are celebrated and rewarded with opportunity and success, while those with a deficit are frowned upon and limited. While not the only dimension, urban-rural status is highly relevant to cultural capital and the resulting hierarchy it creates and maintains.

Chapter Five

The Public Imagination of Rural

In chapter 1 we showed the demographics of the world shifting in an increasingly urban direction, and in chapter 2 we claimed that this has created greater urban-rural epistemic distance. In chapter 3 we suggested that urbanormativity is an ideology that evolved out of this distance in order to serve a purpose—to enable control over rural resources while maintaining legitimacy. Chapter 4, on cultural capital, suggested that urbanormativity devalues rural and celebrates urban, unpacking the formal and informal mechanisms of socialization. This chapter builds on these threads by exploring the popular imagination of rural as can be found in popular media sources. We theorize that epistemic distance opens the door to misinformed stereotypes that degrade the public imagination of rural, which in turn serves to justify economic and cultural domination. Popular media, in turn, promotes stereotypes and images that bolster control over the rural oikos upon which urban populations depend.

Since there are fewer people residing in rural communities, social representations of rural life are being lifted out of direct experience and are becoming increasingly reliant upon secondary sources. Rural images and ideas are embedded in various forms of media that permeate culture. From television and film, to literature and music, the rural theme has maintained a steady presence in most Western cultures, though we focus mainly on the American context. Indications of public opinion research suggest that the public is enamored with a rural mystique (Willits, Theodori, & Fortunato 2016), even as this public becomes more urban and distant from rural reality. This is particularly the case in the United States where several recent studies have shed light on this question. We will examine several examples of popular cultural media dealing with rural themes, relying primarily on research that has already been conducted. Following this, we will review research on public opinions and public views of rural.

TELEVISION AND FILM MEDIA

An ambitious study by Jicha (2016) found that within the last fifteen years, there had emerged 127 rural-themed "redneck reality" television series. Jicha traces the phenomenon to the show, *The Deadliest Catch*, which takes us aboard an Alaskan fishing vessel to negotiates some of the worst natural conditions imaginable—extreme cold, rough seas—to reel in valuable seafood, a form of rural production. The show's focus is on its rural characters, who are both brave and a little rough around the edges—tragically, the captain would go on to die from a stroke, and one of the crew would be found dead in an Alaskan hotel room. The show's attraction to urban audiences is itself a function of alienated rural labor: resource extraction as an economic activity is so remote to the average urban consumer that it now passes for entertainment. The adventure of the fishing trips coupled with the public interest in the peculiarities of rural people drove *The Deadliest Catch* to an extremely high level of popularity. This success did not go unnoticed by television producers, and soon there were multiple attempts to capitalize on the public's penchant for rural. It was followed by such series as *Ice Road Truckers*, *Axe Men*, *Black Gold*, and *My Big Redneck Wedding*.

Jicha discovered several themes in content analyzing this genre of television. One involved what he called "Dangerous and Dirty Jobs" where rural people are shown to be working in some of the worst occupations imaginable. Another theme involved "Rural Law Enforcement" and included such series as *Alaska State Troopers*. The "Rags to Riches" theme plays off the popular imagination of the Gold Rush, where rural people take massive risks to strike it rich. This in some ways is a twist on the first theme. Another set of shows fall within the theme of "Family Values" including the stereotypical *Here Comes Honey Boo Boo* and the hugely popular, *Duck Dynasty*. Part of the overall image of rurality in reality TV involves a high regard for family and morality, and this theme taps into those sentiments. The public also thinks of rural people as survivors, and Jicha's theme, "Backwoods Survivalist" taps into this sentiment, including such series as *Yukon Men* and *Alaska Bush People*. Rural people are usually imagined to be traditionalists, and Jicha finds several shows in this vein, which he terms "Traditional Lifeways." Among the shows in this category are *Amish: Out of Order*, highlighting the conflict of younger people in the Amish community leaving and often not returning. Next, Jicha found several real estate–based shows that he dubs, "Buying Rural," and these include *Buying the Bayou* and *Buying Hawaii*, for instance. This theme is somewhat different as the main characters are usually privileged urbanites looking for a country escape—a theme identified in other studies of rural media. Another category involved "Mystery Hunters," and these series take the viewer on some kind of adventure to find often fictitious creatures like Sasquatch, ushering in an implicit view of rural naivete. *Alaska Monsters* and *Mountain Monsters* exemplify this theme. There is an entire category of "How-to Guides" for those interested in living a rural life. Shows like *Barn Hunters* have titles that play off other series (e.g., House Hunters) while adapting the focus to a rural setting. The last category identified in the analysis by Jicha is the most blatantly stereotypical, and that is "Pure Redneck Reality." The premises of these shows tend to center on the absurdity and inferiority of rural people. The terms hillbilly and redneck are often invoked. For instance, the show, *R U Faster than a Redneck*, plays off the older series, *Are you Smarter than a Fifth Grader*. Much of the content is intended to be comical, just as the material of comedian Jeff Foxworthy and his famous jokes involving the "You might be a redneck . . ." line.

The multiple themes that Jicha (2016) discovered after going through hundreds of recent rural reality-themed shows fill a niche in the urban desire to consume rural. Not all shows are degrading or stereotypical—of course, many depend on this—but what they share are threads that tap into some element of the public imagination or social representation of rurality. The three higher level themes found by Thomas et al. (2011) of rural as wild, simple, and escape apply in different ways to these themes. The more grotesquely stereotypical shows tend to portray rural people as wild. The shows highlighting values of family and tradition, often circle around the notion of simplicity. The real estate and adventure themed shows correspond to rural as escape. Thomas et al. (2011) arrived at these representations after examining a small set of fictional rural media that includes *Northern Exposure*, *Deliverance*, *Twin Peaks*, *Jenny*, and *The Fox and the Hound*. Each of these examples has elements of rural as wild, simple, and escape in different proportions. The most grotesque and stereotypical example is the iconic *Deliverance*. It is thanks to this film that the dueling banjos musical rhythm, "da da de da de da de da de," invokes instantly the thought of the most backward and monstrous redneck imagery possible.

Fulkerson and Lowe (2016) build on this earlier examination, by expanding the range of television series. They begin in the mid-twentieth century by considering the longest running and highest-rated television series in the history of the United States—a Western drama called *Gunsmoke*. The reasons for the show's popularity are not well understood, but as one reviewer suggested, it was the *Odyssey* and the *Iliad* of American history. The notions of frontier life, manifest destiny, overcoming adversity, establishing law and order, had wide public appeal. The rural setting promotes a sense of adventure and danger, and the story lines usually find resolution in the carrying out of justice by the main character, who is the marshall of the town, Matt Dillon (James Arness). Many of these themes and ideas can be found in similarly popular Westerns of the mid-twentieth century, such as *Bonanza* and *Wagon Train*. The Western genre has not gone away, and we continue to see it appear in popular shows like *Deadwood*, *Hell on Wheels*, and the more recent, *Godless* and *Frontier*. These shows combine adventure with a sense of danger and find resolution in the carrying out of justice—often by vigilantes.

Beyond the Western genre, Fulkerson and Lowe (2016) consider popular rural titles from the 1960s and 1970s, including *The Beverly Hillbillies* and *The Andy Griffith Show*—both highlighting the ideas of traditionalism and family values noted by Jicha. In the 1980s and 1990s, rural was not as active as a brand, but shows like *Dallas* kept it alive. By the 2000s rural came back into style, as noted by Jicha. The emerging fictional series took on new flavors, as seen in the comedy series, *Parks and Recreation*, the apocalyptic brand of rural as found in *The Walking Dead* and *Revolution*, and in the fantasy genre, in such shows as *True Blood* and *Sleepy Hollow*. The show *Nashville* harkened back to the nighttime soap opera theme of *Dallas*. In addition to examining the themes of these titles, Fulkerson and Lowe (2016) decided to provide an overall moral valence code. In short, they conclude: "the most popular rural-themed television series are generally cast in a dangerous and negative light, while the most prominent theme is violence and murder" (p. 31).

Lowe (2016) also finds that the rural is a theme that has entered the post-apocalyptic genre. This is evidenced in several series including *Doomsday Preppers* (also a reality show identified by Jicha), the fictional *The Walking Dead* series as well as its less popular spin-off, *Fear the Walking Dead*, and also prominent in *Planet of the Apes*. In each of these examples, the rural takes on a slightly different shade—becoming a haven in the wake of the collapse of urban life. Indeed, for *The Walking Dead*, the series begins with the main characters fighting frantically to escape the city that is "crawling with walkers" following a zombie outbreak.

In recent film, we find the Western genre with its usual characteristic wild and rough characters, who are often violent and unpredictable. In the 1960s, films such as *The Good, The Bad, and the Ugly*; *Butch Cassidy and the Sundance Kid*; or *The Magnificent Seven* (recently remade), use the same recipes of violence, adventure, and justice. More recent popular titles include *Tombstone*, *The Unforgiven*, *Django Unchained*, and the remake of *True Grit*, originally one of many John Wayne films. Recent treatments differ in some important ways, such as the portrayal of violence. Whereas gunfights in earlier films would show an injured person lying on the ground from a gunshot wound, there would be little blood. New films offer a more visceral and graphic depiction of violence. In addition, the dialogue has grown more decidedly profane, with recent Westerns flush with four-letter words, rivaling the dialogue of films in the mafia genre.

The Western genre of television and film sustains an impressive level of public interest, although it has become less mainstream than was the case when *Gunsmoke* won the rating wars for over a decade. The genre has become a niche, although this may simply reflect changes in the way people watch television and film in the age of streaming. Moving away from the question of why, we might simply ask, What do we see as common themes in this genre? As noted, there is excessive violence, increasingly crude language, all coupled with a sense of wild unpredictability, and a great deal of adventure. The public takes away from viewing such material a particular image of rural life—violent, wild, dangerous, and unpredictable. Rural people are viewed accordingly as rough, rowdy, violent, ill-tempered, and dangerous.

The notion of rural people as dangerous and violent has shown up outside of the Western genre in a range of forms. It is particularly exaggerated in the horror genre. The work of Karen Hayden has shed light on this tendency. Such films as the *Texas Chainsaw Massacre* capitalize on the view of rural people offered in the Western genre—as violent, wild, and unpredictable. The only difference is the extent. Rather than operate by a sense of rural justice, the characters in rural horror act out their violence in an unbounded manner, unrestrained by the desire for law and order. It is common in the rural horror genre to infuse the notion of degeneracy (Hayden 2016) into the depictions of rural people. Their wildness and violence becomes a by-product of innate genetic dysfunction, typically resulting from a backstory of excessive inbreeding. The representation of rural degenerates becomes a fanciful one, involving characters with noticeable deformities, open wounds, and often superhuman strength. Much of this draws on nineteenth century images of genetic throwbacks or degenerates that paved the way for the now discredited science of eugenics (real world examples of the state isolating and sterilizing rural people abound in the United States). The horror genre has always been more of a niche than the Western genre that found, at least for a time, mainstream approval. Still, the continual stream of films and shows drawing on images of rural incest, inbreeding, and degeneracy underscores the simple fact that many have developed a fetish for viewing extreme forms of unbounded rural violence.

Characters such as Leatherface (*The Texas Chain Saw Massacre*) embody rustic qualities while wielding rustic objects—such as a chainsaw. The premise is that Leatherface is part of a cannibalistic family—another common rural horror image—that waits for unwitting visitors to come into their presence. The family in the film is visited by a group on their way to see a family homestead—an image that juxtaposes the quaint and idyllic rural against the scene of rural horror. This juxtaposition is often at play in the rural horror genre. It can be found in other horror classics, such as the 1980 *Friday the 13th*, where an idyllic summer camp turns into a scene of violent murder. The image of a rustic cabin in the woods—the iconic image of frontier life— is featured as a scene of horror in films such as the *Evil Dead* series (1981, 1987), in which a group of youth stumble on the Book of the Dead that summons a formless evil energy that begins to surround and hunt them. Another example is a film called *The Cabin in the Woods* (2012), a spoof that both glorifies and pokes fun at the horror scene it creates in the rural setting.

As a case study on this point, Hayden (2016) takes us through a rural horror film series called, *The Wrong Turn*. While lesser known and not widely popular, this film series exemplifies rural horror—a small, but profitable niche. This series takes us through six films that netted roughly twenty-eight million dollars, so they are being viewed by someone (Hayden 2016). The main characters are part of the fully inbred Hillickers family. Three grossly deformed brothers appear as subhuman degenerates, capable only of making grunting sounds. Their degeneracy is also their source of strength as they have an uncanny ability to regenerate their health and feel no pain. These brothers engage in the most gruesome forms of cannibalism as the film series progresses. Hayden notes that these characters are also portrayed as being rooted in place and time—they blend in seamlessly to the surrounding environment, making them excellent hunters (of people). The women in this film series are equally animalistic, but while they have a violent streak, are portrayed mainly as sexual animals, driven by a desire to breed. They are shown at times giving birth to new inbred monstrous offspring. At one point, Hayden notes, the character of Sally engages in forceful sex with an almost dead male victim in the hopes of reproducing. In short, the film series portrays rural males as subhuman degenerate inbred monsters hungry for human flesh and blood, while women gleefully join them, but are further driven by a hyper-sexual desire to create additional offspring. While we are not suggesting that viewers of this content are actively taking notes on rural life, exposure to such images cannot help but take rural representations to new levels of disgust.

PRINT MEDIA

In the world of print media, we find a long-standing and steady interest in the rural countryside and its contrast to the urban cityscape. The acclaimed examination of literature, offered by Raymond Williams (1973), in *The Country and the City*, provides one of the first in-depth and incisive reviews of the rural in Western literature, centered mainly on English sources since the sixteenth century, and found in the works as such authors as Charles Dickens, Herman Melville, and Thomas Hardy. Among his insights, Williams points to the tendency of literature to promote a notion of a Golden Age of rural life, which he critiques as "a myth functioning as a memory." Williams also claims that the rural is characterized as simple, wild, and unadulterated—he did not identify rural as escape. The tendency to romanticize rural life is the overwhelming pattern that Williams finds. In his concluding chapter, he points out that the notions of country and city oversimplify reality where we find social forms that do not fit so neatly into either of these archetypes.

As ideas, the country and city have come to be associated with a complex array of conditions. Williams (1973, p. 291) notes,

> People have often said "the city" when they meant capitalism or bureaucracy or centralised power, while "the country," as we have seen, has at times meant everything from independence to deprivation, and from the powers of an active imagination to a form of release from consciousness.

He goes on to point out that while the country is synonymous with the past, the city is the way of the future, and the present is some indeterminate middle ground. The common sigh of regret is the loss of a traditional rural world that is being supplanted by a modern urban world. Williams admits that at certain times he also shared in this sentiment when reflecting on his own life moving from country to city and reflecting on the history of change in England. Then, later, he realized these ideas were false. As the population of the world continues growing, the role of rural production, rather than fading into obscurity, will, in the future, be more important than ever. The problem is that within the world economy, predominantly rural countries are being exploited at a distance, so that the average consumer in a modern urban country, like England, can enjoy reliable rural products like food without knowledge of their complete dependence on rural producers. Meanwhile, Williams critiques the overconfidence that has prevailed in urban life, just as a crisis of industrial urban life is being realized, particularly in the damage being done to the environment. This work was one of the first challenges to the prevailing urbanormativity of Western cultures and was influential for the authors of this book.

Building on Williams's tradition, Ching (2016) reviews a more contemporary work by Smiley (1995), who wrote a fictional novel about a "Cow College" called *Moo*. Ching examines this comedic and tragic work as a satirical glimpse into the inner workings of the stereotypical land grant university. The popular imagination of the land grant is that they are the rustic alternative in higher education to the far superior and more urbane institutions, imbued with a far greater stock of cultural capital. The campus, building names, and characters in *Moo* are a melding of such institutions. The professors at this land grant university are shown to be engaged in corporate funded research that is driven solely to discover novel uses for corn and more ambitious ways of raising bigger animals, such as pigs, for meat. The popular imagination of the land grant is that they turn out inferior rustic students, as is made clear in the often-repeated jokes, such as "What does the Clemson graduate call the University of South Carolina graduate? Boss" and "Why did MSU change their field from grass to artificial turf? To keep the cheerleaders from grazing" (Ching 2016, p. 111). Ching reminds us, in the same vein as Williams, that urban societies are entirely dependent on rural production and farms. While the nitty gritty of what goes on in land grant research may appear comically pragmatic and utilitarian, without it urbanites could not enjoy the plentiful cheap food supply that exists today. Once again, a challenge to an urbanormative understanding of the world is advanced.

Polly Smith's examination of "Ridgefield Corners" (2014) highlights another recent examination of rural literature and the way it has shaped perceptions of a community over time. The community was first written about by James Fenimore Cooper in his novel, *The Pioneers* (2011 [1823]). The images of the community set forth in this classic novel are of a changing environment, as new villages were popping up and wilderness was coming to be replaced with farmland. The main character, Natty Bumppo, laments these changes and represents one of the first real or imagined voices of rural conservation in American literature. This theme fits neatly into Williams's notion of the "Golden Age." Smith goes on to examine the next era, based on Elaine Dorian's novel, *The Sex Cure* (1962), about a young woman who nearly dies trying to obtain an illegal abortion. The nature of this novel is one of scandal and betrayal, and the community of Ridgefield Corners is shown to be a small town that has lost its innocence and now must negotiate the realities of modern social life. Smith interprets these dual portrayals from Cooper and Dorian using the Thomas et al. (2011) motifs of rural as wild, simple, and escape. Though the image is very different in the 1960s as compared to the 1820s, these themes show remarkable continuity in both portrayals. In either case, Smith points out the features of community as shown in both novels that contradict the more common stereotypes of rural communities. The characters, for instance, represent a rather diverse (not homogeneous) group in *The Pioneers*. The conflict and pains of social change in *The Sex Cure* run counter to the more prevalent view of rural places as unchanging and quaint. The impending problems of modernity are elements in both novels, from the way it reshapes the environment to the new forms of social conflict and tension that arise with modernity.

Turning to the nonfiction realm of newspapers, McKay's analysis (2016) of rural suggests that the ability of rural communities to construct their own narrative though news stories is challenged by more influential, urban-based newspapers that have more readership and reach. As a result, the image of rural communities may be shifting from unique local stories with an insider point-of-view projected outward, to something that is filtered through a more generic urban lens that is imposed on the actual community. In other words, rural people no longer get to tell their own story in news—it is filtered through urban news editors. Part of this trend is driven by the very nature of media markets themselves, as they are overtly defined around urban areas, leaving rural areas as an afterthought. One outcome of this is that the vast majority of stories will revolve around the urban experience, setting the foundation for an urbanormative agenda setting process. Through content analysis, Mckay found that the most commonly reported topic about rural communities from the perspective of urban newspapers was crime, but that there was surprising variability of topics outside of this. What we don't know is if the rural residents, who are the objects of the reporting, would feel like important news stories about their communities were being represented by these urban media outlets. The result of this is that community identity is taken out of the hands of those who comprise the community, as their voice is replaced by that of a distant urban journalist interpreting distant rural events.

PUBLIC OPINION

The above brings us to an important question to consider about the extent to which popular culture translates into public opinion. Do people have a realistic sense of what rural life entails, and do they attach positive or negative sentiments to what they imagine rural life to be? Research on public views of rural has received scant attention, but the work of Willits and colleagues (2016) has blazed a trail in this direction, under the mantle of the "rural mystique." Their research asks how this takes shape in the context of the United States. They divide the American rural mystique along four dimensions: 1) nostalgia for past gemeinschaft-like relationships, (2) Jeffersonian democracy and agrarian values, (3) the frontier experience, and (4) the unspoiled wilderness landscape. They then ask to what extent these appear in public opinion research. Studies of residential preference have found, for instance, an overwhelming and persistent desire to live in small towns or rural areas. Several studies that focused on agrarian values have found widespread acceptance of the Jeffersonian ideal. Several studies from the 1980s through the present—much of it sponsored by Kellogg Foundation—have tackled the place of the rural mystique in American culture more completely. In short, there has been consistent and strong support for the above-mentioned dimensions, though support does seem slightly less in the present. Studies in both Texas and Pennsylvania supported these conclusions. This does not belie the fact that there is a simultaneous trend toward viewing rural people in negative stereotypical terms, as noted earlier in the realms of television and film media. The popularity of redneck reality television would not be possible if the primarily urbane viewer was offended—to the contrary, such portrayals of rural life are held to be a source of great entertainment value. The major takeaway of the research of Willits and colleagues, is that the public view of rural is positive. The majority holds rural people in high regard though this is not entirely without exception or contradiction. Beneath the positive sentiments about rural people are a range of contradictory and negative stereotypes. In the next section we evaluate three myths believed to separate urban from rural people in the area of public opinion.

A Comparison of Urban-Rural Attitudes

In this section we offer a primary comparison of urban-rural views on three popular stereotypes that are generally held to divide residents of city and country. The data that we use for this analysis come from the GSS, or General Social Survey (2016 edition), which employs a nationally representative sample drawn by the National Opinion Research Center (NORC). We examine the following three themes: religiosity, attitudes about gun permits, and attitudes about affirmative action. These correspond to three popular stereotypes that rural people are more likely to be religious zealots, avid supporters of gun rights (and therefore oppose permits), and less accepting of affirmative action policies that help racial and ethnic minorities. In the analysis that follows, we examine results of basic chi-square tests of statistical significance to answer these questions. We then go further to consider the extent to which these differences exist among specific subgroups (if present).

We measure urban or rural residency through the question, "Which of the categories on this card comes closest to the type of place you were living in when you were 16 years old?" This question has the advantage of showing where the respondent lived when they were being raised—meaningful as the place of primary socialization. The disadvantage is that it does not show where they currently live. Unfortunately, there is not a parallel question asked about the present. Rather than a simple urban-rural comparison, we use the several categories of residence at the age of sixteen provided by the General Social Survey. The figure below (figure 5.1) reports the percentage of respondents in each category. The predominant category is small town, which accounts for about a third of the sample. As noted earlier, there is a strong preference for life in small towns in the United States, and this appears to be reflected in the distribution of residency at age sixteen. After that category the next biggest is medium cities, followed by large cities, suburbs, the country (not on a farm), and finally on a farm. This provides a full spectrum within which to explore our research question, rather than a simple urban-rural dichotomy.

We begin by examining the issue of religiosity. The General Social Survey asks people to rate the frequency with which they attend religious ser-

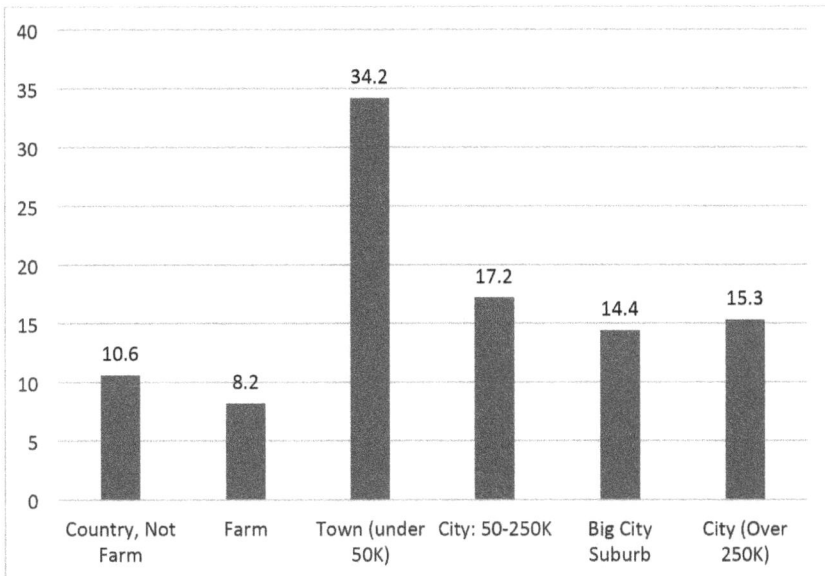

Figure 5.1. Residence at Age 16 (n = 2,861)
The General Social Survey, 2016 edition

vices. The question is, "How often do you attend religious services?" Examining the two variables of religiosity and urban/rural residence (see figure 5.2), we find that there is a statistically significant chi-square test statistic (74.489, p = .000). This means that there are statistically significant differences between the different residential groups in terms of religiosity. When we explore which groups differ, we find that, indeed, the highest level of religiosity is found among those living on a farm at sixteen (37.6 percent) who attend every week or more. Those from the country, not living on a farm, had a far lower level of religiosity (27 percent), however. The lowest overall level of religiosity comes from those living in the suburbs with 17.8 percent attending weekly or more. Those in the largest cities come in at a higher level of 23 percent. From this analysis we see that the reality is more complicated than the simplistic view that rural people are religious zealots. For instance, the gap between the two rural categories of those growing up on or off a farm is larger (difference of 10.6 percent) than the gap between the non-farm rural and small city residents (difference of .2 percent). Thus, the statistical significance is not just along the urban-rural dimension.

Next, we examine the question of attitudes about gun permits. The questions is, "Would you favor or oppose a law which would require a person to obtain a police permit before he or she could buy a gun?" When we examine

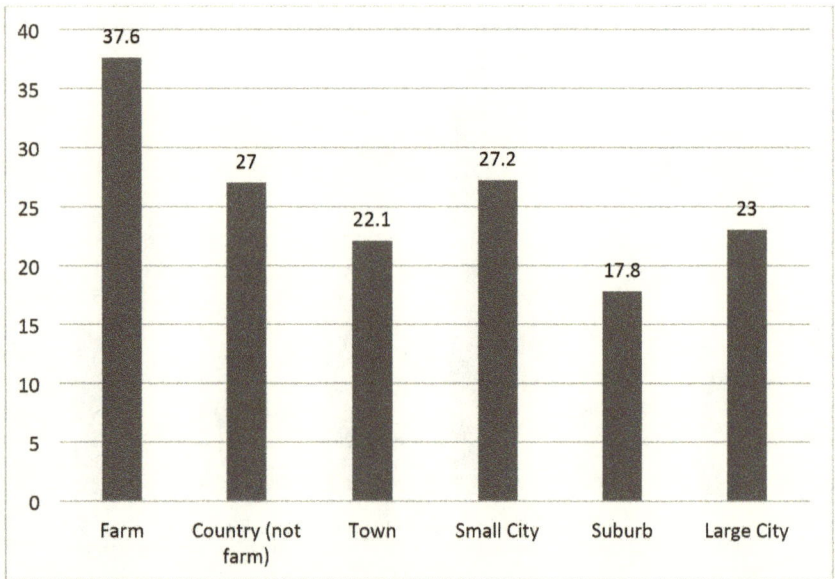

Figure 5.2.   Levels of Religiosity by Residence at 16 (n = 2,846)
The General Social Survey, 2016 edition

this variable for difference along residential lines, we find that there is a statistically significant chi-square statistic (17.141, p = .004). Figure 5.3 reveals a fairly linear relationship. Those living on a farm were similar to those living in the country but not on a farm, and these groups showed lower levels of support than the other categories. The widest gap is from one end to the other, between those living on a farm who had 12.3 percent less support for gun permits than those living in large cities.

Finally, we examined the levels of support for affirmative action policies. The question asked by GSS is "Some people say that because of past discrimination, blacks should be given preference in hiring and promotion. Others say that such preference in hiring and promotion of blacks is wrong because it discriminates against whites. What about your opinion—are you for or against preferential hiring and promotion of blacks?" Figure 5.4 shows how levels of support for this vary by residence at age sixteen. In this case, we found that there was not a statistically significant difference across groups in terms of the chi-square test (20.695, p = .147). That means that the small differences between each category could just as likely be a result of sampling error as opposed to real difference. Nevertheless, we do see a fairly linear relationship with the biggest category being those on a farm, who had the least amount of support for affirmative action policies. The gap between non-

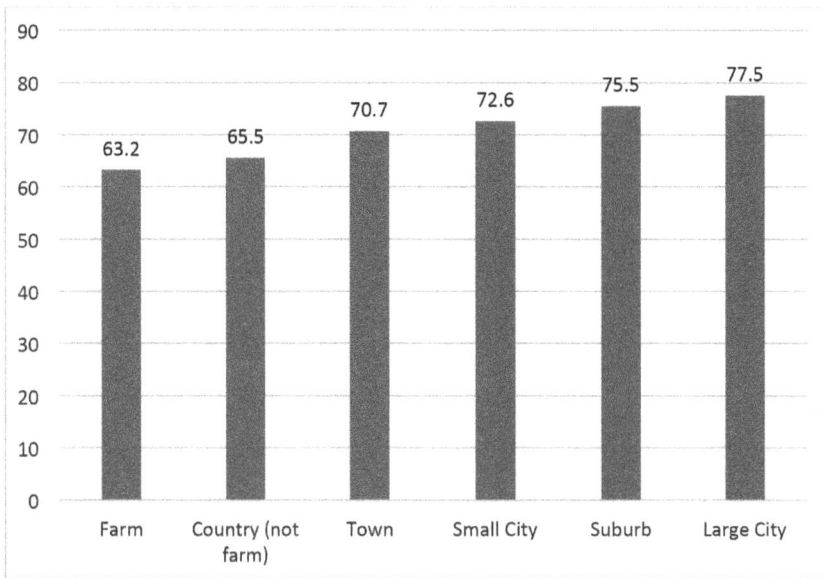

Figure 5.3. Support for Gun Permits by Residence at 16 (n = 1,013)
The General Social Survey, 2016 edition

farm country and big city, however, was only 3.3 percent. Therefore, we do not find evidence for a rural-urban divide on the issue of affirmative action—nearly all groups oppose it.

This brief comparison of attitudes across residential groups from age sixteen provides insight into the urban-rural dynamics of attitudinal difference on important social and political issues. The goal of examining these three items was to evaluate prevailing stereotypes about urban-rural differences, namely that rural people are more religious, more enthusiastic about guns, and less supportive of affirmative action. The results of the analysis showed a complex picture on the issue of religiosity. While the most religious group was the farm population, there was as much internal variation within rural people as there was between urban and rural people. On the issue of supporting gun permits, the relationship was closer to the public perception. The reasons for this may be that people living in a rural setting are more likely to buy and use guns to hunt and therefore want the process to be easier. Still, it should be noted, that every category saw a majority wanting gun permits—it was the size of the majority that differed. The last issue, pertaining to affirmative action support showed little difference across groups—in fact, there was not a statistically significant difference at all. In sum, the

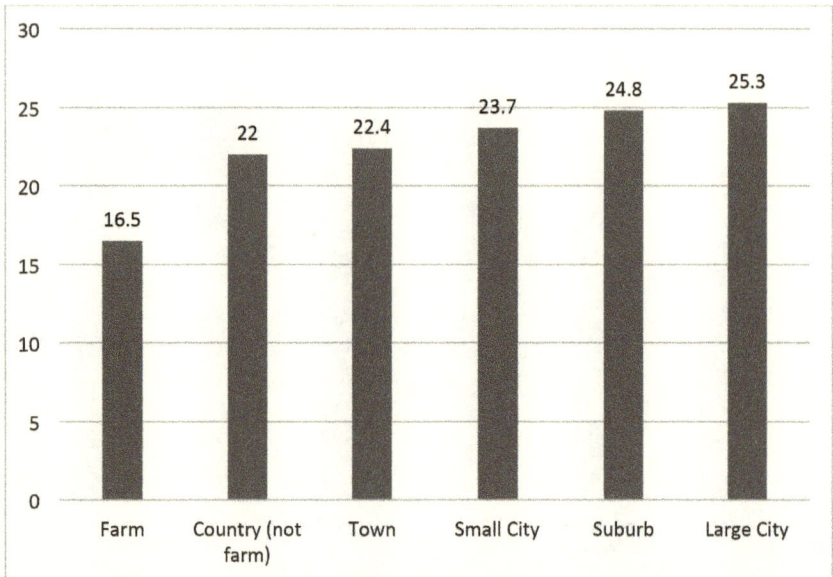

Figure 5.4. Support for Affirmative Action Policies by Residence at 16 (n = 1,176)
The General Social Survey, 2016 edition

public perceptions of rural people that were tested here are overall, gross oversimplifications if not outright myths.

TAKEAWAYS

Popular media of all types project ideas and images on to a social representation of rural that informs the public imagination. Whether thinking about television and film, or works of ancient or recent literature, we see similar themes carried through. The three motifs of rural as simple, wild, and escape (Thomas et al. 2011; Williams 1973) are found in most of the examples of media that has been examined thus far. On top of this, we can note the increasingly fanciful depictions of rural as supernatural, violent, and crude, as is the case for niche-based media that include the rural horror genre and the rural fantasy genre. Even popular rural mainstream television series, studied by Fulkerson and Lowe (2016), were overwhelmingly assigned a negative moral valence.

The problem with the many ways rural has been characterized is that the images, ideas, and messages being transmitted are not filtered through the lens of people directly experiencing rural life—not even news stories about rural communities (McKay 2016). Instead, they become unanchored images attached to the word rural, as most consumers of these cultural artifacts reside at a distance, in an urban setting. Though newspapers were the only media markets researched, nearly all media markets, including radio, are similarly urban-based. Without the benefit of firsthand, direct experience, there is no counterbalance provided, no basis for evaluating the veracity of such images. Epistemic distance has dissolved the real-world knowledge that would normally keep representations of rural in perspective.

Research in the area of public opinion is, however, providing a measure of hope. Though popular media is not promoting positive images of rural overall, the public manages to hold fairly positive sentiments about rural places. Research on the rural mystique in the United States shows support for agrarian values as well as preference for living in a rural area. Willits, Theodori, and Fortunato (2016) note that pro-rural attitudes are on the decline, as compared to earlier studies spanning the last three decades. Perhaps popular media is taking a toll.

Finally, the popular imagination of rural is saddled with a range of rural stereotypes and myths. Our brief analysis of urban-rural differences of attitude found that the popular imagination of rural is largely based on massive oversimplifications and gross characterizations. While the farm population tends to be more religious, the non-farm country population is less religious than people residing in small cities. Differences are significant, but not very large or in the expected pattern. Support for gun permits appeared to line up with popular notions, but in all categories, the majority favored gun permits, and the overall difference was not large. Finally, all groups oppose affirmative action policies with small, non-significant, differences across groups. So much for the myth that rural people are less racially sensitive. As with any stereotype, individual cases may be found, but the overall pattern is not thus represented. In the next chapter, we examine the dynamics of urban/urbane and rural/rustic identity, which is a culmination of cultural capital and social representations.

Chapter Six

Rustic and Urbane Identity

In this chapter we explore the urban-rural dynamics of identity, emphasizing the role of urbanormativity in shaping what is taken to be "normal" versus "deviant." On one hand, urban-rural identity grows out of material conditions (see chapter 3) based on (a) where we live and (b) what we do for a living. On the other hand, it is socially constructed (see chapters 4 and 5)—it has a subjective component that is defined individually and socially, and results from cultural influences through the socialization process. We distinguish the objective component of identity using urban-rural terminology and denote the subjective component with the urbane-rustic terminology, following Ching and Creed (1996). This allows us to recognize the possibility, for example, that a person who lives in an objectively urban place might simultaneously subjectively identify as rustic, or alternatively, for a person engaged in rural work like farming to identify as urbane. As we delve deeper into the dynamics of urban-rural identity, we must address the distinction between objective and subjective conditions that combine to produce identity. This is not the only concern, however, as we must also grant attention to the processes of identity formation. Identity work involves an interplay between the individual, group, and community levels. In some cases, identity fusion takes place, in others there is a partial interaction of identity, and in others, there is a high level of incongruence. There is no straightforward process in which individuals who identify as urbane or rustic will come to be accepted by their home communities. If an urbanite moves to the country, for instance, and claims a rustic identity, this does not automatically lead to social acceptance (Graber 1974). We will attempt to unpack these ideas below.

IDENTITY: OBJECTIVISM VS. CONSTRUCTIONISM
OF SEX AND GENDER

To help orient us to our discussion of identity, let's consider another arena where the distinction between objectivism and constructionism has already been carefully explored: in the study of gender and sex. Sociologists who study sex and gender use the term sex to denote the objective material conditions that refer to differences in anatomy and physiology, including such things as genitals that make one male or female, or in some cases, both male and female or in other cases, neither male nor female. Gender, alternatively, refers to the socially constructed meaning that we attach to sex, categorized through the terms such as masculinity and femininity. The term cis-gendered describes someone whose sex and gender identity align—the dominant group—while the term transgendered describes one who experiences incongruency between their sex (material) and gender identity (construction). It is careless to assume gender identity will automatically align with sex, as this assumption proves to be overly restrictive and oppressive, denying people their right to form an identity that makes them feel complete or whole. From an objectivist perspective, if one were to be born male but identify as female or express feminine qualities, they would be viewed as deviant and perhaps suffering from an identity disorder. Indeed, the diagnostic statistical manual (DSM) that is used by clinical psychologists, offers this very interpretation of a disorder (American Psychiatric Association, 2013, 215–218).

As understanding of the genetic basis for sex has evolved, we now know that sex assignment is largely determined by a single SRY gene (Mukherjee 2017). Even so, this genetic foundation does not account for other physical mutations and changes that may take place during physical development, nor does it explain the far more complex nature of gender identity formation. The danger of advancing knowledge of DNA is that it may bolster the view that sex and gender can be reduced to objective conditions—one's genetic make-up. While genetics may offer a binary switch to be male or female, there is nothing yet identified in our DNA that says we will come to identify as masculine or feminine. This has more to do with the cultural context that transcends the field of genetics belonging to the study of social sciences such as anthropology and sociology.

The constructionist perspective of sex and gender, largely developed by social scientists, is derived from the closest thing we have in sociology to a law—the Thomas (Thomas & Thomas 1928) dictum. This dictum states *that which [men* (sic)*] we define as real, will be real in its consequences.* If someone born physiologically male identifies and defines themselves as female, then per the Thomas dictum, they are female. As we are socialized into a wider culture, we are exposed to ideas of masculinity and femininity and each individual must work out what feels right to them individually. Though there tends to be a high correlation, constructionist definitions are not necessarily anchored in objective conditions. They draw their meaning from the wider cultural context.

As with other dimensions of identity, however, sex and gender are not just an individual matter—they involve social categories. As such, they carry with them a set of socially defined norms, beliefs, and values that are enforced by social sanctions that may be positive or negative. In many cultures, the dominant ideology is patriarchy, wherein males are viewed as superior to females, while masculine qualities are valued over feminine qualities. The belief, for instance, that men are strong, and women are weak, grew out of patriarchal notions of masculinity and femininity. As such, if a male were to exhibit weakness, or a female were to exhibit strength, they would both be in violation of norms and face negative sanctions in the forms of ridicule, disgust, or even bullying or assault. Sex and gender norms are strictly enforced and those who deviate from them often pay a heavy price, as evidenced by the extremely high rate of suicide and substance abuse among the LGBTQ population (see, for example, Mereish, O'Cleirigh, & Bradford 2013), as well as the rate of hate crimes inflicted against this population (see Duncan, Hatzenbuehler, & Johnson 2014).

Evaluating the identity dynamics of sex and gender is informative as we turn our focus to the dynamic interplay of the urban-rural and urbane-rustic qualities of individuals, groups, and communities. There is an objective condition that interacts with a subjective definition to produce different identity outcomes. There is a broader cultural ideology that shapes expectations of normality and deviance, and of superiority and inferiority. We now attempt to outline a parallel view of urban-rural (objective) and urbane-rustic (subjective) identity in a wider context of urbanormativity, which holds urban and urbane as normal and superior.

THE OBJECTIVE BASES OF URBAN-RURAL IDENTITY

Turning our attention urban-rural identity, we observe one difference. Rather than a singular foundation, we find two anchors based on (1) physical place of residence, and (2) forms of work. The first of these is derived from a spatial-demographic perspective that categorizes one as urban or rural based on the level of population density within a given home community. From this standpoint, if you live in a sparse rural area, then you are a rural person. The second anchor is derived from the political-economic perspective, and it categorizes people as urban or rural based on the kind of work in which one is engaged (elaborated earlier in chapter 3). The convenience of the objective perspectives is the ease with which we can categorize people and places in neat and tidy boxes: you either are or you are not. This way of thinking can become blurry, however, when there is incongruency between the anchors. Very simply this means doing urban work in a rural place or doing rural work in an urban place may cause confusion.

The most congruous set of conditions is when rural work happens in rural areas and urban work is performed by those residing in urban areas. If these conditions are met there is little left to interpretation and objective categorization is straightforward. As the world continues to urbanize, however, there has been a decoupling of urban-rural residence and occupation. It is only in the poorest and most rural nations of the world where we find high levels of consistency. According to the CIA World Factbook, in 2017, Uganda saw 71 percent of its population employed in agriculture and they lived among the 76.2 percent of its population residing in a rural area. To be a rural Ugandan is, therefore, almost always to be a Ugandan farmer—the iconic rural occupation (though not the only one). Meanwhile, the vast majority of people living in rural parts of the United Kingdom, for instance, do not engage in any kind of rural work. In 2017, while 16.6 percent of the UK was rural, only 1.3 percent were employed in agriculture. This means that most of the rural population is working in either the service or manufacturing sectors—both of which are urban forms of work. This story is repeated for most of the world's wealthy urban nations. Therefore, the objective foundation of urban-rural identity is more complex than it is for sex, which only has a single anchor—physiology. But even in the case of sex, though rare, we find physiological expressions that blur the boundaries of male and female, as mentioned earlier.

It is quite possible that rural work could be done in urban settings. In fact, urban farming and foraging are becoming a fad in many cities. In a recent study, Ching and Creed (2014) critique the practice of urban foraging, suggesting that it appropriates from rural people the one truly rural occupation—farming—by putting it in the hands of urbanites. Also questioned is the idea that large cities can feed themselves to the point of self-sufficiency—something we have sharply rebuked as well, calling it the myth of urban self-sufficiency (Thomas et al. 2011). The fantasy that urban populations can free themselves from reliance on rural people serves to reinforce a sense of urban superiority while justifying a lack of moral concern or desire to support rural people and rural work. The case of urban farming and foraging, nevertheless, remains illustrative of rural work that is being done in urban areas, even if it is not pragmatic.

The more common incongruency, as noted, is when urban work is taking place in sparsely populated rural areas. It is not at all unusual to find manufacturing in the countryside, nor is it uncommon to find professionals making a living in a way that seems to belong in a city, as architects, scientists, professors, or engineers, for instance. As we define in chapter 3, rural work begins with nature—the energy economy provides the essential material to make life possible for humans (and every other species of life on earth). Urban occupations are identified as those outside of the energy economy. Living in a rural community does not necessarily entail taking advantage of the rich natural resources that are available for food production, or mining, or other rural endeavors. In the United States, many small rural communities were originally founded as a place for farming families to have central place functions and attractor points for social interaction—such as locations for retail, post office, train station, town hall, church, and so forth. As farming declined, and as many of these central place functions and attractor points moved to larger cities, the communities continued to exist only by attracting or retaining people for entirely different reasons. Rather than evaluating such things as the fertility of the soil or the amount of available rainfall, the new residents of these rural communities are more interested in the quality of roads (as they generally commute long distances), the cost of living (usually lower in rural areas), the natural beauty, and the quality of institutions such as schools and hospitals. These institutions may form the foundation of the economy in demographically rural communities, as they support healthcare workers, educators, and administrators, along with a range of support staff. More remote rural communities tend to lack institutions and infrastructure, forcing extreme commutes and bus rides to school, as noted in chapter 4. This is, however, the profile of many contemporary rural communities.

It is the decline of rural work in rural areas that has caused rural scholars to hold a sense of despair and crisis. The objective conditions that so neatly delineated the urban and rural population have been altered. This has been accomplished in part by technological advances that have automated much work in farming, but it is also driven by global trade, as the world's more rural nations now provision urban nations thousands of miles away with rural products such as produce and coffee. Perhaps it is due to a lack of awareness about globalization and automation that rural sociologists, such as Pahl (1966) and Newby (1980), claim that rural is now simply a trivial description of land use, or at worst, an obsolete or archaic term useful only for describing conditions from the past. As the occupation/residency decoupling continues for rural areas, the way of life in urban and rural places is becoming less distinguishable within advanced urban nations. This is not the case for predominantly rural nations, where the distinction is clear. It is hard to imagine a world in which there is no rural work being done in rural areas—our survival as a species depends on it.

As the discussion above makes clear, the objective political-economic reality has changed remarkably for areas that are spatially and demographically rural. This has opened the door to a more politically and economically urban form of rural community. This has a wide range of implications, but for our present purposes, we keep our focus on what this means for identity. How does a person working in an urban profession, while living in a small sparsely populated rural community, think of themselves? Alternatively, how does an urban farmer identify? These questions move us away from the objective conditions of categories toward the subjective constructions of identity.

THE SUBJECTIVE CONSTRUCTION
OF URBANE AND RUSTIC IDENTITY

Bell (1992) claims that, despite the remarkable changes taking place in rural areas in urban society, as described above, the importance of rural has not been diminished as a dimension of identity. His analysis of an English exurban community with the pseudonym, Childerley, finds residents embracing rural identity with a deep appreciation for the natural beauty, quietude, and timelessness of life in the countryside. At the same time, they are regretful of the changing character of their community, the homogeneous sterilization of it, and loss of community identity. Bell concludes, from a constructionist perspective, that regardless of academic confusion and angst, rural (rustic) continues to be meaningful in the everyday lives of Childerley residents. This kind of research validates the need for further examination of urban/urbane and rural/rustic identity.

What it means to be rustic or urbane, is of course, socially constructed and culturally specific, just as the meanings we attach to femininity and masculinity can vary widely from place to place. Most first attempts to pin down the meaning of urbane and rustic begin with stereotypes, such as those reviewed in the last chapter. As we discussed, the public tends to think of rural people and places in contradictory ways. Rural areas are at once romanticized but also feared. Rural people are held up as moral leaders but also despised as degenerate monsters. These mixed conceptions are formed out of a broader ideology of urbanormativity—wherein the invisible referent is the "normalcy" or urban life—and exacerbated by epistemic distance.

Stereotypes aside, rusticity and urbanity are both highly diverse concepts. Even at the subnational level, the meaning of rural can vary quite substantially. Rural identity for two people living in the same community can vary as it comes to intersect with class, race, ethnicity, and gender. Beyond intersectionality are subcommunities within the rural population. Even the basis of subculture can vary; it can be derived from a sport, such as noodling (Grigsby 2012) or it can be derived from religious affiliation, as shown in studies of the Old Order Amish (e.g., Walbert 2002). A central question is what symbols signify membership in the rustic or the urbane world? The answer to this will again be culturally specific. As urbane is generally taken as the hidden referent for normalcy, we focus primarily on rusticity since it is the marked category.

Symbols of Rusticity in the United States

In the United States a deeply controversial and hotly debated symbol of rusticity is the Confederate flag. Those who display this symbol often argue that it represents their identity as a "redneck." It is, of course, also associated with the Confederacy, a failed rogue breakaway nation that fought to maintain the institution of slavery and plantation life in the South. It is therefore, objectively, a racially insensitive symbol that links rusticity to whiteness and white supremacy. This of course ignores the increasing ethnic and racial diversity of rural America (Lichter 2012), including the entire region known as the Black Belt (Wimberley, Morris, & Harris 2014), where rusticity is more closely associated with rural African American experiences. It is important that the social imaginary of rural not render racial and ethnic minorities invisible.

Along with whiteness, rusticity in the United States has also been highly associated with masculinity. Pickup trucks often sport tow hitches decorated with something called "truck nuts," which have the appearance of a scrotum dangling behind the truck. This symbol, of course, simultaneously celebrates masculinity in rustic culture—as does the pickup truck itself. In addition, clothing associated with rural work in terms of farming or hunting—coveralls, camouflage, Carhartt jackets (a rustic brand) and other apparel—signify occupational rusticity. Moreover, bumper stickers that celebrate rustic values typically point to the value of gun ownership, hunting, or other facets of country life.

We might also note that many of the symbols of rusticity in the United States are heavily associated with being in the working class. Much of the pride that rural people express in rustic livelihoods—farming, forestry, fishing, mining, and so on—is based on pride in hard physical labor. Perhaps it is owing to the working-class dimension of rustic identity that Theobold and Wood (2011) find rustics often view their own identity as inherently inferior. Based on a study of educational deficiencies, they (Theobold & Wood 2011, p. 170) note, "Somewhere along the way, rural students and adults alike seem to have learned that to be rural is to be sub-par, that the condition of living in a rural locale creates deficiencies of various kinds." At the same time, rustic identity can provide a sense of dignity, worth, and empowerment (Grigsby 2012). Accepting the role of underdog may explain why people proudly adopt the more derogatory rustic labels of "redneck," "bumpkin," or "hillbilly." This is not unlike the phenomenon of racial and ethnic minorities referring to themselves through racial slurs and epithets.

Rusticity Around the World

The experience in the United States is unique, but there are similar patterns to be found in other contexts. In a pioneering foray into the meaning of urbanity and rusticity, Ching and Creed (1997) assembled a collection of studies that focus on representations of rural people from all corners of the world. We are taken from the southern rural Indian culture of Trinidad (Kahn 1997), to peasant farmers in Central America (Edelman 1997), contrasting images of rural and urban life in James Joyce's Ireland (Sheehan 1997), the rural in Quebec (Guenther 1997), Brittany in France (Maynard 1997), the Israeli Kibbutz (Lees 1997), and on to the idealization of Australian bushmen (Dominy 1997). Each contribution simultaneously reminds us that there is no such thing as a singular "rural" culture or identity, while highlighting the fact that there are patterns of denigration and exploitation that cut across the boundaries of different societies. While the meaning of rusticity is not universal, urbanormativity and rural exploitation are very close to universal.

One of the more hopeful studies is the contribution by Edelman (1997) who finds in Central America that rural campesinos and técnicos have become organized to protect rural interests. Maynard (1997) similarly offers hope in the study of the Brittany in France, where there is a celebration of a unique rural ethnic identity. In contrast, Lees (1997) finds declining support for the rural peasantry in Israel, who were traditionally celebrated and supported through generous outlays of government aid that shored up the Kibbutz communal style of living—something that was central to the success of initial resettlement efforts. Growing resentment on the part of an increasingly urban Israeli population has led to the view that the Kibbutz is a drain on public resources.

An important theme to emerge from this collection is that the intentional, and often well-meaning, "valorization of rural" can imply trapping and limiting the mobility of rustics. Dominy (1997) claims that sheep herders in New Zealand and bushmen of Australia are trapped by the urban imaginary, frozen in time like living exhibits in a museum. Ching and Creed argue that the tendency to romanticize rural reaffirms rustic backwardness. It redirects attention from real problems, such as rural poverty, which do not fit in the romantic ideal and are thus ignored or pushed to the margins. Ching and Creed also conclude that rural people often exaggerate their own rusticity, since using terms like "redneck" is a form of identity work that signifies insider status. These studies suggest that, while rustic identity work may promote a sense of pride and celebration, they may also narrow the possibilities of what it means to be rural and rustic—particularly due to the urban romanticization of rusticity.

CRITIQUES OF OBJECTIVIST
AND CONSTRUCTIONIST PERSPECTIVES

Having reviewed both the objective and constructionist perspectives of ur-ban/urbanity and rural/rusticity, we now evaluate what each perspective pro-vides and what they do not. For this discussion, let's consider some hypothet-icals. For example, an objectivist might argue that an individual living in Manhattan is objectively an urban person, based on their residence. They may also argue that an individual working on a farm is objectively a rural person based on their line of work. Both would be held as true regardless of how these individuals defined themselves. But what if we learn that the individual living in Manhattan identified as rustic since they grew up raising cattle in rural Texas, liked to wear cowboy hats, and enjoyed country music? What if the individual working on the farm identified as urbane because they were raised in a big city, attended prep school, were trained in ballet, enjoyed fine imported wines, and had a master's degree in agroecology? There is no room for nuance in the binaries of the objectivist perspective. Moreover, as noted earlier, the incongruity between place of residence and occupation may call into question the value of the purely objectivist view. While it is sup-posed to be cut-and-dried, the objective approach encompasses ambiguity in categorizing people in terms of urban-rural identity. Yet, before we entirely dismiss the value of objectivity, we might also note that the constructionist perspective is also limited. For example, consider the constructionist view articulated by Supreme Court Justice Potter Steward in his attempt to define hardcore pornographic material without an objective anchor:

> I shall not today attempt further to define the kinds of material I understand to be embraced within that shorthand description ["hard-core pornography"], and perhaps I could never succeed in intelligibly doing so. But *I know it when I see it*, and the motion picture involved in this case is not that (Jacobellis v. Ohio 1964).

Here the objective basis of what constitutes hardcore pornography is so ambiguous that we are asked to ignore it and accept as valid the conclusion *we will know it when we see it*. The objectivist would rightly criticize this as wishy-washy thinking. It leaves too much open to interpretation, and it is likely that this standard would fail to provide a reliable way to categorize films as pornographic, or to adjudicate cases in court dealing with pornogra-phy. Such an ad hoc, purely constructionist, manner of definition—knowing rusticity and urbanity when we see it—would be indefensible. These iden-tities should have an objective anchor to some degree, if they are to make sense as a dimension of identity. At the same time, it would be absurdly rigid to insist on a purely objective understanding that cannot process nuance or clarify ambiguity. The most defensible position falls, alas, somewhere in the middle. It is part objective and part constructed—it is a critical construction-ist definition.

Returning to our example of the Manhattan cowboy and the farming city girl, a critical constructionist perspective might appreciate the fuzziness of the objective anchors of identity without entirely dismissing them as relevant to their subjective identification as urbane or rustic—their upbringing adds new information about their anchors to the objective conditions. The conclu-sion that is reached by Rye (2006a), who studied youth social constructions of rural through personal interviews, is that social constructions tend to be highly rooted in structural conditions. We must therefore improve our ability to identify and understand the complexity in how the objective and con-structed interact to produce different identity outcomes. In the end, it is largely up to individuals to find the identity that feels right, and to force anything else on someone would be unnecessary and oppressive. This bring us to the next segment of our examination of identity—the individual and group level processes that constitute identity formation.

PERSONAL, SOCIAL, AND FUSED IDENTITIES

In his description of the sociological imagination, C. Wright Mills (1959) claimed it was the ability to see how the biography of individuals (personal) could be located within a shared history of a group (social). In the context of American culture, there is a deficiency in sociological imagination. There is a tendency to overemphasize individuals and to reduce all explanations of action to the individual level. Doing so ignores the overarching social and historical processes that shape individual lives and biographies. The funda-mental attribution error refers to the fallacy of attributing success or failure in life to the attributes of individuals, when in reality these are due to social factors such as group membership. When there is a deficiency in the soci-ological imagination, there is a greater likelihood of committing the funda-mental attribution error. While identity formation is largely an individual/ personal matter, it also exists at the social/group level. While personal iden-tity draws upon unique characteristics, such as our personality and experi-ences, social identity grows out of characteristics shared by members in the same group or social category.

Belonging to a social group comes with a set of privileges, and in many cases, a set of challenges. Membership in minority groups—based on race, ethnicity, gender, sexuality, working class status, or being rustic—means going through life as someone viewed as deviant, inferior, or somehow "less than" the dominant group. This is accompanied by a range of stereotypes, prejudice, and, in some cases, discriminatory action. Typically, minority group status forces one to develop a stronger sociological imagination, as there is a constant second-guessing every time something is denied or withheld, if it is based on something entirely individual or if it is, alternatively, the result of group membership. Being denied access to college, getting turned down for a job, or being declined for a loan, among other things, are potentially the result of low grades, lack of qualifications, or bad credit—all individual characteristics. Yet, many people with these same shortcomings find the doors of opportunity sitting wide open—the privilege of dominant group membership. Of course, if one benefits from dominant group status there is little incentive to investigate the social causes of success. To the contrary, people like to congratulate themselves on their accomplishments and take full credit based on the personal action and achievement—yet another commission of the fundamental attribution error.

Identity Conflict and Fusion

In certain cases, individual identity runs against social identity, creating an internal conflict. On this point, DuBois (2017 [1903]) observed that the black population lived with something he called "double consciousness"—an internal conflict that blends together the ability to see the world outwardly and subjectively as a black person, but also view one's self objectively through a white lens—a condition he argued could lead to self-loathing (becoming racist toward oneself). It is possible that a similar dynamic is at play with those who are rural/rustic and living in an urbanormative culture—as observed in the earlier mentioned study of rural educational deficiencies (Theobald & Wood 2011). Not only do you see the world subjectively through the eyes of a rustic, you develop the ability to view yourself from the standpoint of urbanites, perhaps developing a sense of inferiority in the process.

In other cases, personal and social identity do not conflict, finding some level of interplay. The extreme is identity fusion, when individual and social identities become inseparable (Kte-pi 2018). This is something that we find with sports fans, for example, as fans become so highly identified with their teams, they begin to lose sight of their personal identity. They may act in ways that are inconsistent with their own values when immersed in the sports scene. In this context, normally peaceful people engage in physical confrontations and fighting as a result of identity fusion. By the same token, identity fusion in sports fans may allow for unusually high social bonding with strangers due to their shared identity, as when football fans reminisce about past victories or defeats, transforming strangers into close friends instantly. The phenomenon of identity fusion and related outcomes like crowd violence may result from the fact that humans evolved under a system of tribalism, under which humans adapted by protecting other members of the tribe even when personal risks were present (Pinker 2012).

In sum, when group membership becomes the most salient dimension of individual identity, identity fusion may follow. If someone were to devote their life to passionately working for an environmental nonprofit organization, their personal identity may fuse to the identity of being an environmentalist. Other personal interests and values may eventually take a backseat to this master identity. For our current project we ask if rusticity can be elevated to this level. Are there people for whom their status as a rural or rustic person is the most important fact of their life?

Group and Community Identity Work

Understanding identity formation likewise requires examination of group processes associated with identity work (Schwalbe 1996). In her essay on meaning construction among racial, ethnic, and immigrant groups, Lamont (2000) claims that we participate in a form of identity work that has as its goal creating a distinction between those are "like us" and those who are "others." Group identity work is "largely a matter of signifying, labeling, and defining" (Schwalbe and Mason-Schrok 1996, p. 115) so that we can more easily detect the boundaries of group membership. We would expect urban and rural people to engage in a form of identity work that draws an exclusionary line separating insider from outsider. Group identity processes usually carry with them a moral project that celebrates the virtues of a particular identity while demonizing the wickedness of others (Schwalbe 1996). A country song that celebrates rusticity while denigrating the urbane life of cities—a fairly common theme in this genre—would illustrate this fact.

When someone is born into a rural community, they may resist rusticity, behaving in ways that distance themselves from rural life, while promoting an urbane image. Rural youth may exclaim that they hate their hometown, can't wait to leave, and celebrate urban identity and lifestyles. Alternatively, rural youth may embrace rusticity and incorporate it as an important part of their personal identity. Urban people who relocate to rural areas may imagine that they are becoming more rustic. They may begin to refashion their identity in a way that resembles an image of what rusticity looks like. Even if an urbanite were to embrace a rural community, and identify as a rustic, it does not mean that they will be accepted by the community as a member. Relocated urbanites often wish to be granted insider status and to feel a sense of belonging in their new community but may face serious disappointment if this does not come to fruition.

Rural communities are often difficult to penetrate for an outsider, due to the high level of bonding relative to bridging social capital that is typical (Flora & Flora 2015; Wilkinson 1991). There is a well-documented literature in rural sociology on the conflict between "newcomers" and "old-timers" in rural communities that suggests group membership may be difficult to achieve (Graber 1974; Salamon 2003). Much of this literature is focused on how the character of communities is altered. This literature does not hash out the identity dynamics of community membership that distinguishes who these newcomers are—we would hypothesize that an urbane newcomer would have a harder time transitioning compared to a newly arrived rustic person. Suburbanization may bring a mixture, but likely the majority will identify with an urbane identity.

The difficulty in being accepted may explain why some urbanites, seeking to start a new rustic life, opt to join intentional communities instead of organic communities. For example, the Dancing Rabbits are an intentional community that holds a formal vote on whether to accept or reject new members, who go through a formal application process (Sanford 2018). If accepted, new members must make some pretty major changes, such as learning to grow their own food and build their own house, all while taking a vow of poverty. While these costs may be high, the reward is a level of social acceptance and belonging that may be otherwise impossible to achieve in an organic rural community. Eventually, as new members become acclimated to their new way of life and community, their personal identity and social identity as a Dancing Rabbit may begin to fuse into one. It may then be difficult to recall what life was like before making this major change.

The opposite scenario would probably play out differently, as when a rural/rustic person attempts to relocate and become a part of an urban community. Generally, urban areas are not as exclusionary as rural communities, since there is a higher level of bridging relative to bonding social capital (Flora & Flora 2015; Wilkinson 1991). Individuals may come and go relatively unnoticed. Yet, as observed by Simmel, urban areas may leave new residents feeling isolated and lonely, especially if accustomed to having a greater sense of social belonging that comes from small-town bonding ties. Urban people typically do achieve a level of belonging by carving out a social network of support, but this takes time. A rural person may find that they lack the cultural capital it takes to be accepted by urban communities.

Intersectionality

To this point we have discussed the different dimensions of identity—race, ethnicity, sex, gender, class, urban-rural—as separate. What happens when these interact and intersect? As noted above, each individual has membership in a variety of social groups/categories, and these carry a system of privileges and obstacles derived from social location—intersectional identity. Sociologists specializing in intersectional studies have devoted copious research to the examination of intersectionality, but generally to the exclusion of the urban-rural dimension. Ching and Creed (1997, p. 3) state that, "Given the pervasiveness of the rural/urban opposition and its related significance in the

construction of identity, it is remarkable that the explosion of scholarly interest in identity politics has generally failed to address the rural/urban axis."
Are we to believe, for instance, that being a black female in a rural community in the United States is no different than in a black female in an urban
setting? Urban-rural difference can be profound.

An exception is the growing body of work that examines rural-urban
sexuality. Following Gray (2009), Stapel (2014) maintains that the popular
imagination of rural renders nonnormative sexualities—homo, metro, a, or
bi-sexual—invisible. Reviewing the work of rural queer studies, Stapel
(2014) points out that while most of these scholars have employed nuanced
and critical approaches to understanding sexual identity, they have simultaneously embraced the purely objectivist/materialist view of the urban-rural
binary—those based on population density or occupations. He calls for a
move to a more "fluid, subjective, sociocultural rurality" (p. 151), or what we
have been referring to as rusticity. Following Weston (1995), Stapel questions the urbanormative tendency to view cities as safe harbors for the gay
community, while denouncing rural areas as the source of persecution. Once
arrived in the safe harbor of a city, Halberstam (2005, p. 27) observes gay
urbanites may "distance themselves from the horror of the heartlands and
even congratulate themselves for living in an urban rather than a rural environment." This view is highly exclusionary of nonnormative sexualities in
the countryside, and also neglectful of the horrors associated with urban
bigotry.

TAKEAWAYS

In the twenty years following publication of the edited volume by Ching and
Creed (1997), entitled, *Knowing Your Place*, there has been only a minor
level of social scientific attention devoted to the study of urbane and rustic
identity. At the time of writing this volume, we report only a modest level of
change. We hope to see further research on this dimension of identity going
into the future.

The changing realities for many rural areas have led to the
(mis)perception that the relevance of rural life is waning or has already
vanished from significance. While it is true that the countryside has become
more urban and urbane in many respects, it is premature and misguided to
reject the importance or relevance of rural or rustic identity. From a global
perspective, traditional rural conditions that many assume to be dead, remain
alive and well in rural nations such as Uganda. Even with continued movement toward automating rural work, it would be foolish to assume the human
race could continue to survive without the labor of rural workers providing
the basic materials required of our economy. It is also unlikely that people

will ever stop living in sparsely settled rural areas, even if their occupation is not part of the energy economy—there remains a cultural preference for small-town life.

Perhaps more important to note is the fact that identity has an oft-neglected subjective component that is socially defined. As with sex and gender, the objective conditions of rural or urban identity do not always align with the subjective definition of urbane or rustic. Individuals must work through the process of identity formation, and in so doing engage in a certain amount of self-evaluation. This does not happen in a vacuum, but rather within the wider context of social group and even community identity formation. Urbane and rustic identity may be claimed by individuals, but that does not mean that they will be accepted by social groups or communities that claims urbane or rustic identity. Based on the interplay between individual and group processes, some level of identity fusion may be achieved. It is important to likewise consider how the urbane-rustic dimension of identity intersects with all of the other dimensions to create different outcomes. The broader study of intersectionality might follow the lead of the pioneering work on rural sexualities and incorporate this long-neglected dimension.

Part III

Everyday Life

Chapter Seven

Policy and Law

As cultural norms, values, and beliefs begin to align with realities of life in urban society, the rural experience grows increasingly distant and unfamiliar, due to the expansion of epistemic distance. The needs and challenges confronting rural populations become less visible and tangible, while those of the urban population take center stage. As any society determines what priorities it has and how best to meet them, it commences to write or rewrite the rules—that is to say, it begins to implement new policies and laws. When the value system is urbanormative, urban needs are prioritized over rural. Urbanormative laws and policies assume an urban context, so when they are uniformly applied to a rural context, the outcomes often create disparities and inequalities.

Laws and policies operate much like an operating system functions for a computer—providing the necessary rules to coordinate the physical components with the appropriate software. Operating systems are designed based on a set of assumptions about the architecture of a computer—the processor power, the motherboard, the amount of RAM, types of peripherals, and so on. As physical components are replaced by newer models, the operating system requires new rules called hardware drivers. Without them, the system does not function properly. Eventually, the system may need a total upgrade. Installing a modern operating system on a computer with twenty-year-old physical equipment would likely fail, as the assumptions of hardware—processing power, memory, and other variables—would be incorrect. Our guiding question in this chapter is whether the rules designed to guide urban life can successfully operate in the architecture of a rural context.

Most rural communities were, of course, initially operated by the rules of a rural system. A rural system functions, as noted in chapter 3, by coordinating activities associated with life on the front line of the energy economy.

This includes collecting and harvesting food, timber, ores, and other natural resources, and then trading the bounty with urban populations using different transportation networks. In many cases, these functions have been lost and rural communities might come to be operated by urban rules. The problem is that rural communities are less populous, less dense, and more physically distant and spread out than urban communities. They also generally lack much of the retail, communication, transportation, and other kinds of infrastructure that tends to be more developed in a city. When laws and policies are written based on a set of assumptions about the typical citizen, and that is assumed to be an urban citizen with access to urban amenities, it should be no surprise to find dysfunction.

Ideally, policies and laws will be written in ways that accommodate different urban-rural realities. What seems to be happening is the application of a one-size-fits-all urbanormative laws and policies that best serve urban populations and leave rural communities languishing. We will attempt to understand the why and how of this shift to urbanormative and urban-centric rule making, while considering some recent examples. Before getting into specific outcomes, we begin with some historical and contextual background. As law and policy are context-specific, and as there has been limited research on urbanormative law, this chapter will focus primarily on the dynamics unfolding in the United States

HISTORICAL BACKGROUND
OF RURALITY AND POLICY IN THE UNITED STATES

Historically, in the United States, from the time of independence through the period immediately following the Great Depression, politicians understood the need to win over rural populations if they hoped to have a political future. If a candidate did not appear to support pro-rural policies—which were mainly pro-farmer policies—then they would most likely lose, as the farming class made up roughly one third of the electorate (Prasad, 2012). The rural farm constituency was a major political force, with a unified interest in a set of pro-farming policies. Prasad (2012) documents how politicians in the 1930s would strive to win the approval of rural farmers by supporting measures such as production and price controls that would guarantee a fair price for agricultural commodities. They also promised to regulate agricultural trade by providing protections through tariffs that ensured domestic agricultural products would remain competitive in foreign markets. These policies, designed to protect farmers, were routinely touted by politicians across party lines in order to win the rural vote. As we will argue, as the strength of the rural contingency declined, the necessity of pro-rural policies likewise fell by the wayside in place of pro-urban policies.

At this stage, it is worth reflecting for a moment on the historical trajectory of urbanization in the United States. In 1776, when the Declaration of Independence was signed, roughly 5 percent of the country lived in a city. The vast majority of Americans were situated in small towns that served a wider region of farm homesteads. The interests of early voters were, therefore, almost entirely synonymous with the interests of rural farmers. Devising policies that ensure the viability of farming while improving trade networks to serve distant urban populations, were of primary concern. By the Civil War, the urban population had grown to nearly 20 percent—a powerful, but as yet, small minority. The urban population of the United States became a numerical majority in the middle of the twentieth century, and it is at this time that we begin to see remarkable and radical departure from pro-farmer and pro-rural policies to pro-urban and pro-consumer policies.

Moreover, as the population became urban, the unified interest of farmers began to fragment, resulting in competing interests and policy demands for those growing corn, wheat, and cotton (Winders & Scott 2012; Winders 2017). In other words, the already shrinking agricultural population was becoming divided against itself, with different factions calling for wildly different policies that would no longer serve the interests of all farmers equally well (Winders & Scott 2012). After divisions within the agricultural sectors deepened (Winders & Scott 2012), the overall influence of farmers began to decline.

The shrinking of the farm population, coupled with internal fragmentation, spurred the decline of rural influence on national politics. In its place has arisen a new set of rules—a new operating system—based on serving the interests of urbanites. Now political candidates focus on promises geared toward urban consumers, instead of rural producers, with profound consequences, particularly in such areas as agricultural policy. This has, for instance, led to the dismantling of subsidies and controls that support farming, and this has allowed the cost of agricultural goods to plummet. While this has come with a heavy cost for farmers, many of whom would lose their livelihoods in the 1980s farm crisis as commodity prices went into free fall, it also makes for more affordable food products that make urban consumers happy (Lobao and Meyer 2001).

Political realities have followed disparate trajectories at the state level. Urbanormativity in public policy is rarely so blatantly stated as in New York State. Home to the largest city in the country, New York City spews suburbs for over a hundred miles in any direction, resulting in a Combined Statistical Area (CSA) that in 2017 was home to 23,876,155 people in four different states (US Census Bureau 2017). Add to this another three CSAs of over a million people and even smaller metropolitan areas like Syracuse and Utica, and the state is custom-made for a culture of urbanormativity. Even in Albany, the state capital and the center of a CSA of nearly 1.2 million people, it is common for people to refer to "the city" not as Albany but as New York, 150 miles to the south. And so we should not be surprised that urbanormativity is built into the state constitution.

New York is divided into townships, each of which has its own local government. The only municipalities in the state not part of a township are the cities, each of which has its own charter, a right to a share of the county sales tax revenue raised within the city (townships do not), and a variety of public programs not available to townships. Among the towns, however, there is a further distinction:

> In New York towns are classified as either "towns of the first class," which includes any township with over ten thousand residents or those with over five thousand that request such status . . . or "towns of the second class" (NYSDOS 2009, 61). (Thomas et al. 2011, 22)

The state grants less powers to, and retains more powers over, the second-class towns. This includes such basic functions as setting a speed limit.

Arguably, the recent election of Donald Trump as president of the United States was due in part to a gamble he took on trying to win the rural vote. This was done by holding rallies in states and counties that would attract rural voters, where he would make promises to restore such things as coal mining and farming to their former glory. Though this may have seemed like an outdated political strategy, it proved successful. The rural vote—which still makes up a sizable 20 percent of the population—controls a disproportionately high number of electoral votes. This explains why Trump could win the majority of electoral votes but not the popular vote. Perhaps this indicates that politics in the United States have started to come full circle—the rural vote, it turns out, still matters. Promises aside, after decades of change, the overall policy and legal framework has become heavily urban-centric and urbanormative.

THE URBANORMATIVE POLICY CONTEXT

The above background shows the overarching direction of policy in the United States, which started with a strong foundation in rural interest, but by the second half of the twentieth century began to transform to a new urban operating system. We now focus more closely on the changing character of the new policy context. It involves four interrelated patterns of privatization, deregulation, devolution, and fiscal stress. The overall goal of these patterns is captured in the term austerity that aims to replace a public system of administration that is centrally organized and regulated, and which makes heavy investments in local development, with a private, decentralized, and deregulated system with shrinking levels of federal support for local communities. The older model is based on the vision of Franklin Delano Roosevelt's New Deal, which involved heavy federal investments in rural development through outlays that were underwritten by steep taxes on the wealthy. The new model is based on the vision of Ronald Reagan's Free Market, Trickle-Down Economics, which argued that cutting taxes on the wealthy would jumpstart the private sector and eliminate the need for government involvement or regulation. We will now unpack the meaning of these four patterns under the new context of austerity.

Devolution and Fiscal Stress

Devolution refers to the increasing downward pressure that is being placed on local communities to be more economically self-sufficient, as government support is withdrawn. As sources of funding from above—at the state or federal level—are eliminated, we are seeing uneven results across urban and rural places. In theory, the idea of making communities responsible for their own services sounds fair—much like a parent making their children responsible for their own finances. The problem is that not every community (or child) is equally prepared for this transition, and some will not fare well at all. As we will discuss, rural areas are generally least prepared due to—by definition—their small, sparse populations that are spread out over large areas.

Only the most populous, well-resourced urban and suburban communities, can be sustained through self-reliance, since this depends on the ability to create substantial local revenue streams by way of property taxes or perhaps, local income taxes (almost exclusively found in large cities). Indeed, property tax is usually the primary source of revenue for funding local needs, such as school districts, parks and recreational opportunities, and an array of infrastructure. For communities lacking sufficient local revenue— due to small population, low property values, and high poverty and unemployment rates, typical of rural areas—the ability to achieve self-sufficiency ranges from very difficult to insurmountable. It is in such places that we find the problem of fiscal stress, as when local revenue is insufficient for supporting the community's needs. Fiscal stress becomes apparent at the sight of crumbling infrastructure, weakening local school districts, and neglected parks and recreational opportunities.

There is a lot of variation across rural communities, and the problem of fiscal stress is exacerbated by high poverty rates. This can be found in areas where there is a large elderly population living on a fixed income, and generally in communities that are further from urban centers. Aging homes often hold little value, so resulting property taxes are not sufficient to cover what the community requires, which typically involves massive upgrades to aging infrastructure. In the case of local school districts, the pressure is often to shutter the school or consolidate with another community. While this can have positive financial effects, the negative impact of a school closure on rural communities is hard to quantify—beyond the problems raised in chapter 4, it more or less guarantees that families with young children will no longer wish to live there, and this will have dire consequences for future population growth. It will exacerbate the aging problem, further undermining the ability to generate local revenue. As for parks and recreation, the decision is often to simply shut it down or relinquish control to a private entity. A local park may be transferred to the county or state, if possible, but as the general trend is toward devolution this is an unlikely outcome. Organizations that charge membership fees, like fitness centers, may replace public recreational facilities, or communities risk losing their ability to provide recreation—thereby injuring its desirability as a place to live. When it comes to infrastructure, a community may try to transfer control of its local roads to the county, state, or federal levels. If that fails, it may go into decline and become unsafe. Bridges may risk collapse, roads may become dangerously worn, adding to the probability of accidents, water may become unsafe to drink, sewage systems may breach causing contamination, solid waste may become problematic if not contained, and so on. As infrastructure declines, so too does the attractiveness of the community. This further discourages would-be residents from moving in, thereby fueling a cycle of disinvestment. The public sector is simply unable to support itself in the absence of external funds. The choices are: (a) to do nothing and allow the community to slowly decline, (b) to forfeit local control to the state or federal level, wherever possible (the least likely outcome), or (c) to hand control over to private entities either entirely or in partnership with local government. Another possibility, of course, would be to return to Rooseveltian levels of rural investment, but this would require a much bigger change in federal policy.

Privatization and Deregulation

In the area of infrastructure, the dominant trend is toward privatization, or transferring public control to a private company to manage either in partnership with a local government or in a market-based arrangement with no public role. For example, municipalities once provided solid waste removal services to residents. Trash bins would be taken to the curb and the waste would be removed by municipal workers—all paid for with tax dollars. Local communities seeking to reduce their fiscal stress have opted to hand control of solid waste removal over to private companies. Now, residents haul their waste to the curb and receive a monthly bill for the service from a private company. Similarly, as the cost of maintaining water treatment and distribution systems exceeds what communities can support, municipal governments may decide to hand over the water system to a private company. As with the solid waste service, residents are sent a bill for their water use.

The effectiveness of privatization is greatest when households have the resources necessary to pay for all of these additional bills that were once covered by tax dollars. Wealthy households may shrug off a new utility bill, but for many disadvantaged rural residents living on a limited or fixed income, the addition of new bills can be devastating. What privatization does, then, is extend the downward pressure of devolution from the local community to the household level. Once again, this will have uneven outcomes. When a household cannot afford to pay its bills, we begin to see bankruptcy, eviction, abandonment of property, and rising social problems associated with homelessness, food insecurity, and crime, along with personal and domestic stress-induced problems—divorce, domestic violence, mental health problems, and substance abuse.

As the public sector shrinks, the array of services provided disappears, and the value of living in a publicly funded community diminishes. As a result, many wealthy people often choose to live in private, often gated, communities. These are designed to maximize control over how community needs are addressed. In place of taxes, private communities rely on association fees or dues that function like a tax in a private setting—the main difference is that in a private setting, citizens are not guaranteed a voice, and homeowner associations do not necessarily function democratically. Residents in private communities are often upset by their lack of voice in matters that impact the community overall—this was the case, for instance, in Celebration, Disney, where many residents wanted to have more say in how the local school was being run (Bartling 2004). While the quality of life is often impressive in affluent private communities like Celebration—excellent infrastructure, top-notch recreational opportunities, beautiful parks, and high performing schools—it is often achieved at the cost of surrendering the democratic guarantee that comes with living in a public community. In some private communities, the developer retains full control over community affairs under the logic of protecting investment. What is this but a form of totalitarianism?

Not only do the residents of private communities sacrifice democratic process, but by spatially removing themselves from the wider public, they leave those outside their community, who are less affluent, to fend for themselves with fewer resources. No longer are the wealthy underwriting the needs of the poor by enriching public coffers with taxes paid on more expensive property. Losing these tax dollars worsens the problem of fiscal stress. It is also why it not uncommon to find rampant poverty in a city or rural area that lies just beyond the gate of a wealthy private community. Of course, the problems experienced in these neighboring communities have spillover effects, as residents in wealthy communities come to live in fear of nearby impoverished neighborhoods and communities. In the end, many of their problems of crumbling infrastructure, declining schools, and other quality-of-life concerns such as parks and recreation, would be reduced if wealthy households were brought on to the tax rolls.

As privatization takes root, another consequence is deregulation. When a service is public, it must operate in a transparent fashion. Public school districts must present a budget for public approval, for instance. If the public is unhappy with the way the district is doing their job, they can go to the local school board or town council meeting and voice their concerns. This will then be met with some kind of public response. If a service becomes privatized, however, there is no parallel mechanism for local residents to voice their concerns. In other words, deregulation means forfeiting public oversight and becoming non-democratic. There is no such thing as a Freedom of Information Act that applies to private companies, so if its practices are objectionable to the public, or are simply called into question, there is less legal basis compelling accountability and responsiveness. In short, privatizing public services slowly chips away at democratic oversight.

Of course, many will object to this claim, arguing that the government is highly inefficient while the private sector is not. Government at all levels can be very bureaucratic, and that is undeniable. However, government must also be open to the public. Private organizations, which may be equally inefficient and bureaucratic, have no similar legal requirement for transparency and openness. Further, while government can put community needs ahead of profitability, private organizations must necessarily put profits ahead of all else, or they risk going out of business.

The extent to which rural communities become privatized is currently quite variable. Some are more resistant, and others are simply not targeted for private development. While government may invest in all rural communities, private companies will be selective, looking for places that will earn the greatest profit. Profitability requires lots of customers who are able to pay high dollar amounts for services. For example, if a company were to operate the water system of a community of only two hundred people it would stand to make very little money—they would have to charge a lot so the population would need to be affluent. If local water remains easily accessible, it may be profitable to serve a small population, but if it is scarce, as in more arid regions, requiring a great deal of investment in infrastructure, private companies will probably not show any interest. This logic of investment explains why rural communities lag behind their urban counterparts with regard to high speed internet access. Laying down fiber optic cables requires too heavy an investment to serve such a sparse and small population.

Lack of private investment in rural communities explains the decline of public transportation. Rail lines ones traversed much of the United States but have now been almost entirely privatized. Cargo transportation is generally more profitable than passenger service, so private rail companies invest in cargo, while cancelling passenger service. This dynamic is perhaps most obvious with air travel. Since air travel was deregulated in the 1980s, fares have fallen for consumers in large cities traveling to other large cities. Smaller airports have not adapted, and many rural and small metropolitan airports have lost commercial service entirely. This is aggravated by increasing security demands such as checkpoints and new technologies, demands that only larger urban airports can afford to provide. Ironically, even travelers from larger cities are hurt by these forces as they too are now faced with more limited air service and destinations.

As a result, rural communities that were once served by a wide transportation network are suddenly cut off. The transportation needs of communities are no concern for a private rail company or airline, especially as they may not have any local ties, perhaps even based out of a different state or country. This forces rural residents to rely on themselves, and this usually means finding a way to pay for and maintain an automobile—a major expense that the urban poor can often avoid and the rural poor cannot. Again, the needs of local residents are a matter of democratic concern, not of private investment and profit-maximization.

This overview of the current austere policy context—devolution, privatization, deregulation, and fiscal stress—provides a foundation for understanding many of the problems facing rural areas. The downward pressure of devolution causes local communities to offer less support for households. More affluent communities can weather the cost of private services, while the poor and disadvantaged must make the hard choices of canceling services, allowing infrastructure to go into disrepair, consolidating or closing schools, or handing control over to private enterprises (if they are interested). In turn, these unregulated companies are not subject to the same level of transparency, oversight, and public scrutiny as local government. What is the logical conclusion to these trends in the long run? It is hard to say with certainty what will happen in the future, but it is entirely possible that as local governments hand over control to private interests, the autonomy of rural communities will eventually be lost, the sense of place and local community identity will disintegrate, and migration to urban areas will seem the only logical move. In the end, there may be no public sector to speak of, exposing rural citizens to the whims of deregulated private organizations. We now turn to a more specific evaluation of how this plays out across different political and legal areas.

SPATIAL INEQUALITY AND
THE URBANORMATIVITY OF POLICY AND LAW

Spatial inequality refers to the fact that there is a geographic basis for many of the problems facing communities. Unfortunately, as Lobao, Hooks, and Tickamyer (2007) point out, most scholarly studies of social inequality tend to neglect the spatial dimension. To be sure, spatial inequality centers on the urban-rural fault line, in which urbanormative policies systematically privilege urban over rural interests. Below we examine some of the only research that has been conducted on the urbanormativity of law.

Poverty and Welfare

The context surrounding poverty and welfare fits squarely within the earlier noted pattern of devolution—federal programs are disappearing or drying up, state programs are being eliminated, responsibility is being handed down to the county or municipal levels. The local governments adapt by shedding services and handing things over to private companies, and this makes it more difficult for households and the individuals paying to run them. Devolution creates a highly predictable pattern of spatial inequality.

Public opinion surrounding federal welfare policies grew to be antagonistic since the 1980s, when Reagan and like-minded media channels began invoking the stereotypical image of the Welfare Queen, who "is a lazy woman—implicitly black—who continues to have children in order to increase the size of her welfare check. She lives high on the hog at the expense of hardworking American taxpayers" (Pruitt 2016, p. 289). Pruitt (2016) notes that it is possible that Reagan purposely sought to obscure the fact that most poor people were white rural people, previously served by the now defunct New Deal. If the public awareness of poverty had a white rural face, this may have generated empathy for the poor and greater support for the Rooseveltian programs that Reagan wished to eliminate. Yet, the public imagination of white poverty is not always synonymous with empathy either, as the notion of "white trash" serves to undermine empathy by defining poor rural whites as undeserving. Along with decline in public concern for the poor has come decline in financial support for welfare programs.

Tickamyer et al. (2007) find evidence that recent shifts in welfare policy have produced uneven results along spatial lines. Their analysis of Ohio counties found that the more rural Appalachian, southern counties fared far worse than the northern urbanized counties, after responsibility for welfare administration was forced down to the county level. They note that counties hosting large cities, like Cleveland, have far more human, social, and financial capital on which to draw, and therefore enjoy a much greater capacity for administering welfare programs. The southern rural counties were found to have a weak tax base and suffered from an inability to deliver services, leaving their mostly rural residents neglected.

Lobao and colleagues (2007) find similar results in their comparison of two representative Ohio counties—Geauga and Meigs. Although residing within the same administrative structure, the urban Geauga enjoys higher median incomes and lower poverty rates than rural Meigs, located in the Appalachian portion of the state. Consistent with Tickamyer et al. (2007), they conclude that urban communities may find it easier to succeed and thrive in the context of devolution and privatization, while rural communities will need to live with the reality of fiscal stress.

Pruitt's (2010b) analysis of spatial inequality in the state of Montana focused on the delivery of county-level child poverty services. While the Constitution of Montana has an Equal Protection clause, disparities in the ability to deliver services across counties has resulted in unequal outcomes that violate this clause. A central mechanism identified by Pruitt for this disparity is, once again, reliance on local property taxes. Sparsely populated, remote, rural counties suffering from socioeconomic disadvantages are unable to generate the necessary resources through property taxes to support programs. The result is that many rural children are left underserved and unprotected.

Wallace and Pruitt (2012) note that just as levels of financial support for welfare services are disappearing, there has been a concomitant rise in the removal of parent rights from rural parents, who are found by the state to be unfit. As Wallace and Pruitt note, there is hypocrisy in the fact that as the state cancels services that would enable people to be better parents—by providing financial assistance, offering parenting classes and support programs—it subsequently rules against parental fitness and terminates parental rights for those who might have benefitted from the now unavailable services. As counties flounder under a deficient tax base—which is more likely in rural areas—they are forced to withdraw services, leaving households fending for themselves. As poor rural households struggle to make ends meet, anxiety and stress increase, as do the probabilities for a host of problems, from substance abuse to domestic violence.

Gender Rights

As with issues surrounding poverty, spatial inequality has also been detected in analyses of laws and policies that involve gender—such as domestic violence and access to abortion services. Pruitt (2008b) suggests that the phenomenon of domestic violence plays out very differently in rural versus urban contexts. The legal landscape has a hidden urbanormative assumption in how to respond to and prevent domestic violence. Rates are difficult to measure, as there is a known underreporting bias in formal crime statistics.

Yet, as Pruitt (2008b) notes, a recent pioneering study on intimate partner homicide discovered a far greater prevalence in rural areas. Of rural homicides, 18 percent were against an intimate partner, while for urban areas it was only 6 percent. Similar disparities have been detected through research on injuries to intimate partners. Moreover, recent research has shown there is less enforcement of domestic violence laws in rural areas, both in terms of policing and in prosecuting cases in court. Further, there are disparities in the resources available to victims, who are overwhelmingly female. Access to shelters and other support services are far greater in urban settings, leaving rural women underserved.

Statz and Pruitt (2018) and Pruitt and Vanegas (2015) both examine the role of physical distance in creating unequal abortion service access for women living in rural areas. Recent years have seen a large uptick in activity among states implementing restrictions on abortion—205 restrictions were proposed between 2011 and 2013 alone (Pruitt & Vanegas 2015). The constitutionality of these restrictions has been challenged in cases such as *Planned Parenthood of Texas v. Abbott* case. The ruling supported a requirement that abortion providers to have ambulatory access to surgical centers within thirty miles. Other states—Mississippi, Alabama, and Wisconsin—implemented similar requirements. Ultimately, this assumed that women seeking an abortion resided in more populous metropolitan areas. Pruitt and Vanegas (2015) argue that, as a result, such laws place undue burdens on rural and poor women's abortion rights. Ironically, the most at-risk population (rural women) will have the most difficulty obtaining an abortion. They argue that there is a high level of judicial urbanormativity in assuming that most women will have a spatial privilege of living in proximity to the services they require. The 2016 Supreme Court ruling in the case of *Whole Woman's Health v. Hellerstedt* agreed, and the requirement for proximate ambulatory access was found to create an undue burden (Statz & Pruitt 2018). The ruling was, however, too late to save roughly half of the abortion providers in Texas who were shuttered during the years of the restriction. Vast portions of Texas are now underserved.

Legal Rights and Representation

Statz and Pruitt (2018) evaluate the role of physical distance in creating inequalities in the realm of voter ID laws. They note that the requirement to obtain legal identification forces people in rural settings to traverse greater distances than their urban counterparts in order to obtain the documentation necessary to vote, and therefore, to participate in the political system. It is hard to imagine a more direct assault on democracy than creating barriers to the ability of citizens to exercise their basic rights of voting.

Another right that is under assault is the right to representation. Pruitt and Showman (2014) consider the spatial challenges rural people face when it comes to finding and accessing legal services. They find that less than 2 percent of small law practices exist in small towns and rural areas, despite the fact that roughly one-fifth of the population lives in these locations. In other words, the rural population is being underserved with regard to the availability and provision of legal services. They further observe that even where services do exist, the ability of rural people to physically and financially access these services is undermined by widespread regional poverty. So there is a two-part problem: (1) providing incentives for small legal practices to locate in rural areas, and (2) providing assistance to those rural citizens in need of legal services. The recent and innovative Project Rural Practice initiative, implemented in the state of South Dakota, seeks to address the first of the problems, but as Pruitt and Showman observe, it will be hard to succeed without a second program addressing the other part of the problem—providing aid to citizens in need of legal services.

Education

As noted in chapter 4, reliance on property tax as the mechanism for funding schools often results in uneven outcomes. Pruitt (2010b) found this to be the case in Montana, where, again, the Equal Protection clause of its constitution is being violated by the inability to ensure children are provided equal access to quality schooling. The uneven education outcomes combine with the unequal delivery of child poverty programs to create a higher probability of children becoming at-risk. This may mean dropping out of school or engaging in risky behaviors that can lead to additional problems, such as mental illness, teen pregnancy, homelessness, and substance abuse.

For those rural schools that remain operational, inequalities are exacerbated by an education policy that promotes urbanormative curricula. This urban curriculum emphasizes the accomplishments and importance of distant urban-based civilizations, while simultaneously neglecting the historical importance of the local community. This has the effect of reinforcing the sense that the local community is unimportant and why many rural people claim to be from the "middle of nowhere."

Perhaps the greatest evidence of urbanormativity in education is the mass migration of talented rural youth to urban centers near and far, as noted in the influential work by Carr and Kefelas (2009), *Hollowing Out the Middle*. Students are divided between the "achievers" and the "stayers." The most talented youth are lured to larger cities to pursue the educational and career goals, while the less successful students remain in the community. This depletion of human capital over time has been referred to as the "brain drain." Perhaps, if the importance and value of a rural community were taught, many of the more successful students would find a way to be a high-achieving stayer.

The notion of Place Based Education (Avery & Sipple 2016), introduced in chapter 4, has been offered a way to counter the hegemonic and homogenizing qualities of current educational curricula. There is a marked deficiency in the area of STEM jobs in rural communities, so many students find little value in excelling in STEM content. If rural communities were to host a well-educated population trained in STEM areas, they may hold greater appeal to potential employers in the STEM fields.

Health

A final area with the potential for disparate urban-rural outcomes, owing to spatial inequalities, is health. Earlier we discussed the issue of abortion access for rural women, and this was an example of the kind of potential health inequality that exists. We now extend the discussion to include mental health and substance abuse. As noted by Pruitt (2009b), rural adolescents are at the greatest risk for developing a substance abuse problem, when compared to their urban counterparts. This is in spite of the fact that the stereotypical understanding of drug use is of an urban problem. The development of adolescent substance abuse in rural areas may be exacerbated by the presence of other problems stemming from endemic poverty and disadvantage, coupled with diminished support services, lower levels of law enforcement, and a lack of mental health infrastructure that could address or prevent such problems (Pruitt 2009b; Zians 2016). The invisibility of rural substance abuse problems—due to epistemic distance—may explain why policies appear to be written with an implicit assumption that people live in an urban place. One-size-fits-all policies developed for urban areas do not translate well to the rural context where there are a host of different factors at play. It is the wrong operating system.

In the broader context of mental health prevalence and treatment, Zians (2016) contends that not only is the supporting infrastructure lacking to provide services, there is also a greater social barrier to seeking help in rural communities. Zians suggests that in rural communities, the values of individualism, self-reliance, autonomy, and "bootstrap pulling" are more common. The idea of asking for help may, therefore, be viewed as weak and unacceptable. Zians summarizes challenges to mental health treatment with the three A's: accessibility, availability, and acceptability. Even if services are locally available, which is unlikely, rural residents are often unable to pay for services and are also less likely to be insured. If services were both available and accessible, they would still need to be viewed as acceptable, and, as noted above, this may not be the case. Zians finds that many mental health clinicians are not trained to understand the unique context that a rural area presents, so he makes the case that cultural diversity training should begin taking rural awareness into consideration. Finally, while Zians notes that mental illness prevalence and treatment rates are not well documented, the conditions found in rural communities will likely translate into greater prevalence coupled with a proportionately lower rate of the mentally ill receiving treatment (including substance abuse).

TAKEAWAYS

As urbanization and urbanormativity continue to expand, a new political and legal landscape has taken shape. The political influence of rural people, once the foundation of American politics, has been eclipsed by urban interests over the last several decades. The generous federally-supported New Deal policies of rural investment have been supplanted by Trickle-Down policies of austerity—devolution, privatization, deregulation, and fiscal stress. The outcomes have been uneven with the most deleterious effects flowing to disadvantaged rural communities and most beneficial outcomes flowing to urban (and suburban) communities.

The hidden presumption that law designed for an urban population will work equally well for rural people has proven false and has left many rural people underserved. We found evidence of urban-rural disparities in the areas surrounding poverty, gender, legal rights and representation, education, and health. In each case, rural populations fared worse than their urban counterparts, due in large part to a system that requires local self-reliance.

We also tried to point out the interconnectedness of the policy disparities. If poverty is untreated, households may experience more problems with mental health, substance abuse, and domestic violence. Young people, who have more vulnerability from poverty may suffer unwanted pregnancies, thereby creating a demand for abortion services that are difficult to receive. The distance traveled to and from school, and the quality of schooling may undermine the potential for educational success. Communities may see their youngest generation leaving, and with them, the future of the community.

Reversing course will mean developing policies and laws that consider and adapt to variations along the urban-rural continuum. It may require a modern New Deal that restores investment in rural communities that are not likely to find a way to pull themselves up by their bootstraps. Preserving the public funding of communities is the best way to protect democratic oversight and process as well as public protections. In the next chapter, we turn to a discussion of how urbanormativity has changed rural communities in ways that transcend law and policy.

Chapter Eight

Urbanormative Communities

This chapter examines the many ways in which the ideology of urbanormativity is reshaping and changing rural communities. The ideas, images, and values that comprise this ideology do not simply exist in the minds of urbanites—they find physical expression, particularly when reinforced with laws and policies as reviewed in the last chapter. Place-structuration refers to the process through which values, norms, and beliefs become encoded into the built and natural environments of communities (Fulkerson & Thomas 2014; Seale & Fulkerson 2014; Thomas 2014a). Through this process, the character and tradition of communities are remade into an idealized form (Molotch, Freudenburg, & Paulsen 2000) that meets urban expectations.

The relationship between culture and structure in a community is complex. To inform our understanding, Giddens (1984) offers the notion of *structuration*, whereby the rules of social life—its structure—are constantly made and remade to fit new and evolving cultural realities. As norms and values evolve, so too do the rules of social life. A modified version of this concept, *place-structuration*, was introduced by Molotch, Freudenburg, and Paulsen (2000) that adds the benefit of including a spatial component. Their comparison of two California communities, Ventura and Santa Barbara, illustrates how different values about the economy and environment result in different structural and spatial outcomes. Ventura would pursue traditional economic development based on oil production, while Santa Barbara would develop as a tourist destination, making use of its rich environmental amenities. In the case of Ventura's extractive community, economic growth superseded the value placed on environmental protection; for Santa Barbara, these priorities were reversed. Through place-structuration, the physical communities evolved to encompass different characters—as embodied in the physical landscape.

The term rural simulacrum refers to an object, symbol, or activity that simulates rural or rustic qualities, based on representations (see chapter 5) held by urbanites that are informed by cultural resources (see chapter 4), including popular media (Thomas et al. 2011). One can imagine the sight of a horse-drawn carriage lying in wait to provide a simulated rustic experience, or a storefront sporting a sign that reads "General Store," where rustic items such as cowboy hats, boots, spurs, and so forth, may be purchased. Rural communities that appeal to urbanites reflect not the local history or traditions of the community but a generic and idealized rustic quality that meets the aesthetic and social expectations of urbanormative rural representations as the process of place-structuration proceeds (Seale & Fulkerson 2014). Seale and Fulkerson (2014) outlined more precisely the process that reveals how abstract social representations become encoded into the character of communities. Their model begins from above, where mass culture, imbued with urbanormative ideology, creates rural representations. These representations reflect the themes of rural as simple, wild, and escape (Thomas et al. 2011). From the representations come rural simulacra as objects, activities, and symbols. Finally, as the presence of these simulacra accumulate, the character and tradition of the community are gradually transformed—with consequences for the community's cultural capital. The irony is that beneath the resulting simulation of rural life is a traditional authentic rural community with a specific local history and level of importance that may be gradually erased or rewritten.

As rural tourism and migration bring hordes of urbanites to the countryside, the disruption and restructuring of local economic and social life continues. In most cases, traditional rural work and history are eclipsed for the generic, Disney-fied version of rural life. Urban societies, like those found in Scandinavia, the United States, and the United Kingdom, have responded by enacting different development strategies with varying priorities assigned to expanding the rural economy versus protecting the environment. Before examining these, let's consider what we mean by traditional rural communities.

TRADITIONAL RURAL COMMUNITIES

Historically, rural communities were defined not just by spatial demographic characteristics of small and sparse populations, but by political and economic functions—they participated on the front line of the energy economy (defined in chapter 3). While the popular imagination of traditional rural communities often paints a rosy and quaint picture, the realities are often much harsher. Disasters such as floods that destroyed the coal mining towns of Buffalo Creek, West Virginia (Erickson 1978; Schwartz-Balcott 2008), and contamination in Centralia, Pennsylvania (Kane & Thomas 2016), remind us of the dangers and risks rural people face collecting and harvesting the resources in the energy economy that will later be traded to and consumed by the urban population. Rural communities must deal with a rash of harmful consequences from agriculture, deforestation, strip mining, mountain top removal, and energy extraction.

McKinney's (2016) analysis of Evangeline, Louisiana, sheds light on this issue. In Evangeline, the twin industries of extracting oil and treating wood (for such purposes as railroad ties), operated from the 1940s through the 1980s. As these industries declined it was discovered that dangerous levels of known carcinogens—arsenic, pentachlorophenol, and polycyclic aromatic hydrocarbons—were contaminating the water and land. This would lead to the declaration of a Superfund Site by the Environmental Protection Agency. McKinney observed urban bias in the way the EPA handled this disaster, neglecting input from the rural community, announcing public meetings in the nearby urban newspaper of the community of Jennings—reflecting the pattern observed by McKay (2016) of urbanormative news coverage. The concern of the EPA was clearly not for the health of the local population of Evangeline, but that the risk of contamination might spillover to the community of Jennings. For McKinney, rural people like those in Evangeline, are victims of environmental injustice. Their communities are damaged by harmful enterprises that expose local populations to tremendous risks, all for the purpose of providing urban populations with products they need and wish to consume. In return, they are shown little concern or regard, often met instead with moral indifference (chapter 2) or urban resentment for the damages that are incurred. In short, rural populations are blamed for damaging the environment to conduct these important economic functions. Similar examples could be provided of rural communities located near massive CAFOs (Contained Animal Feeding Operations), where animal waste lagoons threaten air and water quality with damaging bacteria, or communities located in places dealing with the side effects of mountain top removal for coal or hydraulic fracturing for natural gas.

Devaluing Rural Production and Places

Urbanormative ideology does not acknowledge or fully grasp urban dependency, and consequently those who subscribe to it assign little or no value to rural production. The dim understanding of urban reliance on rural production comes into clear focus, however, after a shortage. Painful reminders were felt in the post-war United Kingdom and Great Depression-era United States, where food crises cut away urbanormative illusions of security. The UK government enacted land use restrictions designed to preserve rural agricultural lands to ensure food security. The measures did not, unfortunately, include provisions to protect rural farmers or communities responsible for the food production (Marsden et al. 1993). In the United States, the government enacted production and price controls that would shore up the economic viability of farmers. This was effective in the beginning for pulling rural people out of the Depression, but by mid-century, these policies were getting watered down and were eventually fully repealed. This would lead to another farm crisis in the 1980s. The oil shortage of the 1970s similarly reminded urban populations in Western countries of their reliance on rural extractive industries.

Nations that become fully urban often lose the capacity for rural production, such as Singapore and Saudi Arabia, due to ecological constraints—arid conditions, lack of arable land, and so forth. Some have innovated new forms of urban agriculture, but technology has not yet reached a point where it can overcome the limits of urban environments, offering only a limited capacity to feed the population. Though urban agriculture may help lessen the depth of urban dependency, most fully urban nations are turning to land grabs to ensure food security, whereby they sign century-long lease agreements to farm foreign lands (Brown, 2011). This exploitative practice calls into question the national sovereignty of host countries, which tend to be predominantly poor and rural (mostly in Africa) and already struggling to feed themselves.

Rural production remains vitally important to the well-being of urban populations. Yet, as the pain of shortage fades from memory in urbanormative society, the value placed on rural production subsides. In turn, the tolerance of rural production in rural places, perhaps ironically, diminishes. Urbanites who visit the countryside for the sake of tourism or permanent migration do not wish to witness deforestation, to see or smell CAFOs, or breath in toxic materials from mining activities. Instead, they wish to experience the rustic charm of an idyllic life.

REVALUING RURAL FOR URBAN CONSUMPTION

The low value placed on rural productive activities does not mean that urbanormativity attaches little value to the experience of visiting or living in the countryside—although it may shun life in a traditional rural production-oriented community. The terms that describe the positive feelings people have about rural people and life, as discussed in chapter 5, are the rural idyll and the rural mystique. What these scholars find is a cultural theme that is surprisingly robust across cultural contexts, involving a romantic nostalgia for the rural past. Even the act of romanticizing this past does an injustice to the trials and problems that rural people have endured through time.

Urbanormativity prioritizes urban over rural life—there is a longing to escape the constant overcrowding, traffic, hurried, and expensive cost of living found in cities and suburbs near the urban core. The inner city is especially known to play host to some of the worst social conditions that urbanites wish to escape—substandard housing, high crime, alienation, mental illness, decrepit infrastructure, and so forth. Paradoxically, many of these same conditions can be found in struggling traditional rural communities, making them unfit as rural getaways. The rural idyll/mystique ensures a high demand for the rural brand, but it is a sanitized problem-free and highly managed version. In other words, rural has become a brand that can be bought and sold—it has been commodified such that, as Urry (2012) claims, we are consuming the countryside. It has been transformed from a site of production to one of consumption. In order for a rural community to achieve idyll status, a great deal of intentional planning must be undertaken as it is not at all a typical outcome for traditional rural communities to accidentally transform into charming country getaways.

Proliferation of Rural Simulacra and Creation of Rural Hyperreality

In their study of Cooperstown, New York, Fulkerson and Seale (2012) discovered many of the hallmarks of a simulated rural experience. When entering the village, for instance, one sees a welcome sign situated on finely groomed grass that describes the community as "America's Perfect Village." As you enter the business district, you find a General Store, and catch a glimpse of such things as a horse and buggy available for the public to ride. Down the road from the business district is the Farmer's Museum—itself a simulated rural village set in the nineteenth century. Within this museum is a working farm, operated by an array of workers who are all dressed in period-appropriate costumes, and are prepared to give a presentation on the historical facts that surround their corner of the Farmer's Museum, such as the printing press, the blacksmith, and the law office. Fulkerson and Seale compare the community of Cooperstown to the Farmer's Museum, as a similarly managed and highly maintained community—Cooperstown is nearly a museum unto itself (see also Anania 2016; Thomas 2003).

While rural simulacra are created to captivate and please urban visitors and newcomers, as they accumulate, entire communities may be transformed into a hyperreality of rural life. Traditional rural communities are notable, in contrast, for precisely the opposite: they are completely unmanaged. Not surprisingly, the lack of concern with pleasing urban visitors solidifies the future of many traditional communities as something other than a residential or tourism destination. The unsightliness may be a calculated action, designed to prevent the takeover of the community by urbanites with delusions of rural grandeur. In Bennett-Knapp's (2016) examination of Adirondack communities, she identified many that lacked the signs of urban interest—

they were missing rural simulacra and had less desirable aesthetic qualities, making them unsuccessful for tourism.

One might define the development of traditional rural communities by their general lack of direction and random land use patterns. Driving down a country road one might find a magnificent rural mansion with a carefully manicured lawn situated next door to a dilapidated single wide with a rusted-out vehicle up on blocks. Next might be an aging farm with a collapsing barn, followed by semi-forested or grassy landscape, filling in where a farm once stood. The unmanaged countryside may reflect a rural norm that celebrates individual freedom—a libertarian ideal, perhaps. In the absence of any overarching rules or regulations imposed from above, landowners are free to do with their land as they wish.

Desirable idyllic rural communities try to anticipate the expectations of urban visitors and newcomers, and in turn, strive to create and simulate the conditions that mark them as idyllic. The hyperreal rural community is highly managed. The residents may enforce strict zoning regulations, limit or prevent conventional rural economic activity, privilege activities that enhance rustic charm, and devise building codes that keep homeowners in line with the managed character of the community. Insisting that houses be stick built with clapboard siding, for instance, helps maintain the bucolic feel. The end result of this intentional management may be a spike in the value of local properties. This may be so successful that it drives out the original population, as they watch their property tax bills elevate to unbearable levels. Eventually, the community may be completely remade with an entirely new permanent or seasonal urban population, as we explore below.

Rural Gentrification

Given the difficult realities that many rural people endure in traditional rural communities, when they are joined by urbanites these new arrivals are quite often disapproving. A view toward a romantic rural life does not include images of dilapidated homes, rusting automobiles, or other outward signs of struggle and desperation. If enough urbanites decide to inhabit a traditionally depressed rural area, there are usually major changes brought about through a process that could be labeled rural gentrification. This form of gentrification is not exactly the same as urban gentrification, but the result is similar.

In urban gentrification, a portion of a city that has fallen on hard times is typically reduced to rubble and rebuilt in the form of expensive housing and luxury amenities like fine restaurants, high-end stores, and art galleries. The old inhabitants of a rebuilt gentrified neighborhood typically get pushed out due to rising rents and cost of living. In rural gentrification, the old inhabitants are similarly pushed out, but the nature of the gentrification is different. In place of the high-density development of restaurants, stores, art galleries, and the like, the rural environment is remade in the image of a romantic rural village. Broken concrete sidewalks might be replaced with an old Western style boardwalk. Bars may adopt the façade of a Western saloon with swinging doors. Interior design shops might sell rustic furniture. Outside of the downtown, failing farms with dilapidated barns are replaced with neatly mowed lawns that lead to refurbished or replaced farmhouses, usually surrounded by beautiful gardens. The country "mini estate," as we have come to label them, typically have large lots of 5–15 acres, and host some aesthetically pleasing feature, such as a mountain view or a pristine pond or lake. There is also a new generation of highly educated urbanite farmers that grow specialty items that may appeal to the demand for locally produced goods, such as hops used by local breweries.

Who would not like to live in this charming country setting, beholding the natural beauties of the rural landscape, living the quaint life of a rural farmer? The ability to live in the gentrified rural community depends, of course, on being independently wealthy or having the means to earn an urban living without the requirement of a physical presence in the urban setting. This luxury, not unlike the gentrified urban downtown neighborhood, is limited to those of a higher socioeconomic status atypical of most traditional rural communities. Traditional rustics, who have labored under difficult conditions to achieve a life that is at or just above the subsistence level, do not have access. The life offered by a gentrified community—urban or rural—can be wonderful, but it is not available to the original inhabitants who must now move on to new locales where they can afford to live and make a living. Of course, many rural producers lack the ability to relocate their productive means—one cannot pick up a farm and move it, for example—and thereby may altogether lose economic viability as a result of being pushed out by rising taxes and land values.

Rural gentrification, like its urban counterpart, is a form of development that maintains a certain amount of concern for the local environment and economy, but little to no concern for local equity issues. The previous inhabitants, who perhaps created the town, are looked upon as obstacles, nuisances, or degenerates, just as inner-city counterparts are subjected to a range of socially denigrating attitudes—often with a strong racial tone in the United States.

Second Home Ownership

Much of the transformation of rural communities to gentrified idyllic simulations is driven by second home ownership. Adjacent rural communities may be brought into the commuting zone of distant metro areas, becoming exurbs, so that residents may drive to work in a city while residing in a rural place. Eventually some of these may become fully suburbanized, especially when the adjacent city is expanding outward. This completes the process of bringing the community into the urban fold. Those further afield may be connected via telecommuting or by temporary residence, such as having a weekend country home. Advances such as internet-based communication and productivity allow many to engage in urban work in a more remote rural setting, provided there is connectivity. In any case, the urbanite continues to enjoy the benefits associated with the urban economy, while simultaneously enjoying the desirable aspects of rural life—the great outdoors, slow pace of life, rural recreation (hunting, golfing, camping, etc.). Moreover, rural communities are often the location of well-developed recreational tourism economies that tend to increase other amenities, such as bars and restaurants. These are the more objective conditions that make second home ownership possible, but we should not dismiss the more subjective constructionist considerations, as they are crucial for understanding the decision for second home ownership (Farstad & Rye 2013; Rye 2011).

Clearly, the behaviors of individuals are guided, at least to some extent, by social psychological and cultural constructions of urban and rural. What draws people to the city, or to the country, are a set of expectations that may or may not have a basis in reality—they derive from social representations (Halfacree 1993, 1995). These representations may be derived largely from popular media accounts (Seale & Fulkerson 2014), but direct contact from epistemic closeness plays a more prominent role the more someone experiences rural life firsthand (Farstad & Rye 2013).

In his analysis of Norway, Rye (2011) discovered a somewhat unique and complex situation. Here, urbanites have traditionally maintained a second seasonal home devoted to supporting work in agriculture and fishing. Rural Norway is not monolithic, however, hosting a great deal of diversity related to social class. In turn, attitudes about second home ownership are not uniform—those at the very top and very bottom of the social class hierarchy are most favorable, while those in the middle are heavily resistant (Van Auken & Rye 2011). Farstad and Rye (2013) find that second home owners often become the most protective of rural communities, resisting change or ambitious development projects. In other words, they want to be accepted into the community, but do not want to leave the door open for other urbanites to follow in their path.

Studies of rural youth perceptions highlight early-life migration intentions (Rye 2006a, 2006b; Rye & Blekesaune 2007). This is a critical topic as many rural areas continue to suffer from the brain drain as rural youth in an urbanormative culture develop negative views of country living. Rye (2006a) maintains that social constructions of rural are an important factor and adds that these are highly conditioned by structural constraints like social class position. His study also highlights the importance of intersectionality. Being a young working-class rustic male will influence migration decisions very differently than being a young working-class urbane male.

An interesting follow-up question to ask, related to chapter 6, is when do the so-called "newcomers" to rural communities, who are clearly urbane, make the transition to becoming rustics? One may find that the relocated urbanite is quick to adopt an objective view—"I live in a rural area; therefore, I am rustic." This may not be accepted, however, by the community to which the urbanite has relocated. To the contrary, such individuals may never be accepted as a true member of the rural community. Again, it is important to remember that the process of identity work is a group process. The ability to signal membership as a rustic depends on more than simply owning property in a rural community. Nobody is more aware of that than the already established rural population. This does not mean that it is impossible to transition from urbane to rustic, but the process may be long and difficult. When rural gentrification is advanced, however, the question of being accepted may become moot, as the population is completely remade by an urbane influx. The social resistance to newcomers may become a motivation for new arrivals to ramp up gentrification efforts.

Rural Tourism

Apart from second home ownership, consuming the countryside is accomplished in large part through rural tourism. Rural communities offer a variety of amenities that appeal to urbanites. Generally, they appeal to the "rural as escape" sentiment by managing a charming rural landscape. The ecological aesthetic of a mountain or lakeside community may entice visitors from long distances to visit and enjoy the scenery. Bennett-Knapp's (2016) study of Adirondack communities notes that traditional rural production in agriculture, forestry, fishing, or hunting is nearly gone, making up a modest 5 percent of population's workforce. Tourism has become the dominant sector. By conducting storefront coding in eleven separate communities, she found that the more successful communities had a much larger presence of food and restaurant fronts, in addition to a range of other tourism-oriented businesses. The most successful community was Lake Placid, which gained visibility and prominence after the 1932 and 1980 Olympics. The community has capitalized on its Olympic reputation by continuing to offer activities such as skiing and luge racing.

Like Lake Placid, Cooperstown benefits from a long historical popularity, only in this case, it is due to the writings of James Fenimore Cooper, who wrote long ago about the beauty of Glimmerglass Lake (Otsego Lake) as well as the Baseball Hall of Fame (Seale & Fulkerson 2012). Tourists began filling a large stately resort hotel as early as 1908 to experience Cooper's delight. Then, in the aftermath of the Great Depression, like many rural tourism destinations, Cooperstown went into crisis following a sharp decline in tourism. The innovation that rescued Cooperstown was the Baseball Hall of Fame that is now the central attraction drawing large crowds of tourists—roughly four hundred thousand each summer (Thomas 2003; Anania 2016). Although Cooperstown is a success story as a tourist destination, the seasonality of the economic activity is difficult for small businesses to endure and there is a high level of turnover and poverty among workers. The weakness of the tourism economy, even when it is successful, is something corroborated in Vieira's (2016) study of the Jay Peak Ski resort in Vermont, where she found seasonal employment to be highly unstable and poorly compensated.

Agritourism

The phenomenon of agritourism represents another possible pathway toward development that may be a compromise between traditional and urban ideals for rural community life. Urbanites might pay to stay on a farm, often at a country bed and breakfast, where they are treated to farm fresh food as they take in the scenery of the lush pastoral landscape. In some cases, the guests may be invited to help milk the cows or engage in some other form of agricultural labor like harvesting fruit. The balance here depends on maintaining an acceptable aesthetic of the farm, while allowing enough productive activity to remain profitable. Highly productive rural economic activity is often unsightly, environmentally damaging, and thus not typically the object of desire on the part of urban tourists. There is a reason bed and breakfasts are not set up on CAFOs (Contained Animal Feeding Operations), where the highly productive raising of livestock for meat and dairy purposes takes place. As Steel (2013) notes, the ability for an urban society to be food secure by feeding massive urban populations, depends to a large degree on this kind of undesirable but highly productive work.

Agritourism does not always involve a long-term stay, as much of it is restricted to a single day of activities that include fruit picking, selecting a pumpkin out of a pumpkin patch, or cutting down a Christmas tree, for instance. As result, much agritourism takes place within a short drive of the metropolitan fringe. Wright and Eaton (2018) offer an excellent analysis of cider mill agritourism that underscores the active maintenance, on the part of the operators, in managing the idyllic rural image urbanites wish to experience. Wright and Eaton (2018) note that while agritourism offers rural communities economic opportunity that hinges on the ability to give urbanites an experience that satisfies their taste for the rural idyll, even as the experiences may serve to reinforce an out-of-touch image of rural life. The less desirable aspects are carefully hidden from view.

RURAL COMMUNITIES AND IMMIGRATION

The dynamics of newcomers and old-timers assume new dimensions when rural communities are the site of international migration. The urbanormative history of US immigration is centered around urban destinations, such as New York City, and does not consider what a traditional rural community has to offer. Minority groups—whether immigrant or not—that reside in urban areas are often the target of prejudice and discrimination. In some cases, the potential for building bridging-ties across racial and ethnic lines is greater in small rural communities that are more personal than large cities, as we discussed in chapter 2. It is hard to remain unnoticed in a town of a few hundred people, for instance.

A recent documentary, by Jessica Vecchione (2011), about the rural community of Fleischmanns, New York, offers an insightful immigration story. Several Mexican immigrants, who at first arrived in New York City, later moved into the city of Newburgh in search of a better life but found life difficult and oppressive. They decided they would prefer to live in the serene rural Catskill community of Fleishmanns. The community, predominantly white upon arrival, was experiencing a range of challenges typical of rural communities—the decline of rural production, an aging population, flagging school enrollments, and an uncertain future. It was once a tourist destination that collapsed and never recovered after the Depression. While the stereotype of traditional rural communities is that they are homogeneous and closed off to outsiders, this did not prove to be the case for Fleischmanns. Residents began to notice the presence of their new Mexican neighbors after a new restaurant and store (tienda) opened on Main Street, which for the most part, had been completely vacated. These businesses served as new attractor points, which brought new life and social interaction to a flagging community, providing a space for old-timers and newcomers to become acquainted. One of the central connection points facilitating the integration of this newly arrived group was the school. School teachers—particularly ESL teachers— were instrumental in making young immigrants feel like they were part of the community. Within a few years of arrival, commencement speeches were being given in both Spanish and English, while one-third of the graduating class were the children of Mexican immigrants. It is worth noting that, had the local school been shuttered, this positive outcome may not have developed.

While the case of Fleischmanns provides hope for the unique potential of rural communities to integrate new immigrants, this is not always the case, as noted by Pruitt (2009a). She observes that, in general, the homogeneity of rural communities can work against immigrants in such areas as community policing. Members of immigrant groups tend to stand out more obviously in small homogeneous towns, where the potential for profiling is greater. This is not inevitable, but the potential is there. Consistent with observations made by Vecchione, Pruitt finds that the Latinx population is simultaneously re-making and revitalizing rural communities across the Southern United States at a time when they most need it. How these rural communities respond to their new arrivals will depend on levels of trust, attitudes about immigration, supportive institutions such as schools, and opportunities for interaction.

Not all immigration to rural communities follows the same path. Vieira (2016) brings our attention to the EB-5 program that was designed to pro-mote international investment and a chance to obtain citizenship in the Un-tied States for its investors. The program was used to generate start-up capital to build the Jay Peak Ski Resort in Vermont. As Vieira notes, this was essentially funding rural investment by selling citizenship to those who could afford it. Unlike the example of Fleishmanns, where the immigrant group became integrated to some extent, investors in the EB-5 program remained external and separate from the community. This is not unlike the tourists who come in short visits to consume the resort, physically separated from the surrounding community. At best, the resort provides a small economic op-portunity for the community, providing low-paying, seasonal work that is less than ideal.

TAKEAWAYS

As traditional rural production declines as a source of employment in rural communities, often what remains are the economic and social problems asso-ciated with poverty, unemployment, and long-term environmental damage associated with the energy economy through agriculture, forestry, mining, extraction, hunting, and fishing. In the absence of some form of external intervention or rural development strategy like that which was enacted fol-lowing the Great Depression, many rural communities will languish. Some will turn to bolstering tourism and second home ownership by commodifying rusticity. Others, if adjacent to cities, may experience suburbanization to some extent. In each case the community will experience the process of place-structuration—transforming the character and tradition of the commu-nity.

When the latter strategy of commodification is pursued, rural gentrifica-tion is often the result, leading to highly managed rural simulations that resemble life in a museum (not unlike the Farmer's Museum)—creating a Disney-fied version of rural life. The proliferation of rural simulacra will accumulate and create a rural hyperreality, carefully managed through mech-anisms such as restrictive zoning and building codes. The simulated idyllic rural community will attract urban migration, second home ownership, and tourism. This population brings substantial resources and investment that drive up property values and may inadvertently drive out the older residents who can no longer afford the increased taxes. The newly arrived residents may become some of the most politically active members of the community, protecting the newly created idyllic character (Rye & Blekesaune 2007). While the resulting community may be charming and desirable, the economic benefits of a tourism economy are limited (Vieira 2016), while the initial problems facing the original rural populations remain unaddressed and simply displaced.

The positive impact of new immigrant populations on declining rural communities is notable, as was discovered in the case of Fleishmanns, New York. Further examination of this phenomenon is certainly warranted. One key characteristic of Fleishmanns is tied to age structure, as the new immigrants were generally younger and had small children that could fill schools and become workers in the local economy at small independently owned businesses. Alternatively, research might identify when the experience is not successful, leading to such outcomes as profiling. We suspect the role of attractor points and associated supportive institutions, such as schools, will be a requirement for successful immigration outcomes.

In summary, as we think about the future of rural communities in urban society, it will be important to understand the processes outlined in this chapter and how they connect to the wider urbanormative ideology. Allowing traditional rural communities to continue suffering from long-term losses strikes us as equally unacceptable as leveling and replacing these communities with a playground for urban enjoyment. Perhaps there are more just development strategies that can simultaneously support traditional rural endeavors while opening the door to tourists and part-time residents. Agritourism provides one potential avenue in this direction, but much depends on how it is carried out. The ultimate goals of equity and justice should be maintained as we explore in the next chapter.

We have admittedly devoted less attention to predominantly rural societies in this chapter, as they have not yet experienced the brunt of advanced urbanization. Nevertheless, they can anticipate similar futures, and already witness early urbanormative changes that we have described. Less developed nations in Asia and Africa, in particular, have been viewed as urban playgrounds, with tourism becoming a growing part of the economy. The Western European notion of "going on Safari," for instance, reflects a particular urbanormative view toward a rural nation, its people, its wildlife, and its environment. What separates these from more urbanized nations, is that a large part of the population remains engaged in rural activity. This is a crucial time to decide on policies that might support this population, ensuring such things as food security, while limiting the rural-urban migration flows by making life more bearable and satisfying in the countryside. The reality of urban dependency on the global scale implies an increasing need for traditional rural economies to have a thriving future. After all, a world that is fully urbanized is not only unsustainable, but we would argue it is also impossible. Rural people and rural work deserve both recognition and support for what they contribute.

Chapter Nine

A Rural Justice Ethic

Having considered many of the different aspects of urbanormativity and the way it serves to disadvantage rural people and communities in previous chapters, this chapter pivots us in the direction of envisioning a just response. We begin with the construction of a rural justice ethic that might provide some basic principles to inform a new agenda. We will first consider the meaning of justice by comparing dominant frameworks, while offering critique. Following Pruitt (2011) we arrive at what we think is the most fruitful direction based on the notion of capability maximization, relying on the ideas of Amartya Sen (1999). We apply this framework to the urban-rural dimension and evaluate barriers to its realization. These are divided between (a) rural residence and spatial disadvantages, and (b) rural work and the devaluation of rural products. While the former applies to nearly all rural people around the world, the latter impacts a shrinking number, the majority of whom live in less developed nations dealing with the realities of extreme poverty. We will suggest that in order to enhance rural capabilities, we will need to find a way to address spatial inequality and revalue rural work. Ultimately, we call for a revalorization of the rural (Seale & Mallinson 2018).

WHAT IS JUSTICE?

The contested concept of justice has a long history of debate carried out through various religious and philosophical perspectives since ancient times. Central questions surround the morality of human action that provide frameworks to enable the best courses of action. The goal of developing a rural justice ethic is to identify the most appropriate framework for action that overcomes rural injustices. Before we can arrive at such an ethic, we must take a more general tour through some of the dominant justice frameworks in existence.

Contemporary discussions of justice often begin with utilitarianism as a baseline (Bentham 2015 [1780]). The notion of utilitarian justice is relevant as it continues to inform much political and social thought with real legal and political consequences. It is based upon the principle of maximizing utility—the greatest well-being—for the greatest number of people. It is derived from a form of hedonism, under which utility is found as the sum of pleasure minus the cost of pain that a particular action brings about. The choice of which course to pursue is thereby judged according to the consequences of action. Utilitarianism takes inspiration from Aristotle's notion of eudaimonia—that the highest human good is the ultimate purpose of human action. It is a blending of these philosophies that gives us the more colloquially recognized version of the *greatest good for the greatest number*. As a philosophy, utilitarianism is more than hedonism, as it is not focused exclusively on individuals. Rather, the core focus is on maximizing utility at the aggregate level. Bentham envisioned a system of justice carried out by government wherein offenses would be punished in proportion to the pain and suffering that they cause—both the immediate, first-order, and more distant, second-order effects.

Utilitarianism, on its face, may appear to be a reasonable framework. Perhaps, in a homogeneous context it is effective, since most people define utility along the same lines. The problem is, most societies are diverse with respect to the definition of utility, and it is here that problems start to arise, as divergent factions come into conflict over what they value. Under utilitarian logic, when there are numerous groups with conflicting values, the smaller minority groups will most likely be silenced. In other words, the utility of the majority will overrule the utility of minority groups—a condition referred to as the "tyranny of the majority" by John Stuart Mill (1869 [1859]). We would point out that the de facto urbanormative justice ethic has a strong utilitarian logic.

As it allows a tyrannical majority to legitimately marginalize minority groups, the utilitarian framework should not be taken as the final word in the justice debate. A major advance that eliminates the problem of the tyrannical majority was offered by John Rawls (1972), based on three principles. The first—the greatest equal liberty principle—states that each person, rather than having access to maximum utility or happiness, should have access to maximum liberty, and that this liberty must be equally compatible with the maximal liberty of others. In this way, the meaning of utility is an individual matter and that privileging any individual or group over another is judged to be unacceptable. The second—difference principle—stipulates when violations of the equal liberty principle may be tolerated. It holds that inequality may be justified if it brings benefits to those who are the least advantaged, since this may increase their opportunities. Finally, the third—equal opportunity principle—is derived from the difference principle, stipulating that inequality may be tolerated only when all positions and offices are equally open to all. Rawlsian justice elevates the primacy of equality in both liberty and opportunity and abandons a uniform notion of utility. Further, it does so at the individual, rather than the aggregate level, thereby departing from the greatest number principle. Rawlsian justice makes a case that each individual should have opportunities—that no one need sacrifice opportunity for the greater good.

While Rawls greatly improved upon utilitarian logic, he left a remaining concern unaddressed—it surrounds the issue of capabilities. In short, though it is important for opportunities to be available to all, this alone does not guarantee that everyone will be equally capable of taking advantage of opportunities. For example, minority group members are often deprived access to quality education. If a job opening is announced as being available and open to all, thus meeting the Rawlsian criterion of equal opportunity, if it requires a level of education or a formal degree that the disadvantaged are less capable of achieving, the actual openness of the position may be called into question. If everyone were to be given the same capability of accessing quality education in the first place, then the equality of opportunity would be meaningful. This belies the basic problem of imposing a meritocracy on an unequal society—equal opportunity does not mean equal capability. This is where the insights of Amartya Sen take us one step further than Rawls.

In *Development as Freedom*, Sen (1999) claims that we should be focusing on maximizing capabilities. Like Rawls, he departs from utilitarianism through the rejection of a uniform system for determining utility—each individual's preference is taken to be an external private matter (a common assumption in economics). Rather than focus on the outcome or consequence of utility that bringing pleasure or pain, Sen focuses on the processes within which action takes place. It is in the process of individuals striving to satisfy their own interests that we find the problem of *capability deprivation*. Sen defines freedom as the maximization of capabilities, and poverty as the deprivation of capabilities. On this basis, Sen outlines three areas of concern. Like Rawls, Sen shares concern with the equality of opportunity—only now it implies the equal opportunity to maximize capabilities in order to achieve that which people desire in life. Equal opportunity without capability is empty. Second, Sen asserts that in order to maximize capabilities, priority must be given to political freedoms and transparency. If someone lacks political freedom, it would impinge on their capabilities to act as citizens, and in turn, they would be unable to advocate for laws and policies that best represent their interests. Third, capability maximization depends on protection from hardship such as economic poverty and unemployment. Sen was a proponent of social safety net programs that supplement incomes or offer employment to those in need. Thus, standing on the shoulders of Bentham and Rawls, Sen advances a justice ethic that transcends them both. Our question now is how all of this translates into a *rural* justice ethic.

JUSTICE FOR RURAL COMMUNITIES

Our overview of competing justice frameworks provides a foundation on which to construct a justice ethic appropriate for remedying rural injustices. Though it has only been the case for a few years, the global rural population has become a numerical minority. For some urbanized nations, rural became a minority long ago. From a utilitarian perspective, maximizing the utility of the urban population to the exclusion of the rural may be justified since *the greatest number* is served, but it is only served at the expense of individual-level capabilities of rural people. The dominance of urban utilitarianism is evident in two ways: (1) the devaluation of rural production and workers and (2) the exacerbation of spatial inequalities. The global rural population is a diverse lot, yet they hold in common many of the same challenges born out of residence in a sparsely settled place or engagement in rural production (in the energy economy).

Closing the capabilities gap for rural residents will mean finding mechanisms that overcome spatial disadvantage by devising policies and laws that accommodate rural spatial realities. Further, mechanisms must be discovered that will revalue rural labor. The current trend is toward devaluing rural production to the point that rural workers are finding it difficult to meet their basic subsistence needs. Global markets are not setting a price that is fair, adequate, or just, and the economic hardships that this creates lead directly to rural capability deprivation. A rural justice ethic would ensure that rural populations are given the same opportunities and capabilities as their urban counterparts.

Capability Deprivation and Rural Work

With the viability of rural work hanging in the balance, the weight of increasing urban dependency will exact even greater pressure on the remaining rural population over the coming decades. In predominantly urban nations, the segment of the population employed in rural work has already largely vanished, leaving the expanding urban population more vulnerable and dependent than ever before. Rural communities that were designed for rural work are being transformed into urbane residential zones. The character and tradition of these communities may gradually erode, along with the legacy of its original community members. Other rural communities may fail to attract urban residents or tourists, and in these cases, the declining tax base will combine with devalued rural production to create fiscal stress and all the associated challenges that brings, such as school closures and deteriorating infrastructure.

In predominantly rural nations, where rural workers comprise a numerical majority, their economic worth pales in comparison to what is enjoyed by the urban population. In 2017, for instance, the country of Chad saw 80 percent of its labor force employed in agriculture, but it generated only 52 percent of GDP (Gross Domestic Product). Unsurprisingly, Chad's poverty rate is nearly 47 percent, impacting almost half of the population. With an urbanization rate of 3.88 percent, it is clear that the citizens of Chad are responding to capability deprivation, as is common in rural nations, by abandoning rural for city life. While this may be a wise move in the short-run at the individual level—and even applauded by those holding an urbanormative ideal—the long-run aggregate effect is continued deterioration of the world's rural foundation, not to mention the array of problems stemming from the proliferation of population in already overcrowded cities.

Once again, the global economy, as described in chapter 3, is an energy economy that begins with rural producers, who gather and harvest that which nature provides. Urban production picks up where rural production ends, leading to a variety of manufactured and finished products that enhance the lives of those in urban society. The urban "free hand" population is removed from the land, along with the long hard hours endured by the rural "cultivator" population, which, if not adequately compensated, will look for a way out. Why engage in this harshly difficult work if there is no reward? Yet, if all rural workers decide to quit, the rural circuit of production will fail, and with it the global economy would cease to function. It is a collective action problem: what is rational for the individual rural worker is irrational for the wider global urban-rural system.

Global markets set price levels that theoretically reflect the balance of supply and demand. One way to ensure artificially low prices is thus to create an oversupply of rural goods. The market's pricing mechanism has no inherent directive to ensure the integrity of the overall system or basic level of support for its workers. If prices fall to a level that undermines the viability of rural work, productivity will grind to a halt while supply—which includes such basic necessities as food and fiber—will eventually become scarce. The result will be food and textile prices that make urban life expensive and difficult to attain. Theoretically, rural production would resume once prices rise, but as the knowledge and memory of farming fades into obscurity, the now-urban population will find that it has become ill-equipped to feed itself. The upshot of this is that today's rural capability deprivation may eventually translate into tomorrow's urban capability deprivation. Developing and acting upon a rural justice ethic is, therefore, not a simple act of charity or kindness, but a crucial step toward long-term well-being for both urban and rural populations.

If we hope to operate on the basis of a rural justice ethic, a critical step moving forward will be to acknowledge the reality of urban dependency on rural resources and the people who grow, collect, and harvest them. This includes, but is not limited to, agriculture for food and clothing, energy for heat, electricity and transportation, timber for constructing shelter and the built environment, mineral resources for a range of products such as batteries and electronics. Paradoxically, some of the most resource-rich rural areas are also some of the poorest places on earth due to devalued rural production. How can we ensure that rural people are fairly compensated for continuing to provide these critical elements to the global energy economy?

It is important to note, at this stage, that the devaluation of rural products is presently so extreme that a revaluation would not likely result in any noticeable price increase for consumers. Take the example of coffee—the most heavily traded commodity in the world, second only to oil. A kilogram of green coffee beans will currently fetch an Ethiopian farmer the equivalent of about 29 cents (Maasho & Hunt, 2019). Once roasted and ground, this kilo of coffee can produce roughly eighty cups of coffee. Each cup can be sold in a standard Western coffee shop for about $3–$4. The net retail cost therefore ranges from $240–$320. The share of this earned by the farmer ranges from .001 cents (.29/240) to .0009 cents (.29/320). This means that a hundred-fold increase in the value of the green coffee beans would yield $29 for the farmer but would only add 9 to 12 cents to the cost of a cup of coffee for consumers ($29/$240 = .12, and $29/$320 = .09). While this would radically improve the lives of coffee farmers, like Gafeto Gardo in Ethiopia (Maasho & Hunt 2019), who is struggling to get by, it may go entirely unnoticed by the consumer. The math in this example suggests that a rural justice ethic may be within reach without necessitating any radical sacrifices or compromises. It implies that urban-controlled companies and commodity chains must study and reconsider the level of rural exploitation that is embedded in their practices and profit-maximizing behavior.

Capability Deprivation and Rural Space

For many rural areas, the cause of capability deprivation is physical space (Lobao, Hooks, & Tickamyer 2007). What might be a simple walk or quick trip on public transportation in an urban setting translates into an onerous, difficult trek for a rural resident. In predominantly urban society, the continued consolidation of schools has rural students traveling further and further afield, leading to reduced capability to participate in extracurricular activities, lowered academic performance from lost study time, and increased exposure to problems such as bullying from extended bus travel. Rural buses traverse difficult, rough, unpaved roads, and risk getting into accidents in a place that is far from any emergency services. Students in predominantly rural nations must reconcile vast spaces without the luxury of buses—engaging in long walks of several miles, to and from school. Again, the extended travel limits availability for study or for work at home as many such students are relied upon for their labor. Moreover, prolonged foot transportation in public exposes rural students to risks, such as sexual violence against girls. Acknowledging the spatial barriers that rural people face could lead to more responsive decision making—perhaps school consolidation would be rejected, or more rural schools should be built once the negative costs of space are factored.

Another spatial problem that disproportionately impacts rural residents, perhaps ironically, is food deserts. A food desert refers to the condition wherein ready access to the food required for daily caloric intake is impeded. Rural residents in predominantly urban societies are generally disengaged from the practice of food production, such as maintaining animals for meat, gardens for produce, or field crops such as grains. Instead, they rely on grocery retail stores to provide what is needed. The problem is that the desirability of small rural communities for food retailers is limited due to their small population sizes. For a grocer to be profitable in the rural context, very little food can be lost to spoilage, and with the reality of low volume sales, this means that fresh food will be hard to find. Further, as grocery store chains have merged over the past twenty years, there is less competition within urban settings and thus little incentive to explore more marginal locations that offer lower profit margins. Not unlike rural residents in urban societies, those from predominantly rural and agricultural societies may also suffer from the pangs of living in a food desert. In this case, the practice of food production may be alive and well, but desperate rural farmers prioritize the production of commodities over food. Crops that may be equipped to feed a family may not yield much economic value and will therefore be avoided. Even if desirable food products are produced, to consume them would mean losing trade revenue, so the decision may be made to accept short-term hunger for long-term economic returns. This dynamic is what underlies the fact that most famines have occurred in nations that are net exporters of agricultural products. Observing this led Sen (1981) to later develop the justice ethics that we now draw upon.

To complicate things further, the low price paid to rural farmers for their harvest is often itself a function of spatial inequality—the distance between the point of production and the market place where so-called "middle men" offer very low prices, only to turn around and sell for a profit. This business model depends on exploiting the spatial barriers of farmers and is the first crucial step in a long line of exchanges. Providing alternative means for trading agricultural products with buyers in distant markets, such as through farmer cooperatives and use of Fair-Trade labels, may go a long way in revaluing rural work. Moreover, promoting the practice of agrarian self-sufficient farming may help to alleviate the problem of food deserts for rural residents living in either rural or urban societies.

Spatial inequality thus leads to a host of access problems, many of which were discussed in the previous chapter. The inability to receive medical attention in a timely manner, for instance, could be the difference between life and death. The same could be said for other emergency services like fire fighting and policing, where the difference between saving someone or something is determined by response time—time that is often lost traveling to and from the point of need.

URBANORMATIVE BARRIERS TO RURAL JUSTICE

One of the most common urbanormative responses to the challenges of rural work and rural space is, "why don't you just move!?" Of course, that is exactly what many rural residents are doing, as evidenced by the extremely high rates of urbanization found in the most rural nations on earth. This solution, however, only serves to exacerbate the reality of urban dependency. Below we question the urbanormative meaning of development as well as the limitations imposed by the urban imaginary.

Rethinking Development

The dominant way of thinking about national development since the middle of the twentieth century revolves around modernization theory and faith in the urban transition (see So 1991 for a review). Modernization scholars cast rural people as backward facing remnants of an archaic and obsolete world. The challenges facing rural people were seen as short-term consequences of living an outdated rural life with all it implied about being uneducated, rigid, and unwilling to change. Rural people were viewed as needing a modern form of education and training that would prepare them for life in an urban society. Any failures to adapt would be interpreted as a by-product of the inherent limitations of rural people.

Building on this theory, proponents of the Green Revolution argued that if rural people were to remain farmers, they would need to give up their old ways of doing things and adopt modern scientific practices that could generate enough production to support the urban and rural populations (Jain 2010). While there were some success stories in terms of improvements to yields, the Green Revolution has had several unintended negative consequences that ultimately undermined the capabilities of many rural farmers. The application of pesticides, for instance, caused irreparable damage to ecosystems that disrupted natural cycles once responsible for feeding the local population. The over-irrigation of crops led to water shortages. The over-farming of soil led to desertification and soil loss. On the whole, the sacrifices of rural farmers during the Green Revolution were accepted as justified since it sustained the growing urban population—an indication that the utilitarian ethic was dominant. Modern agriculture accelerated the transition from self-sufficient subsistence farming to commodity farming for trade that led to the ironic coexistence of gross food exports and famine within the same rural societies, as observed by Sen (1981). In a sense, the generation of rural surplus for the benefit of urban populations not only went unchallenged, but the intensification of rural labor was seen as central to a better world. In the process, however, increased productivity actually weakened rural communities as less labor was necessary for production, and the surplus workers moved to the cities to exacerbate the problem of urban dependency.

Over the remaining decades of the twentieth century, and now into the twenty-first, the dire conditions of rural life, coupled with the enclosure and privatization of agricultural lands under neoliberal austerity policies, would drive the rural population to migrate to cities. Within the modernization paradigm, the rapid rate of urbanization was taken as a sign of progress—that the nation was beginning to outgrow its archaic past and join the ranks of other modern urban societies. Those that have succeeded have become focal points in the global economy as emerging markets. Left behind are those nations that continue to house a large rural population—interpreted through the modernization paradigm as stuck in the past.

As dependency (Frank 1967) and world-system scholars (Wallerstein 1987) have pointed out, many of these forgotten societies were prevented from modernizing and urbanizing, because they were depended upon by more powerful nations for their cheap rural products and labor. These scholars argued that it was a fallacy to ignore the international dynamics linking modern urban and traditional rural nations together. We echo the point that successful urban nations owe their success to their ability to forge advantageous trade relation with rural nations, who provide what they need in the form of rural products. This is the basic structure of international urban dependency—a structure that came into existence thousands of years ago (Thomas 2010).

Rethinking development means challenging the urbanormative assumption that urbanization equals progress. If every nation were to fully urbanize, as noted throughout this book, the global economy would collapse—the reality of urban dependency is inescapable. A more sustainable approach to development would embrace the notion of capability maximization for rural nations by embracing some of the ideas we offer, which may serve to preserve and protect the highly productive and undervalued rural laborer living with the realities of vast physical space.

Rethinking the Urban Imaginary

Another barrier to rural justice may be found in the urban imaginary, where rural people are often frozen in time (Dominy 1997). The iconic images of rural people as rustic cattle ranchers, farmers, and coal miners, while histori-cally accurate, usually ignores the ugly side of poverty and environmental destruction surrounding this rural world, nor is it compatible with a world of urbane lawyers, doctors, accountants, and architects who now find a home in a rural place. The romanticization of rural and rustic traps rural people in the past, ignoring the social problems as well as the changes that have taken place in rural communities. This ignorance, coupled with epistemic distance and moral indifference, impedes progress toward a rural justice ethic. A parallel view may be observed in the way Native Americans are often ex-pected by white Americans to live as they did two hundred years ago. The so-called "noble savage" stereotype romanticizes a rustic version of Native American life that leaves no space for contemporary livelihoods or the many challenges facing the various Native American tribes across the continent.

Owing to romantic rustic images of the urban imaginary, many urbanites wish to live in rural places for a better quality-of-life than the city or suburb can offer. This does not mean they wish to move to a rural area that is saddled with rural work and persistent poverty, as may be found in the Appalachians, the Black Belt South, or Brown Belt Southwest. In the United States, as in other urban societies, the devaluation of rural has very nearly played out to the logical end—the total devastation of rural work and com-munities. Rural communities that do "best" are not surprisingly closer to metropolitan areas, ideally along interstate highways so that the rural life-style can be quickly escaped when a "big box" store or exotic food choice is desired (Thomas 2003). Often, rural communities in urban societies escape poverty by becoming satellites—as exurbs or tourist towns—of urban life.

Activities, such as rural gentrification, serve not to glorify and vindicate the rural that already exists—it attempts to replace it with a sterile, artificial, and highly simulated countryside borne out of the urban imaginary. In many respects this is a colonial act. It does not go unnoticed by rustics, who may, in turn, exaggerate their identity as a form of resistance. This may mean engaging in activities that subvert the romantic ideal sought by urbanites, such as showcasing their poverty, making it highly visible—parking a car on blocks curbside for all to see, for instance. Lacking a language of resistance that parallels the labor movement or the civil rights movement, blanket sym-bols of resistance, such as the Confederate flag, are utilized to voice disgust at "liberals," locally defined not as a set of political policies but as an ethnic slur uttered against the educated and the urbane who have minimized their plight.

In contrast to the rural romantic is the alternate side of rural as "deplorable" or backward, as a population blamed for damage to the environment, bent on its own destruction politically, one that embraces racism and sexism, and that is utterly hopeless. It is a population of uneducated white men dressed in camo, wielding heavy firepower, driving pickup trucks, and planning the next McVeigh-style Oklahoma attack. Just as the media sensationalizes and stokes fear of urban minority gang thugs, so too does it sensationalize the image of rural deplorables. As with any stereotype, one can usually point to exemplars—there are individuals who appear to match the crude portrait. The problem with stereotypes, of course, is that they isolate extreme cases that embody the most loathed qualities and presents them as typical. Once accepted, all the hatred and vitriol against the entire group seems justified. As the Democrats discovered in 2016, calling people names is not a winning strategy.

Rural Resistance

Rural people are aware of the urban imaginary. A major theme in the country music genre is rural resistance to urbanormative disdain. Hank Williams Jr. capitalized on the sentiment with his popular, *A Country Boy Can Survive*, as evidenced by his chorus lines, "Because you can't starve us out and you can't make us run, 'Cause we're them old boys raised on shotguns, And we say grace and we say Ma'am, If you ain't into that we don't give a damn." The lines imply an assault on a rural way of life in the urbanizing world, a fierce determination to push back, and a strong sense of preserving rustic cultural values. As noted by Ching and Creed (1996, p. 28–29), rural people wish to gain recognition and value in the wider urban imaginary:

> While simple rural conservatism may support the status quo, the idea that rural life and rustic lifestyles are valid and valuable, that what the world needs is a few more rednecks, is a radical attempt to upset existing cultural hierarchies, or at least to prevent further devaluation of rusticity.

The appeal of artists like Hank Williams Jr., is that they clearly understand and give voice to widely held rural sentiments that grow out of anger toward an urbanormative culture that not only pervades the city but has now found its way to the countryside and is intent on claiming it.

President Trump routinely channeled this sentiment to marshal support for his successful campaign in 2016. In a speech to the Farm Bureau, he noted that no president had spoken to them for the past twenty-five years: "Where are they? Where did they go?" he asks, implying that previous presidents did not care enough about rural people to visit them. In the background is a banner with a slogan that reads, "Rebuilding Rural America." The speech glorifies the role of farmers in building the country—"farmers have always led the way," Trump states. The crowd responds very warmly and excitedly to this. His speech then goes on to celebrate the values of hard work and grit found in farmers. Regardless of the actual helpfulness of Trump's policies for rural people—arguably they work in the opposite direction by promoting the interest of the mostly urban elite—he clearly understood how to gain respect and admiration of rural Americans by validating their feelings of exclusion, alienation, and anger at being the target of urbanormative stereotypes (Full President Trump Speech 2016).

In a comedy routine that reflects upon an exchange he had with poor rural whites, comedian Dave Chappelle points out the dissonance between what Trump says and what he does, imploring, "You are poor. He's fighting for me!" Then, in an expression of understanding, Chappelle goes on to state, "I didn't see one deplorable face in that group." The reference refers to a claim made by Hillary Clinton that Trump's supporters were a basket of "deplorables." It was read by many as a backhanded jab against undesirable rural people. The term deplorable would go on to become a rallying cry against Clinton that ignited a political backlash many believe delivered the 2016 election to Donald Trump. Now, two years later, conservative commentators and Facebook posts continue to invoke the "deplorable" comment as an insensitive and bigoted slight against rural people and, increasingly, an urban working class in deindustrialized cities. Chappelle's insightful statement acknowledges the validity of rural resentment and expresses understanding as to why rural people voted for Trump—even though he does not agree with them politically. As an African American, Chappelle knows all-too-well what it is like to face stereotypes and discrimination. His compassion is perhaps a model that could inform the practice of a rural justice ethic in everyday life.

CORPORATE CONCENTRATION AND URBAN DECLINE

It is important to note that a rural justice ethic will challenge the urban production dynamics that are just as harmful to many urbanites as they are to rural residents. In "second-tier" cities that are former manufacturing power-houses whose best days are gone, corporate concentration of urban production has led to empty storefronts and vacant lots. The decline of small-town banks, for example, were often the result of considerable concentration in the financial industry. Thomas (2003) relates the rise of Oneida National Bank in Utica, New York—a deindustrialized city that was also home to the world's first commercial computer: the Univac. Oneida National was founded to serve a budding textile industry in the 1830s and grew after World War II by acquiring one small-town bank after another in central New York. The towns not only lost a community institution, but also the impressive incomes of bank executives who now worked in Utica. In 1970, this would have seemed like a problem for "rural communities," but by the late twentieth century it was Utica's turn: Oneida National was bought first by Albany-based Norstar, which was subsequently bought by Providence-based Fleet, and then Boston-based FleetBoston. It is now part of the aptly named Bank of America. In Utica, seven stories of downtown office space sit vacant, the only identifiable benefit for the community being the parking lots that serve a local theater. In many of the little towns where Oneida National operated, the local branch is now the only bank in town—corporate concentration has deprived millions of rural people a degree of choice with whom they can do business. Simply enforcing anti-trust regulations with an eye toward rebuilding local institutions would help both rural people and those in second-tier cities alike.

The issue is not just in finance: in industry after industry, corporate concentration has advantaged large cities over smaller cities and towns. In 1900 the local electricity supplier would likely have been headquartered in town or perhaps in a nearby city. In upstate New York, a series of regional suppliers eventually merged into Syracuse-based Niagara Mohawk, and in cities such as Utica the former headquarters went empty (although now is a healthy office building). Corporate concentration has led many companies to be acquired as commodities on a global market, and whatever local control is now located in distant cities. Niagara Mohawk is today owned by London-based National Grid plc, itself the result of the breakup of the British national electricity system.

At times, federal policy has aided this assault on local communities. The Telecommunications Act of 1994 implemented a system in which cable companies received local monopolies in given municipalities. Cable provider must regularly, by law, renegotiate the terms of their contract with local officials, and the scene in these negotiations is telling. Local officials are often offered free internet and phone services in town facilities, and in exchange are granted a monopoly over the municipality in question. This might seem to be a good deal for the town in question, but local officials are at a substantial disadvantage in negotiations. The cable provider owns the lines, so a failure to reach agreement would result in town residents losing communications until resolved. In effect, the town would need to order the company to sell its lines, but such systems typically span multiple jurisdictions so that even if a buyer could be found the satellite receivers for the system might not be part of the deal, requiring the new owner to invest in a new receiver. Because the municipality has no real negotiating power, a requirement to improve service or increase the number of homes in the system is easily fought by the cable provider. As a result, the more densely settled areas of town often have cable and high-speed internet, but the sparsely settled areas do not. The digital divide is thus highly localized, with some members of the community living a full twenty-first century lifestyle while neighbors a mile away struggle with high-priced satellite versions with poor service or, often, do without. As the same market failure for the digital divide applies to cellular phone coverage, residents of rural areas often require the "wired" phone service that is often more expensive than cellular plans but, ironically, is less likely to drop service.

The end result of corporate concentration is a landscape dotted by the hollowed shells of local firms now headquartered elsewhere, a gestalt of decline that permeates the environment but is unnoticeable to economic statistics. One may still be employed, but the nearest grocery store is two towns away and the nearest metropolitan center is a sea of empty lots and broken windows. Corporate concentration tends to begin with the consolidation of rural and small-town industries into smaller cities, which in turn lose those industries to larger cities. Ultimately, the winners are the largest global cities, where major industries are based.

To seek rural justice does not necessarily involve turning the clock back to coal production and does not require companies to ignore the obvious fact that robots exist. It does require that the wealth of the nation be more equitably spread throughout both the population and across the landscape—the tendency of urban production to concentrate wealth runs against this need. What the above points to is a need to revalorize the rural, as suggested by Seale and Mallinson (2018). It is a call to overcome the long-standing stereotypes that have fueled urban disdain for rural deplorables, without resorting to the equally disillusioned image of the romantic rural, trapped in time. Both images are constraining in their own way, denying the agency of rural people. Acts of rural resistance, as voiced in song, or as votes cast at the ballot box, demonstrate that rural people are not rolling over. Yet, there remain real challenges for rural people, based on spatial inequality and the devaluation of rural work, so the ability to exercise agency is hindered. A rural justice ethic would empower and activate the agency of rural people, attempting to understand everyday challenges, while offering legitimate policy solutions that can help to overcome them. To a large degree, a rural justice ethic will lead to more sustainable policies in terms of equity, environment, and economy (Edwards 2005). The benefits of the rural justice ethic do not simply flow to rural people, but to everyone in the urban-rural system. As noted in the discussion of corporate concentration, the urbanormative dynamic eventually inflicts harm on smaller and less central urban areas as well, as the example of Utica reveals.

TAKEAWAYS

In summary, after considering the limitations of the utilitarian justice framework that dominates the urbanormative ideal, we suggest a capabilities-based approach to rural justice (Sen 1999). Though the rural experience is highly variable and diverse, the realities of vast physical space and the difficulties of rural work unite rural people in a shared set of challenges that translate into capability deprivation. The challenges of physical space are based on un-equal access to goods and services. Because of physical space, rural people wind up living with disparities in education, health, and basic needs such as food. The challenges of rural work are rooted in fundamental dynamics and exploitative practices of the global economy that presently devalue rural products and fail to reward rural workers for the fruits of their labor.

Before the challenges of rural space and work can be addressed, several urbanormative obstacles must be addressed. This starts with questioning the dominant paradigm surrounding the issue of national development that privi-leges urban populations and encourages continued urbanization. This only amplifies the problems of rural people who are taught to abandon a tradition-al way of life, including the practice of subsistence farming. New ways of thinking about development that embrace the capabilities approach will go far in changing this ideal. Arguably, however, there is a parallel need to rethink general cultural attitudes at the core of urbanormativity that devalue the inherent worth of rural people as our discussion of "deplorables" sug-gests. Rural people are fully aware of how they are devalued within the wider cultural hierarchy, and rightfully push back against it through different ex-pressions of resistance. Changing the cultural tide will mean a revalorization of rural that transcends the simplistic rustic images that threaten to trap rural people in the past like exhibits in a museum.

Conclusion

As the world urbanizes, it develops what the United States did years ago: an urbanormative culture. Urbanormativity involves a set of beliefs, values, and practices that place the worth of urban life above rural and is the foundation of a cultural hierarchy that has become nearly universal across nations. These include beliefs about the inferiority, backwardness, and horror of rural cultures, the underlying assumption that social progress equals urbanization, expectations that rural societies should aspire to become urban, and beliefs that rational rural actors should see the logic in migrating to an urban area. The urbanormative context creates spatial inequalities and devalues rural production and workers. In turn, hours of difficult and dangerous work on the front line of the energy economy are poorly compensated, often below the level of subsistence.

Urbanormative culture assumes the natural normalcy of urban life. In doing so, it not only portrays rural life and people as different, but as defective. For example, a story on the website Buzzfeed (Buzzfeed 2019) titled "17 People who Dramatically Changed after Moving to a Bigger City" featured ordinary people who transformed after moving to a larger city. Cognizant of the implication, the author noted, "for clarification, this doesn't happen to everyone and I'm not saying cities are better than small towns or anything." Nevertheless, the implication was evident: becoming urbane is a form of self-improvement for rustics.

Urbanormative culture often becomes policy and law that privileges urban populations. The pervasive spread of urbanormative policy through various national governments and international development agencies remains largely unchallenged and even unnoticed, while entire communities are being transformed to fit with urbanormative standards. This is what prompted us to write this book. We have attempted to open a line of investigation into the how and why of urbanormativity with the hope of bringing attention to several patterns that have long been in motion, while seeking to alter its trajectory. In this conclusion, we will attempt to briefly summarize key ideas that we raised.

THE RISE OF URBANORMATIVITY
AND URBAN-RURAL SYSTEMS

Though urbanormativity is a cultural ideology and a social construction, it does not evolve accidentally or in a vacuum—it exists for a reason. It grows out of and accelerates the process of urbanization itself. In chapter 1, we sought to describe the current state of urbanization in the context of global social change and development. We pointed out that the world is already predominantly urban and is projected to continue urbanizing long into the foreseeable future. While the global rural population should hold steady at about three billion, the global urban population will continue its linear climb toward the seven billion mark, becoming an even larger majority—mainly from rural-urban migration. The most rural nations, found primarily in central Africa, are experiencing the fastest rates of urbanization, and it will not take long for them to complete the urban transition. Nations that are further along the urban transition are finding an optimal level to be in the range of 80–90 percent urban. Few nations—apart from a few city states that have no hinterland, such as Singapore—will reach full urbanization. Nations that are home to vast natural resources and fertile lands typically maintain at least some interest in maintaining priorities such as food security requiring sufficient agricultural productivity. These factors should continue to support at least some rural work in urban nations even with automation. Further, the majority of urban nations have a surplus of mobile urbanites who wish to own a piece of the countryside for the setting, the scenery, or for recreational purposes. They will either visit as tourists, purchase second homes, or fully relocate. These patterns point to a different kind of urbane future that may become entirely disengaged from rural production, radically changing the character and traditions of existing rural communities.

The significance of the global urban transition is often overlooked. It is the culmination of thousands of years of trial and error. Humans were originally foraging creatures that began experimenting with stable settlements over twenty thousand years ago during the Paleolithic, when Ohalo II emerged as a modest site of a few permanent structures. From there it would be another ten thousand years before the emergence of Neolithic agrarian settlements in the Fertile Crescent. The urbanization of the planet is partly a function of the way the global economy has come to devalue rural production, destroying the viability of rural life. While historically pro-rural policies were implemented, such as the New Deal in the United States following the Great Depression, such protectionist policies have largely vanished in the present era of austerity. The tendency has been a movement toward urban-centric policy. We would point out, however, that urbanites remain vulnerable and trapped in the endemic state of urban dependency—inescapably relying on the products of rural labor. Understanding this vulnerability requires elaboration of urban-rural dynamics.

The core dynamics that constitute complex adaptive urban-rural systems begin with the environmental dynamics that encompass a world of energy that humans, like all life on earth, must tap into if they wish to survive and thrive. From this world springs forth economic dynamics, or strategies humans use to harness the planet's energy. Importantly, the energy economy is the foundation of all life—human and non-human. Within the human *species economy* it is rural (not urban) workers who hold the direct line to nature, much like their predecessors, the nomads and agrarian farmers. In order to secure access to stores of energy in the absence of a direct line, urbanites have resorted to various political and cultural dynamics in order to achieve control. Politically, coercive strategies have given rise to forceful conquest, often through violent encounters, followed in many cases by policies involving land enclosures that confiscate rural lands. As we noted, this is a costly strategy in the long run, as the threat for retaliation is ever-present. The more effective strategy is cultural, and this is where the rationale of urbanormativity comes into play. Under this ideology, the goal is for everyone to become convinced of the inferiority of rural life, so the exploitation of rural lands and peoples appears to be just. As the values of urban superiority become widely adopted, among both urban and rural populations, any actions that privilege the urban population appear as legitimate and righteous. Rustics indoctrinated with urbanormative ideology may develop the kind of self-shame or self-loathing that resembles the condition that DuBois called "double consciousness."

In chapter 2 we elaborated the role of distance and interaction as mechanisms that make urbanormativity possible. Physically separating humans into urban and rural spaces creates divergent contexts for socialization wherein alternative epistemologies and identities can be formed. Those raised in a rural setting are less familiar with urban life, while those raised in urban settings often remain uninformed of rural life. This is not totally equivalent, however, since urban and rural people experience the *settlement space* of the other differently through their *viable spaces*. It is far more common for rural residents to travel great distances to visit urban spaces—often as a matter of routine for work, school, or other needs. Urban residents, conversely, may find that it is unnecessary to ever travel outside of their settlement space enabling them to remain oblivious to rural realities. The broad viable space of rural residents typically makes them more aware of urban life.

Differential spatial experiences lead to alternate identities and social psychological outcomes, such as the development of the blasé attitude among urbanites, as observed over a century ago by Simmel. The intense overstimulation of urban spaces overrun with activity and population impacts the nature of social interaction, giving it a more rational and transactional tone. Urbanites may be less comfortable or patient with the kind of qualitative social interaction that unfolds in rural settings, where things may be more personal and have more depth and content. Patterns of interaction, in turn, influence the prevalence of strong and weak ties so that rural communities tend to have a higher prevalence of strong ties, while urban communities tend to support a prevalence of weak ties.

Ultimately, the bifurcated urban-rural spatial experiences lead to attitudes, ideas, and beliefs that are worlds apart socially, so that even if physical separation were to be overcome, the ability to interact smoothly would remain hindered by social distance. This social distance makes the formation of urban-rural social ties less likely. This is consistent with Mayhew and Levinger's (1977) *Law of Distance-Interaction* as we all as Zipf's (1949) *principle of least effort* hypothesis. If urban people migrate to the country, or rural people migrate to the city, then the dynamics of distance begin to shift, as social representations come to be replaced by direct experience. Identities may be altered, as social ties develop between rustic and urbane people. In the absence of something like a migration event, however, the epistemic distance between urban and rural remains great, leading to urban moral indifference—enjoying the fruits of rural labor while ignoring its true cost is one unfortunate result.

Chapter 3 took a deeper dive into the dynamics of the energy economy— the oikos of urban-rural dynamics. Urban dependency emerged with the first urban-rural system and remains with us through the present. Early Neolithic farmers in the Fertile Crescent attempted to be fully self-sufficient but often continued relying on hunting for meat. It would take another five thousand years to create a prototype of what we call an urban-rural system—the first of which emerged in the Euphrates Valley of Iraq around 5500 BCE. While agrarians seek self-sufficiency, urban-rural systems thrive on the exchange of rural and urban products between settlements. The first rural villages remained highly self-sufficient but generated enough surplus that they could trade for complex goods assembled in larger market towns. The first urban market towns relied heavily on the import of rural products for such necessities as food and textiles. This was the birth of the "freehand" and "cultivator" classes described by Sir James Steuart in the late eighteenth century. It has since evolved into the present, as a global system centered on gigantic global cities that draw resources from both urban and rural places all over the world. Many rural settlements are today entirely dependent on exporting their surplus, having given up self-sufficiency altogether. Others dream of a return to agrarian self-sufficiency in the hope that basic nutritional needs can be met, as trade with the urban world is proving inadequate.

While technological improvements may enhance the productivity of rural work, the ability to keep up with the swelling urban population is increasingly difficult—perhaps we are approaching a global carrying capacity. *Rural production* is responsible for gathering what is natural and putting it into a form that can be either consumed or traded; *urban production* begins with rural products and either consumes or transforms them into other products— some simple, others more complex. In a world that is 50 percent urban, the ratio of rural to urban residents is 1:1—for every urban "freehand" there is a rural "cultivator." When the world hits a ratio of 2:1—expected by 2050— the weight of urban consumption and rural exploitation will double. Whether this can be sustained is a fundamentally important question that must be answered in years to come.

CULTURAL VALUE, REPRESENTATION, AND IDENTITY

The ability to justify rural exploitation and inequality culturally is the core function of urbanormativity. In the second part of the book, we divided the cultural dynamics of urbanormativity into three components—cultural capital, rural representations, and identity. In chapter 4, we attempted to outline a framework for thinking about the value of rural versus urban drawing on Bourdieu's notion of cultural capital. Every culture assigns privilege to those who embody certain characteristics deemed to be desirable. The privilege structure of institutional cultural capital then becomes the skeleton of the wider cultural hierarchy. Though it is not the only dimension, urban-rural identity is surprisingly universal across nations, and the associated cultural hierarchy overwhelmingly tends to privilege the urban population. This was true as early as the dawn of urban society itself. In the Sumerian *Epic of Gilgamesh*, the hero-king looks upon the city walls of third millennium BCE Uruk as the height of human achievement. In a similar vein, urban elites in second millennium BCE China dismissed the rural peasantry as implicitly inferior "black haired people" (Keay 2009). This is similar to the hierarchy based on gender inequality that is embedded in patriarchal societies, where masculine qualities are valued above feminine cultural qualities—whatever each of these may entail.

In urbanormative society, being perceived as urban or urbane is a source of cultural capital (and therefore, privilege), and this opens the door to institutional forms of cultural capital—like attending a prestigious school or working for a prestigious firm. Being rural or rustic may, alternatively, create barriers to advancement. Cultural capital, in other words, has significant implications for economic class and related outcomes. What is unique about the urban-rural dimension is that it is not limited to individuals, as it also describes geographic spaces. Entire communities may come to be perceived as urbane or rustic, composed of signifying objects such as rural simulacra—buildings that resemble log cabins or have other rustic facades, for instance. As a result, entire communities may be located within the urban-rural cultural hierarchy. On the lower end, communities acquire a stigma that may be inherited by its members, as discovered in Hayden's study of Seabrook. The community was widely viewed as a backwater, and its residents often acquired the nickname, "Brooker," to denote their backward rusticity. Language is another important indicator in which rustic dialects generate a negative form of linguistic capital.

An important follow-up to the discussion of cultural capital and cultural hierarchy, is the consideration: How do people come to hold normative evaluations of urban and rural? In chapter 5 we sought to answer this question through a review of work on rural representations. The notion of a rural representation was introduced in our discussion of epistemic distance—as an often-uninformed social representation of rural life held by urbanites. In place of direct experience and observation, the ideas that comprise rural representations are taken from such popular media as television, film, and music. Prior research has shown emergent themes to include rural as simple, wild, and escape. There is also growing evidence of a fourth theme of rural horror. The urban imaginary has been exposed, in the United States for instance, to such images as the romantic rustic life of Mayberry in the *Andy Griffith Show*, as well as to the horror of insane, inbred, cannibalistic murderers in the *Wrong Turn*. These images are contradictory but share in the urbanormative belief that the rural other is unreal—idealized characters representing the best and worst of rural life.

The contents of rural and urban images inform our discussion of rustic and urbane identity in chapter 6. Here the construction of identity is presented as individual, group, and community-based processes—when they align there is identity fusion. There are objective anchors to identity, but ultimately, identity is a social construction. We noted the tendency to reduce urbane and rustic identity to its two objective anchors: residency and work. We compared this to the fallacy of reducing gender identity to the biological sex of male or female that one is assigned at birth. While most people who are born anatomically male identify as masculine, there are those who identify as feminine, for instance. Similarly, there are people living in rural areas that are urbane and people living in urban areas that are rustic. We hope to advance the study of urban-rural identity beyond reductionist tendencies. Further confusion arises when the objective anchors do not align, as when, for instance, one lives in a rural community but is employed in urban work (the second circuit of the energy economy, discussed earlier). In urban societies, this is not at all uncommon as more and more urbane people populate rural communities. This led us to raise questions about when one might be accepted by a wider community as rustic or urbane. Clearly, the analysis of rustic and urbane identity needs further investigation, but the existing literature on old-timers and newcomers is informative. While scholars have been slow to take this up, the salience and importance of this dimension of identity remains important for everyday citizens, as noted by scholars like Bell. Of further interest will be explorations into the intersectionality of urbane-rustic with dimensions of identity such as race, ethnicity, gender, sexuality, and social class. Scholars like Stapel have noted the fact that nonnormative sexualities—homo, metro, bisexual—are typically identified with the urban experience, rendering rustic people with nonnormative sexuality invisible. We extend this to include remaining dimensions of identity that are associated with urban experience, including race and ethnicity. The tendency to associate rural with whiteness in the United States, renders racial and ethnic minorities—who are a growing segment of rural communities—invisible.

THE CONSEQUENCES OF URBANORMATIVITY

The third part of the book examined the consequences of urbanormativity in everyday life. In chapter 7, the focus turned to policy and laws that have an urbanormative bias. We began in chapter 7, with a discussion that explores what a policy is, in terms of a rule within a wider operating system. Our position is that the policy-scape is being written based on the assumption of urban conditions. When rural conditions are present, the operation of the system falls apart, leaving rural residents at a disadvantage. This is analogous to a computer operating system that does not have the correct drivers to initialize older components. Historically, taking the United States as an example, we maintain that pro-rural policies were enacted as a response to the power of the rural vote. In a democracy, the majority determines political outcomes, such as the winner of elections to various political offices. Politicians seeking to earn the rural vote promised policies that would, for instance, make farming less risky and more rewarding economically. As the size of the rural vote demised, so too did its power and influence. Gradually, policy shifted toward exclusively urban voters. As the power and influence of the urban vote spread to encompass more of the political framework, the pervasiveness of urbanormative law has grown.

The overarching neoliberal policy shift toward deregulation, devolution, privatization, and fiscal stress, is one that favors urban society. As support for local communities dwindles, it is left to such mechanisms as property tax to meet the needs of the community. The small, scattered population of a rural community is far less prepared to rely on such a mechanism, in comparison to a large, dense, and well-resourced urban settlement. To be fair, inner city urban populations have not been able to weather the shift either, as resources move within the urban region from the center to the suburban fringe. In our model, suburbs are a functional part of urban settlements, somewhat unique to contemporary settlements primarily found in North America. The end result is an overall urban settlement that is faring better than the rural—that does not mean urbanites share advantages equally. Rural communities that are proximate to larger urban areas are often transformed into exurbs or suburbs. When this happens, it ceases being a rural settlement space. We also note that as current policy trends become more advanced, the privatization of community life will become increasingly undemocratic, serving the wishes of private companies over citizens.

The broader urbanormative neoliberal shift is now manifest in an array of concrete policy outcomes. The decline of state support for welfare—though it was framed in a way that antagonized the inner-city poor (minority) population—actually cut support for many rural communities in regions where the economy had been lagging for decades. Old farming and mining communities, for instance, are heavily reliant on receiving economic assistance in its various forms, from cash to food aid. Entire regions, such as the Appalachians and Black Belt South have suffered from chronic structural economic hardship for several decades and include the majority of persistently poor counties in the country. Forcing such places to provide for their own schools and infrastructure, while eliminating support, is a double blow that secures an even more difficult and arduous future. These conditions have been conducive to a range of ills from substance abuse to mental health problems and domestic violence. The rights of women have suffered since parental rights are revoked when poverty is coupled with these resultant problems. Access to health services, including family planning and abortion rights are diminished for rural women. Access to legal representation is lower for rural residents, so if there is a legal problem, rural people have fewer choices. As the demand for mental health services has increased, availability has become strained.

In chapter 8 we noted that the consequences of urbanormativity extend to entire communities. As participation in the energy economy subsides, spatially rural communities wind up either languishing under fiscal stress or else experience place structuration—transformations to their character and traditions—as they are increasingly guided by an urbane population. This means that rural representations begin informing the local character and tradition, often incorporating rural simulacra, to create an idyllic rustic charm simulation. This is, after all, what many urbanites are in search of finding, and what motivates them to visit or move to the countryside in the first place. The expectation for a quaint rural life runs counter to the experiences of many traditional rural communities, who as noted in the chapter on policy, suffer chronic poverty and its attendant social problems.

Traditional rural communities are those that remain embedded in the energy economy, performing rural work, accessing natural resources for the purpose of trade with urban populations, who are struggling with a global devaluation that creates hardship. In addition to the economic crisis, extractive processes of intensive rural production also carry heavy environmental costs, as noted in the example of the Superfund site in Evangeline, Louisiana, and also in the case of the Buffalo Creek mining disaster. These atrocities are left out of the urban imaginary when urbanites dream of a quiet, simple, and romantic country. Traditional communities contradict these aspirations and are thus ignored out of moral indifference.

The idyllic rural community is much like a museum exhibit that captures various images and objects associated with the rural experience. Successful communities, like Cooperstown or Lake Placid, New York, are washed clean of the problems of traditional rural communities, while offering the rural experiences and simulations urbanites crave. They become communities of consumption rather than production (Urry 2012). The process of transformation is not unlike another familiar form of gentrification found in the inner-city, where years of disinvestment leads first to decline, and later to re-investment that creates new and beautiful spaces and homes out of low-cost properties. The chief difference is that it takes place in the country—it is rural gentrification. Such communities typically offer a combination of tourist opportunities and second home ownership options, but many urbanites will choose to relocate permanently. In any case, though gentrification may beautify the façade of the community, it generally does so by pushing out original inhabitants, replacing them with more affluent households who assume, among other things, control over local politics. Once under control, regulations may be enacted to ensure that place structuration moves forward through policy mechanisms like building codes and zoning laws. Property values will increase in cases of successful rural gentrification, driving up property taxes and pushing out old-timers. Though they may be attractive aesthetically, their seasonal nature limits economic viability for those operating local businesses. This coupled with higher taxes may make it hard to survive unless one is independently wealthy.

Throughout the discussion of urbanormativity offered in the preceding chapters, we have routinely come back to the many forms of inequality experienced by rural people and places. In chapter 9 we offered a discussion of rural justice that suggests that the current context is aligned with a utilitarian logic—the urban majority enjoys privilege and success, while the rural minority sacrifices for the greater good. We reviewed the logical flaws of utilitarian justice in general, and reviewed advances made first by Rawls, and later by Sen. Ultimately, we adopt the ethic offered by Sen with his emphasis on capability maximization.

While there are no easy answers for rural communities dealing with the costs of the energy economy—exacerbated by urban dependency and rural devaluation—the notion of maximizing capabilities provides freedom to develop as members of rural communities see fit. A one-size-fits-all policy will not succeed across places, where unique demographic and political economic factors call for a more carefully tailored approach. In the end, the best judges for what to do with rural communities are the members of those communities. That does not mean that all of the responsibility should fall on their shoulders—indeed that is part of the problem. Offering greater support services and aid that can empower rural people will ensure capability maximization.

WHERE DO WE GO FROM HERE?

This volume had a singular goal: to bring popular and academic attention to the cultural phenomenon of urbanormativity. In examining this concept from different perspective, we have chosen to sacrifice depth for breadth. We imagine that each individual chapter could be elaborated into a book length analysis. Indeed, we hope they will! Research should develop on the topic of urban-rural systems—the arrangement responsible for the creation of urbanormativity. The underlying system dynamics need a more careful and historical comparative treatment. We (the authors) are in the process of developing an analysis. We also have ambitions of elaborating on the meaning and functions of the energy economy. We hope that other scholars will focus more deeply on the study of the three central facets of urbanormativity: cultural capital, rural representations, and identity. Investigations of urban-rural socialization and the associated stigma of rusticity may help identify ways to expand institutional access for rural youth. Studies of rural representations should continue exploring a range of media from different cultures, emphasizing urbanormative trends in television, film, music, art, news, and other venues. Analysis of urbane and rustic identity should continue as a devoted area of study, as well as part of a wider intersectionality agenda that has long neglected this dimension. More research is needed to illuminate the mechanisms by which rural cultures and languages are being eclipsed for a generic urbane alternative, such as the edited volume by Seale and Mallinson on *Rural Voices*.

Beyond academic pursuits, we also have some pragmatic recommendations. We believe there is a need to create intentional cultural sensitivity programs that emphasize the value and worth of diverse rural experiences—often misunderstood through the lens of stereotypes that devalue and homogenize rural people and places. Such a program might incorporate an intersectional approach, while considering other important factors—race, gender, social class—as they play out in both urban and rural settings. This will be especially useful in the arena of community development, where practitioners and change agents are immersed in the work of supporting and guiding rural communities through a host of challenges. Apart from formal community development, are individuals working within different institutions that include education, healthcare, and criminal justice. Gaining awareness of the broader patterns of urbanormativity and the neoliberal package of austerity policies—devolution, fiscal stress, privatization, and deregulation—may encourage sensitivity to the unique challenges rural communities face. Leaders in these fields may innovate ways to provide better access and availability to services that contribute to improved education, health, and security outcomes.

Leaders in private industry should investigate the tendency to devalue rural work and production, searching for mechanisms that will ensure fair compensation for rural workers, preserve the rural foundation of the global economy, while slowing the speeding global urban transition. The Fair-Trade label may offer at least one model for adding value to rural work. Political leaders will ideally investigate existing mechanisms and come up with new policies that ensure rural production is not exploited. This will not necessarily translate into a return to New Deal policies—the 1930s were very different from the present. Yet, there should be a review of New Deal intentions and an attempt to apply programs that ensure greater protection and support of all citizens—urban and rural.

Finally, we hope that the urban population will read the ideas in this volume and accept the challenge of overcoming urbanormativity. This will mean second guessing rural stereotypes, reflecting on urban dependency and the global need for rural production, it will require moving past moral indifference and toward a rural justice ethic that seeks to maximize the capabilities of all. It will mean developing a more sensitive approach to responsible rural tourism and residency that sustains concern and provides a place for older traditions and community members, who should in turn have a voice in discussions about the changing character of communities. Politically, it will mean thinking about the needs of rural communities and people and supporting programs and policies that avoid intensifying spatial inequalities. It is only after overcoming the cultural deficiencies of urbanormativity that the structural conditions of urban-rural systems will improve, along with the everyday experiences of rural people.

References

Adams, R. M. (1966). *The evolution of urban society*. Chicago: Aldine.

American Psychiatric Association. (2013). *Desk reference to the diagnostic criteria from DSM-5*. Washington, DC: American Psychiatry Publishing.

Anania, J. (2016). Main Street metamorphosis: The impacts of baseball tourism in Cooperstown, New York. *Middle States Geographer* 49: 84–91.

Araghi, F.A. (1995). Global depeasantisation, 1945–1990. *The Sociological Quarterly, 36,* p. 337–368.

Auclair, E. & Vanoni, D. (2004). The attractiveness of rural areas for young people. Pp. 74–104 in Jentsch, B. & Shucksmith, M. (eds.), *Young people in rural areas of Europe*. Ashgate, Aldershot.

Avery, L. & Kassam, K.-A. (2011). Phronesis: Children's local rural knowledge of science and engineering. *Journal of Research in Rural Education*, 26, 2, pp. 1–18.

Avery, L. & Sipple, J. (2016). Common core, STEM, and rural schools: Views from students and states. Pp. 123–146 in Fulkerson, G.F. & Thomas, A.R. (eds.), *Reimagining rural: Urbanormative portrayals of rural life*. Lanham, MD: Lexington Books.

Bartlett, L.J., Williams, D.R., Prescott, G.W., Balmford, A., Green, R.E., Eriksson, A., Valdes, P.J., Singarayer, J.S., & Manica, A. (2015). Robustness despite uncertainty: Regional climate data reveal the dominant role of humans in explaining global extinctions of Late Quaternary megafauna. *Ecography*; DOI: 10.1111/ecog.01566.

Bartling, H. (2004). The Magic Kingdom Syndrome: Trials and tribulations of life in Disney's Celebration. *Contemporary Justice Review*, 7, 4, pp. 375–393.

Beck, U. (1992). *Risk society: Towards a new modernity*. London: Sage.

Becker, H. (2007). *Writing for social scientists: How to start and finish your thesis, book, or article (2nd edition)*. Chicago: University of Chicago Press.

Bell, D. (1997). Anti-idyll: Rural horror. Pp. 94–108 in Cloke, P.J. & Little, J. (eds.), *Contested countryside cultures*. London: Routledge.

_____. (2006). Variations on the rural idyll. Pp. 149–160, in Cloke, P., Marsden, T., & Mooney, P.H. (eds.), *The handbook of rural studies*. London: Sage.

Bell, M. (1992). The fruit of difference: the rural–urban continuum as a system of identity. *Rural Sociology*, 57, pp. 65–82.

_____. (1997). The two-ness of rural life and the ends of rural scholarship. *Journal of Rural Studies*, 23, pp. 402–415.

Bennett-Knapp, S. (2016). What do they do up there? A look at two non-metropolitan counties in New York. Pp. 149–160 in Thomas, A.R. & Fulkerson, G.M. (eds.), *Reinventing rural: New realities in an urbanizing world*. Lanham, MD: Lexington Books.

Bentham, J. (2015 [1780]). *An introduction to the principles of morals and legislation.* Create-Space Independent Publishing Platform.

Bjaarstad, S. (2003). Osloungdommers forestillinger om bygda. En studie av unges stedsforsta° else, tilhørighet og identitet (Youth in Oslo and representations of the rural. A study of young people's understanding of place attachment and identity). Oslo, Norway: University of Oslo.

Bourdieu, P. (1980). Le capital social : Notes provisoires (in French). *Actes Recherche Science Social*, 31, p. 2–3.

———. (1983). The forms of capital. Pp. 241–58 in Richardson, J.G. (ed.), *The handbook for theory: Research for the sociology of education.* New York: Greenwood Press.

———. (1984). *Distinction. A social critique of the judgement of taste.* London: Routledge.

Brown, D. & Schafft, K. (2019). *Rural people and communities in the 21st century: Resilience and transformation* (2nd edition). Medford, MA: Polity Press.

Brown, L.R. (2011). *World on the edge: How to prevent environmental and economic collapse.* New York: W.W. Norton.

Bunce, M. (1994). *The countryside ideal: Anglo American images of landscape.* London: Routledge.

Calhoun, J. B. (1962). *The ecology and sociology of the Norway rat.* Washington, DC: U.S. Government Printing Office.

Caplow, T. & Forman, R. (1950). Neighborhood interaction in a homogenous community. *American sociological review*, 15, pp. 357–366.

Carolan, M. (2006). Do you see what I see? Examining the epistemic barriers to sustainable farming. *Rural Sociology*, 71, 2, pp. 232–60.

_____. (2016). *The sociology of food and agriculture* (2nd edition). New York: Routledge, EarthScan.

Carr, P.J. & Kefalas, M.J. (2009). *Hollowing out the middle: The rural brain drain and what it means for America.* Boston: Beacon Press.

Castells, M. (1977). *The urban question: A Marxist approach.* Cambridge, MA: MIT Press.

Cauvin, J. (2000). *The birth of the Gods and the origins of agriculture.* Cambridge University Press.

Cavalli-Sforza, L.L. & Cavalli-Sforza, F. (1996). *The great human diasporas: The history of diversity and evolution.* Translated by Sarah Thorne. New York: Perseus.

Childe, V.G. (1950). The urban revolution. *Town Planning Review* 21, pp. 3–17.

Ching, B. (2016). Cow college. Pp. 111–122 in Fulkerson, G.M. & Thomas, A.R. (eds.), *Reimaging rural: Urbanormative portrayals of rural life.* Lanham, MD: Lexington Books.

Ching, B. & Creed, G.W. (1997). *Knowing your place: Rural identity and cultural hierarchy.* New York: Routledge.

_____. (2014). Eaten up: Urban foraging and rural identity. Pp. 111–128 in Fulkerson, G.M. & Thomas, A.R. (eds.), *Studies in urbanormativity: Rural community in urban society.* Lanham, MD: Lexington Books.

Cloke, P. (1997). Country backwater to virtual village? Rural studies and "the cultural turn." *Journal of Rural Studies*, 13, pp. 367–375.

_____. (2006). Conceptualizing rurality. In Cloke, P., Marsden, T., & Mooney, P. H. (eds.), *The handbook of rural studies*, pp. 18–28. London: Sage.

Cloke, P., Marsden, T., & Mooney, P.H. (2006). *The handbook of rural studies.* London: Sage.

Cloke, P. & Little, Jo. (1997). *Contested countryside cultures: Otherness, marginalisation, and rurality.* London: Routledge.

Cloke, P. & Milbourne, P. (1992). Deprivation and lifestyle in rural Wales: Rurality and the cultural dimension. *Journal of Rural Studies*, 8(4), pp. 71–76.

Cloke, P. J. & Thrift, N. (1990). Class and change in rural Britain. Pp. 165–81 in Marsden, T., Lowe, P., & Whatmore, S. (eds.), *Rural restructuring: Global Processes and their responses.* London: David Fulton Publishers.

Coleman, J. (1988). Social capital in the creation of human capital. *American Journal of Sociology*, 94 (supplement), pp. S95–S120.

Cooper, J.F. (2011 [1823]). *The pioneers.* Cambridge: Harvard University Press.

Deavers, K. (1992). What is rural? *Policies Studies Journal*, 20, 2, pp. 184–189.

DeYoung, A.J., & Howley, C.B. (2009). The political economy of rural school consolidation. *Peabody Journal of Education*, 67, 4, pp. 63–89.

Dominy, M.D. (1997). Pp. 237–266 in Ching, B. & Creed, G.W. (eds.), *Knowing your place: Rural identity and cultural hierarchy*. New York: Routledge.

Dorian, E. (1962). *The sex cure*. New York: Universal.

Dubois, W.E.B. (2017 [1903]). *The souls of black folk*. CreateSpace Independent Publishing Platform.

Duncan, D.T., Hatzenbuehler, M.L., & Johnson, R.M. (2014). Neighborhood-level LGBT hate crimes and current illicit drug use among sexual minority youth. *Drug and Alcohol Dependence*, 135, pp. 65–70.

Durkheim, E. (1984). *The division of labor in society* (translated by Hall, W.D). New York: The Free Press.

_____. (2001 [1912]). *The elementary forms of religious life*. New York: Oxford University Press.

Edelman, M. (1997). Pp. 131–148 in Ching, B. & Creed, G.W. (eds.), *Knowing your place: Rural identity and cultural hierarchy*. New York: Routledge.

Edensor, T. (2006). Performing rurality. Pp. 355–364 in Cloke, P., Marsden, T., & Mooney, P.H. (eds.), *The handbook of rural studies*. London: Sage.

Edwards, A. (2005). *The sustainability revolution: Portrait of a paradigm shift*. Gabriola Islands, BC: New Society Publishers.

Emery, M. & Flora, C.B. (2006). Spiraling up: Mapping community transformation with community capitals framework. *Community Development*, 37, pp. 19–35.

Erickson, K.T. (1978). *Everything in its path: Destruction of community in the Buffalo Creek flood*. New York: Simon & Schuster.

Farstad, M. & Rye, J.F. (2013). Second home owners, locals and their perspective on rural development. *Journal of rural studies*, 30, pp. 41–51.

Feig, E., Kulzer, R., Winston, S., & Gilbert, B. (Producers), Schmidt, R. (Director). (2003). *Wrong Turn*. United States: 20th Century Fox.

Feig, E., Kulzer, R., & Freilich, J. (Producers), Lynch, J. (Director). *Wrong Turn 2: Dead End*. (2007). United States: 20th Century Fox.

Feig, E., Kulzer, R., Beach, J., & Roth, P. (Producers), O'Brien, D. (Director). (2009). *Wrong Turn 3: Left for Dead*. United States: 20th Century Fox.

Feig, E., Kulzer, R., & Todd, K. (Producers), O'Brien, D. (Director). (2011). *Wrong Turn 4: Bloody Beginnings*. United States: 20th Century Fox.

Feig, E., Kulzer, R., Beach, J., & Roth, P. (Producers), O'Brien, D. (Director). (2012). *Wrong Turn 5: Bloodlines*. United States: 20th Century Fox.

Feig, E., Kulzer, R., Beach, J., & Roth, P. (Producers), Milev, V. (Director). (2014). *Wrong Turn 6: Last Resort*. United States: 20th Century Fox.

Ferguson, T., Page, B., Rothschild, J., Chang, A., & Cheng, J. (2018). The economic and social roots of populist rebellion: Support for Donald Trump in 2016. *Institute for New Economic Thinking*, Working Paper #83, http://ineteconomics.org/workingpapers.

Ferrier, J.F. (1854). *Institutes of metaphysic: The theory of knowing and being*. Edinburgh: William Blackwood and Sons.

Festinger, L., Schachter, S., and Back, K. (1950). *Social pressures in informal groups*. Stanford, CA: Stanford University Press.

Flannery, Kent. 1969. *Origins and ecological effects of early domestication in Iran and the Near East. The domestication and exploitation of plants and animals*, eds. Peter J. Ucko and G.W. Dimbleby (Chicago: Aldine Publishing Co., 1969), pp. 73–100.

Flora, C.B. & Flora, J.L. (2015). *Rural communities: Legacy and change* (4th ed.). Iowa State University: Waveland Press.

Frank, A.G. (1967). *Capitalism and underdevelopment in Latin America*. New York: Monthly Review Press.

Fulkerson, G.M. & Lowe, B. (2016). *Representations of rural in popular North American television*. Pp. 9–34 in Fulkerson, G.M. & Thomas, A.R. (eds.), Reimagining rural: Urban-ormative portrayals of rural life. Lanham, MD: Lexington Books.

Fulkerson, G.M. & Seale, E.K. (2012). The case of Cooperstown, New York: The makings of a perfect village in an urbanising world. Sociological Research Online, 17, 4, 9.

Fulkerson, G.M., & Thomas, A.R. (2014). Urbanization, urbanormativity, and place-structuration. Pp. 5–30 in Fulkerson, G.M. & Thomas, A.R. (eds.), *Studies in urbanormativity: Rural community in urban society*. New York: Lexington Books.

_____. (2016). *Reimagining rural: Urbanormative portrayals of rural life*. Studies in Urban-Rural Dynamics Book Series (eds. Thomas, A.R. & Fulkerson, G.M.). New York: Lexington.

Fulkerson, G.M. & Thompson, G.H. (2008). The evolution of a contested concept: A meta-analysis of social capital definitions and trends (1988–2006). *Sociological Inquiry*, 78, 4, pp. 536–557.

Full President Trump Speech at the Farm Bureau Rebuilding Rural America Conference w: Time Tabs. (2016). Retrieved 1/31/2019, from https://www.youtube.com/watch?v=UEHPfTPN8eg.

Gans, H. J. (1962). *The urban villagers*. Glencoe, IL: Free Press.

Garreau, J. (1992). *Edge city: Life on the new frontier* (1st Anchor Books ed.). New York: Anchor Books. ISBN 978-0385424349.

Gell-Mann, M. (1994). Complex adaptive systems. Pp. 17–45 in Cowan, G.A., Pines, D., & Meltzer, D. (eds.), *SFI Studies in the Sciences of Complexity, Proc. Vol. XIX*. New York: Addison-Wesley.

Giddens, A. (1984). *The constitution of society: Outline of the theory of structuration*. Cambridge: Polity Press.

Gottdeiner, M. (1994). *The new urban sociology*. New York: McGraw Hill.

Graber, E.E. (1974). Newcomers and oldtimers: Growth and change in a mountain town. *Rural Sociology*, 39, 4, pp. 504–513.

Graeber, D. (2012). *Debt: The first 5,000 years*. New York: Melville House.

Granovetter, M. (1973). The strength of weak ties. *American journal of sociology*, 78, 6, pp. 1360–1380.

Gray, M. (2009). *Out in the country: Youth, media, and queer visibility in rural America*. New York: New York University Press.

Grigsby, M. (2012). *Noodlers in Missouri: Fishing for identity in a rural subculture*. Kirksville, MO: Truman State University Press.

Guenther, B. (1997). Pp. 171–194 in Ching, B. & Creed, G.W. (eds.), *Knowing your place: Rural identity and cultural hierarchy*. New York: Routledge.

Halberstam, J. (2005). *In a queer time and place: Transgender bodies, subcultural lives*. New York: New York University Press.

Halfacree, K. H. (1993). Locality and social representation: Space, discourse and alternative definitions of the rural. *Journal of Rural Studies*, 9, 1, pp. 23–37.

_____. (1995). Talking about rurality: Social representations of the rural as expressed by residents of six English parishes. *Journal of Rural Studies*, 11, pp. 1–20.

_____. (2006). Rural space: Constructing a three-fold architecture. Pp. 44–62 in Cloke, P., Marsden, T., & Mooney, P.H. (eds.), *The handbook of rural studies*. London: Sage.

_____. (2007). Trial by space for a "radical rural": Introducing alternative localities, representations and lives. *Journal of Rural Studies*, 23, pp. 125–141.

Hall, P. (1998). *Cities in civilization*. New York: Pantheon.

Harper, K. (2017). *The fate of Rome: Climate, disease, and the end of an empire*. Princeton, NJ: Princeton U. Press.

Hayden, K. (2014). Stigma, reputation, and place structuration in a coastal New England town. Pp. 67–86 in Fulkerson, G. & Thomas, A. (eds), *Studies in urbanormativity: Rural community in urban society*. Lanham, MD: Lexington Books.

_____. (2016). Inbred horror revisited: The fear of the rural in twenty-first century backwoods horror films. Pp. 59–72 in Fulkerson, G.F. & Thomas, A.R. (eds.), *Reimagining rural: Urbanormative portrayals of rural life*. Lanham, MD: Lexingtong Books.

Heberlein. T.A. (2012). *Navigating environmental attitudes*. New York: Oxford University Press.

Hinrichs, C.C. (1996). Consuming images: Making and marketing Vermont as distinctive rural place. Pp. 259–278 in Vandergeest, P., & Du Puis, E.M. (eds.), *Creating the countryside: The politics of rural and environmental discourse*. Philadelphia: Temple University Press.

Hipp, J.R. & Perrin, A.J. (2009). The simultaneous effect of social distance and physical distance on the formation of neighborhood ties. *City & Community*, 8, 1, pp. 5–25.

Husserl, E. (1973 [1900]). *Logical investigations*. Translated by Findlay, J.N. London: Routledge.

Isenberg, N. (2017). *White trash: The 400 year untold history of class in America*. New York: Penguin Books.

Jacobellis v. Ohio. No. 11 (1964). Retrieved: March 16, 2019, from https://case law.findlaw.com/us-supreme-court/378/184.html.

Jain, H.K. (2010). *Green revolution: history, impact and future*. Houston: Studium Press.

Jentsch, B., Shucksmith, M. (eds.). (2004a). *Young people in rural areas of Europe*. Ashgate, Aldershot.

_____. (2004b). Introduction. Pp. 1–7 in Jentsch, B. & Shucksmith, M. (eds.), *Young people in rural area of Europe*. Ashgate, Aldershot.

Kahn, A. (1997). Pp. 39–70 in Ching, B. & Creed, G.W. (eds.), *Knowing your place: Rural identity and cultural hierarchy*. New York: Routledge.

Kane, C.L. & Thomas, A.R. (2016). Centralia, Pennsylvania: Disaster or apathy? Pp. 99–112 in Thomas, A. R. & Fulkerson, G. M. (eds.), *Reinventing rural: New realities in an urbanizing world*. New York: Lexington.

Kapoor, D. (ed.). (2017). *Against colonization and rural dispossession: Local resistance in South and East Asia, the Pacific, and Africa*. London: Zed Books.

Kasarda, J.D. & Janowitz, M. (1974). Community attachment in mass society. *American Sociological Review*, 39, pp. 328–339.

Kaufman, A. (2013). Why we need to invent words. *The Guardian* (March 11). Retrieved 1/5/19 from https://www.theguardian.com/culture/2013/mar/11/why-we-need-invent-new-words.

Keay, J. (2009). *China: A history*. New York: HarperCollins.

Kte'pi, B. (2018). Identity fusion. *Identity Fusion—Research Starters Sociology*, pp. 1–4.

Lamont, M. (2000). Meaning-making in cultural sociology: Broadening our agenda. *Contemporary Sociology*, 29, 4, pp. 602–607.

Lansing, J.S. (2003). Complex adaptive systems. *Annual Review of Anthropology*, 32, pp. 183–204.

Lee, E. (1966). A theory of migration. *Demography*, 1, pp. 47–57.

Lees, S.H. (1997). The rise and fall of "peasantry" as a culturally constructed national elite in Israel. Pp. 219–236 in Ching, B. & Creed, G.W. (eds.), *Knowing your place: Rural identity and cultural hierarchy*. New York: Routledge.

Leicht, K.T., Jenkins, C.J. (2007). New and unexplored opportunities: Defining a spatial perspective for political sociology. Pp. 63–84 in Lobao, L., Hooks, G., & Tickamyer, A. (eds.), *The sociology of spatial inequality*. Albany: State University of New York Press.

Lichter, D. (2012). Immigration and the new racial diversity in rural America. *Rural Sociology*, 77, pp. 3–35.

Little, J. (1999). Otherness, representation and the cultural construction of rurality. *Progress in Human Geography*, 22, 3, pp. 437–442.

Little, S.E. (2000). Networks and neighborhoods: Household community and sovereignty in the global economy. *Urban studies*, 37, 10, pp. 1813–1825.

Lobao, L., Hooks, G., & Tickamyer, A. (2007). *The sociology of spatial inequality*. Albany: State University of New York Press.

Lobao, L. & Meyer, K. (2001). The great agricultural transition: Crisis, change, and social consequences of twentieth century US farming. *Annual Review of Sociology*, 27, pp. 103–124.

Logan, J. R. & Molotch, H. (2012). *Urban fortunes: The political economy of place* (25th anniversary edition). Berkeley: University of California Press.

Lomnitz, L. (1977). *Networks and marginality: Life in a Mexican shantytown*. New York: Academic Press.

Lowe, B. (2016). Reconsidering the rural in the end: Rural representations in post-apocalyptic settings. Pp. 73–94 in Fulkerson, G.F. & Thomas, A.R. (eds.), *Reimagining rural: Urbanormative portrayals of rural life*. Lanham, MD: Lexingtong Books.

Maasho, A. & Hunt, W.M. (2019). Coffee price slump leaves farmers earning less than a cent a cup. *Company News* (January 14). Retrieved 1/16/2019 from https://www.reuters.com/article/coffee-farmers/coffee-price-slump-leaves-farmers-earning-less-than-a-cent-a-cup-idUSL8N1YJ4D2 .

Mactaggart, F., McDermott, L., Tynan, A., & Gericke, C. (2016). Examining health and well-being outcomes associated with mining activity in rural communities of high-income countries: A systematic review. *Australian Journal of Rural Health*, 24, 4, pp. 230–237.

Maher, B. (2017). The country mouse and the city mouse. *Real Time with Bill Maher* (22 Sept). Accessed 1/3/2019, https://www.youtube.com/watch?v=S3aQYfmBV_A.

Maisels, C.K. (1999). *Early civilizations of the old world*. New York: Routledge.

Mann, C.C. (2012). *1493: Uncovering the new world Columbus created*. New York: Vintage.

Mann, Michael. (1986). *The sources of social power:* Volume 1, *A history of power from the beginning to AD 1760*. New York: Cambridge U. Press.

Marches, J.R. & Turbeville, G. (1953). The effect of residential propinquity on marriage selection. *American Journal of Sociology*, 58, 6, pp. 592–595.

Marsden, T., Lowe, P., & Whatmore, S. (eds). (1990). Rural restructuring: Global processes and their responses. London: David Fulton Publishers.

Marsden, T., Murdoch, T., Lowe, P., Munton, R., & Flynn, A. (1993). *Constructing the countryside*. London: University College London Press.

Marx, K. (1990 [1867]). *Capital: The process of production of capital*. Volume I. London: Penguin Books.

Massey, D. (1988). Economic development and internal migration in comparative perspective. *Population and Development Review*, 14, pp. 383–402.

_____. (2005). *Strangers in a strange land: Humans in an urbanizing world*. New York: Norton.

Maxwell, W.J. (1997). Is it true what they say about Dixie? Richard Wright, Zora Neale Hurston, and rural/urban exchange in modern African-American literature. Pp. 71–104 in Ching, B. & Creed, G.W. (eds.), *Knowing your place: Rural identity and cultural hierarchy*. New York: Routledge.

Mayhew, B.H. & Levinger, R.L. (1977). Size and density of interaction in human aggregates. *American Journal of Sociology*, 82, pp. 86–110.

Maynard, D. (1997). Pp. 195–218 in Ching, B. & Creed, G.W. (eds.), *Knowing your place: Rural identity and cultural hierarchy*. New York: Routledge.

McKay, P. (2016). Urbanormativity in news coverage of rural life. Pp. 95–110 in Fulkerson, G.M. & Thomas, A.R. (eds.), *Reimaging rural: Urbanormative portrayals of rural life*. Lanham, MD: Lexington Books.

McKinney, L. (2016). Reinventing rural environmental justice. Pp. 57–76 in Thomas, A.R. & Fulkerson, G.M. (eds.), *Reinventing rural: New realities in an urbanizing world*. Lanham, MD: Lexington Books.

Mereish, E.H., O'Cleirigh, C, & Bradford, J.B. (2013). Interrelationships between LGBT-based victimization, suicide, and substance abuse problems in a diverse sample of sexual and gender minorities. *Psychology, Health & Medicine*, 19, 1, https://doi.org/10.1080/13548506.2013.780129.

Merton, R.K. (1968). *Social theory and social structure*. Free Press.

Mill, J.S. (1869 [1859]). *On liberty* (4th ed.). London: Longman, Green, Reader, and Dyer.

Mills, C.W. (1959). *The sociological imagination*. New York: Oxford University Press.

Mingay, G.E. (1989). *The rural idyll*. London: Routledge.

Moloo, Z. (2017). All that glitters: Neoliberal violence, small-scale mining, and gold extraction in northern Tanzania. Pp. 296–314 in Kapoor, D. (ed.), *Against colonization and rural dispossession: Local resistance in South and East Asia, the Pacific and Africa*. London: Zed Books.

Molotch, H., Freudenburg, W., & Paulsen, K.E. (2000). History repeats itself, but how? City character, urban tradition, and the accomplishment of place. *American Sociological Review*, 65, pp. 791–823.

Moore, A., Hillman, G., & Legge, A. (2000). *Village on the Euphrates: From foraging to farming at Abu Hureyra*. New York: Oxford U. Press.

Mormont, M. (1990). Who is rural? Or how to be rural? Pp. 21–44 in Marsden, T., Lowe, P., & Whatmore, S. (eds.), *Rural restructuring: Global processes and their responses*. London: David Fulton Publishers.

Morris, D. (1996). *The human zoo: A zoologist's classic study of the urban animal*. Reprint Edition. New York: Kodansha Globe.

Moscovici, S. (1988). Notes towards a description of social representations. *European Journal of Social Psychology*, 18, pp. 211–250.

_____. (2001). *Social representations: Explorations in social psychology*. New York: New York University Press.

Mukherjee, S. (2017). *Gene: An intimate history*. Scribner.

Munton, R. (ed.). (2008). *The rural: Critical essays in human geography*. New York: Routledge.

Murdoch, J. & Pratt, A.C. (1993). Rural studies: modernism, post-modernism and the "post–rural." *Journal of Rural Studies*, 9, 411–427.

Nadel D. (ed.). (2002). *Ohalo II, A 23,000-year-old fisher-hunter-gatherers' camp on the shore of the Sea of Galilee*. Hecht Museum, Haifa University.

Nadel, D., Tsatskin, A., Belmaker, M., Boaretto, E., Kislev, M., Mienis, H., Rabinovich, R., et al. (eds.). (2004). On the shore of a fluctuating lake: Environmental evidence from Ohalo II (19,500 B.P.). *Israel Journal of Earth Sciences*, 53, pp. 207–223.

Newby, H. (1980). Trend report: Rural sociology. *Current Sociology*, 28, pp. 3–41.

NYSDOS (New York State Department of State). (2009). *Local Government Handbook*. Albany: NYS Department of State.

Pahl, R.E. (1966). The rural–urban continuum. *Sociologia Ruralis*, 6, pp. 299–327.

Pinker, S. (2012). *The better angels of our nature*. New York: Penguin Books.

Prasad, M. (2012). *The land of too much: American abundance and the paradox of poverty*. Cambridge, MA: Harvard University Press.

Pruitt, L.R. (2008a). Gender, geography, and rural justice. *Berkeley Journal of Gender, Law, and Justice*, 23, pp. 338–391.

_____. (2008b). Place matters: Domestic violence and rural difference. *Wisconsin Journal of Law, Gender, and Society*, 23, pp. 347–416.

_____. (2009a). Latina/os, locality, and law in the rural South. *Harvard Law Review*, 12, pp. 135–139.

_____. (2009b). The forgotten fifth: Rural youth and substance abuse. *Stanford Law and Policy Review*, 20, pp. 359–404.

_____. (2010a). How you gonna keep her down on the farm? *UMKC Law Review*, 78, pp. 1085–1099.

_____. (2010b). Spatial inequality as Constitutional infirmity: Equal protection, child poverty, and place. *Montana Law Review*, 71, pp. 1–114.

_____. (2011). Human rights and development for India's rural remnant: A capabilities based approach. *UC Davis Law Review*, 44, pp. 803–857.

_____. (2016). Welfare queens and white trash. *Southern California Interdisciplinary Law Journal*, 25, pp. 289–312.

_____. (2017). The women feminism forgot: Rural and working class women in the era of Trump. *University of Toledo Law Review*, 49, pp. 537–604.

_____. (2018). To recognize the tyranny of distance: A spatial reading of *Whole Woman's Health v. Hellerstedt*. *Environment and Planning A: Economy and Space*, 0, pp. 1–22.

Pruitt, L.R. & Showman, B.E. (2014). Law stretched thin: Access to justice in rural America. *South Dakota Law Review*, 59, p. 466–528.

Pruitt, L.R. & Vanegas, M.R. (2015). Urbanormativity, spatial privilege, and judicial blind spots in abortion law. *Berkeley Journal of Gender, Law, and Justice*, 30, pp. 76–153.

Rabrenovic, G. (1996). *Community builders*. Philadelphia: Temple U. Press.

Ravenstein, E. (1889). The laws of migration. *Journal of the Royal Statistical Society*, 52, p. 41–301.

Rawls, J. (1999 [1972]). *A theory of justice*. Belknap Press: An Imprint of Harvard University.

Rodrigues, G. (2007). *Walking the forest with Chico Mendes: Struggle for justice in the Amazon*. Translated by Rabben, L. Austin: University of Texas Press.

Rodriguez, R.M. (2017). Lumad anti-mining activism in the Philippines. Pp. 145–163 in Kapoor, D. (ed.), *Against colonization and rural dispossession: Local resistance in South and East Asia, the Pacific and Africa*. London: Zed Books.

Runciman, Walter G. (1966). *Relative deprivation and social justice: A study of attitudes to social inequality in twentieth century England*. Berkeley: U. California Press.

Rye, J.F. (2004). Constructing the countryside: Differences in teenagers' images of the rural. Paper 3/04. *Centre for Rural Research*. Norway, Trondheim.

Rye, J.F. (2006a). Rural youth's images of the rural. *Journal of Rural Studies*, 22, pp. 409–421.

_____. (2006b). Leaving the countryside: An Analysis of rural-to-urban migration and long-term capital accumulation. *Acta Sociologica*, 49, 1, pp. 47–65.

_____. (2011). Conflicts and contestations: Rural populations' perspectives on the second homes phenomenon. *Journal of Rural Studies*, 27, p. 263–274.

Rye, J.F, & Blekesaune, A. (2007). The class structure of rural-to-urban migration: The case of Norway. *Nordic Journal of Youth Research*, 15, 2, pp. 169–191.

Salamon, S. (2003). From hometown to nontown: Rural community effects of suburbanization. *Rural Sociology*, 68, 1, pp. 1–24.

Sampson, R.J. (1988). Local friendship ties and community attachment in mass society: A multilevel systemic model. *American Sociological Review*, 53, pp. 766–779.

_____. (1991). Linking the micro- and macro-level dimensions of community social organization. *Social Forces*, 70, pp. 43–64.

Sampson, R.J., Raudenbush, S.W., & Earls, F. (1997). Neighborhoods and violent crime: A multilevel study of collective efficacy. *Science*, 277, pp. 918–924.

Sanderson, D. (1938). Criteria of rural community formation. *Rural Sociology*, 3, 4, pp. 373–384.

Sanford, A. W. (2018). *Living sustainably: What intentional communities can teach us about democracy, simplicity, and nonviolence*. University Press of Kentucky.

Sassen, S. (1992). *The global city: New York, London, Tokyo*. Princeton University Press.

Schafft, K. & Jackson, A. (2011). *Rural education for the twenty-first century: Identity, place, and community in a globalized world*. University Park: Penn State University Press.

Schwalbe, M.L. (1996). Unlocking the iron cage: The men's movement, gender politics, and American culture. New York: Oxford University Press.

Schwalbe, M.L. & Mason-Schrock, D. (1996). Identity work as group process. *Advances in Group Processes*, 13, 113–147.

Schwartz-Balcott, T.P. (2008). *After the disaster: Re-creating community and well-being at Buffalo Creek since the notorious coal-mining disaster in 1972*. Amherst, NY: Cambria Press.

Seale, E.K., & Fulkerson, G.M. (2014). Critical concepts for studying communities and their built environments. Pp. 31–42 in Fulkerson, G.M. & Thomas, A.R. (eds.), *Studies in urbanormativity: Rural community in urban society*. Lanham, MD: Lexington Books.

Seale, E.K. & Mallinson, C. (2018). *Rural Voices: Language, identity, and social change across place*. Lanham, MD: Lexington Books.

Sen, A. (1981). *Poverty and famines: An essay on entitlement and deprivation*. New York: Clarendon Press, Oxford.

_____. (1999). *Development as freedom*. New York: Oxford.

Serpell, J. (2017). *The domestic dog: Its evolution, behavior and interactions with people* (2nd edition). New York: Cambridge U. Press.

Shandra, J. and London, B. (2003). Environmental degradation, environmental sustainability, and overurbanization in the developing world: A quantitative, cross-national analysis. *Sociological Perspectives*, DOI: https://doi.org/10.1525/sop.2003.46.3.309.

Sharp, J. & Adua, L. (2009). The social basis of agro-environmental concern: Physical versus social proximity. *Rural Sociology*, 74, 1, pp. 56–85.

Sheehan, E.A. (1997). Pp. 149–170 in Ching, B. & Creed, G.W. (eds.), *Knowing your place: Rural identity and cultural hierarchy*. New York: Routledge.

Short, B. (2006). Idyllic ruralities. Pp. 133–148 in Cloke, P., Marsden, T., & Mooney, P.H. (eds.), *The handbook of rural studies*. London: Sage.

Short, J. (1991). *Imagined country*. London: Routledge.

Simmel, G. (1971). The metropolis and mental life. In Levine, D. (ed), *Georg Simmel: On individuality and social forms*. Chicago University Press.

Sipple, J.W. & Brent, B.O. (2015). Challenges and opportunities associated with rural school settings. Pp. 612–629 in Ladd, H.F. & Fiske, E.B. (eds.), *Handbook of Research in Education Finance and Policy* (2nd edition). New York: Routledge.

Smiley, J. (1995). *Moo* (reprint edition). New York: Anchor.

Smith, Michael E. (2009). V. Gordon Childe and the urban revolution: A historical persspective on a revolution in urban studies. *Town Planning Review*, 80, 1, pp. 1–29.

Smith, P.J. (2014). Return to Ridgefield Corners. Pp. 163–180 in Fulkerson, G.M. & Thomas, A. (eds.), *Studies in urbanormativity: Rural community in urban society*. Lanham, MD: Lexington Books.

Snir, A., Nadel, D., Groman-Yaroslavski, I., Melamed, Y., Sternberg, M., Bar-Yosef, O., & Weiss, E. (2015). The origin of cultivation and proto-weeds, long before neolithic farming. *PlosOne*, https://doi.org/10.1371/journal.pone.0131422.

So, A. (1991). *Social change and development*. Newbury Park, CA: Sage.

Stapel, C. (2014). "Fagging" the countryside. Pp. 151–161 in Fulkerson, G. & Thomas, A. (eds), *Studies in urbanormativity: Rural community in urban society*. Lanham, MD: Lexington Books.

Statz, M. & Pruitt, L. (2018). To recognize the tyranny of distance: A spatial reading of Whole Woman's Health vs. Hellerstedt. *Environment and Planning*, DOI: 10.1177/03085 18X18757508.

Steel, C. (2013). *Hungry city: How food shapes our lives*. London: Vintage.

Stopera, M. (2019). 17 people who dramatically changed after moving to a bigger city. Retrieved 1/27/2019 from https://www.buzzfeed.com/mjs538/people-who-have-experienced-the-big-city-glow-up.

Swidler, A. (1986). Culture in action: Symbols and strategies. *American Sociological Review*, 51, 2, pp. 273–286.

Tajfel, H. & Turner, J.C. (1986). The social identity theory of intergroup behavior. Pp. 7–24 in Worchell, S. & Austin, W.G. (eds.), *Psychology of intergroup relations*. Chicago: Nelson-Hall.

Talen, E. (2001). School, community, and spatial equity: An empirical investigation of access to elementary schools in West Virginia. *Annals of the Association of American Geographers*, 91, 3, pp. 465–486.

Tattersall, I. (2013). *Masters of the planet: The search for our human origins*. New York: St. Martins.

Temin, P. (2017). *The Roman market economy*. Princeton, NJ: Princeton U. Press.

Theobald, P. & Wood, K. (2011). Learning to be rural: Identity lessons from history, schooling, and the U.S. corporate media. Pp. 17–33 in Schafft, K.A. & Jackson, A.Y. (eds.), *Rural education for the twenty-first century: Identity, place and community in a globalizing world*. University Park: The Pennsylvania State University Press.

Thomas, A.R. (1998). *Economic and social restructuring in a rural community*. PhD Dissertation: Northeastern University.

_____. (2003). *In Gotham's shadow: Globalization and community change in Central New York*. Albany, NY: SUNY Press.

_____. (2005). *Gilboa: New York's quest for water and the destruction of a small town*. New York: University Press of America.

_____. (2010). *The evolution of the ancient city: Urban theory and the archaeology of the Fertile Crescent*. Comparative Urban Studies. Lanham, MD: Lexington Books.

_____. (2012). Urbanization before cities: Lessons for social theory from the evolution of cities. *Journal of World Systems Research*, 18, 2, pp. 211–235.

_____. (2014a). Historic Hartwick: Reading civic character in a living landscape. Pp. 43–66 in Fulkerson, G.M. & Thomas, A.R. (eds.), *Studies in urbanormativity: Rural community in urban society*. New York: Lexington Books.

_____. (2014b). Urbanization as the Cause of Cities: Notes from the Near East and the Northeast. *Comparative Sociology* 13: 639–663.

Thomas, A.R. & Fulkerson, G.M. (2016). *Reinventing rural: New realities in an urbanizing world*. Studies in Urban-Rural Dynamics Book Series (eds. Thomas, A.R. & Fulkerson, G.M.). New York: Lexington.

Thomas, A.R., Lowe, B.M., Fulkerson, G.M., and Smith, P.S. (2011). *Critical rural theory: Structure*space*culture*. Lanham, MD: Lexington Books.

Thomas, W.I. & Thomas, D.S. (1928). *The child in America: Behavior problems and programs*. New York: Knopf.

Thorburn, J. (2018). "Losing our Inuttitut": The intersection of language shift and language attitudes in Nain, Nunatsiavut. Pp. 23–44 in Seale, E. & Mallinson, C. (eds.), *Rural voices: Language, identity, and social change across place*. Lanham, MD: Lexington Books.

Tickamyer, A., White, J.A., Tadlock, B.L., & Henderson, D.A. (2007). The spatial politics of public policy: Devolution, development, and welfare reform. Pp. 114–139 in Lobao, L., Hooks, G., & Tickamyer, A. (eds.), *The sociology of spatial inequality*. Albany: State University of New York Press.

Tilly, C. (1974). Do communities act? Pp. 209–240 in Effrat, M.P. (ed.), *The community: Approaches and applications*. New York: The Free Press.

Timberlake, M. & Kentor, J. (1983). Economic dependence, overurbanization, and economic growth: A study of less developed countries. *The Sociological Quarterly*, 24, 4, pp. 489–507.

Todaro, M.P. (1976). *Internal migration in developing countries: A review of theory, evidence, methodology, and research priorities*. Geneva: International Labor Organization.

Tönnies, F. (2000). *Gemeinschaft und geschellschaft*. Cambridge University Press, New York

Turner, J.C. & Tajfel, H. (1982). Toward a cognitive redefinition of the social group. Pp. 15–40 in Tajfel, H. (ed.) *Social identity and intergroup relations*. Cambridge University Press.

United Nations. (2014). *World urbanization prospects*. United Nations, Department of Economic and Social Affairs.

Ur, J.A. (2002). Settlement and landscape in Northern Mesopotamia: The Tell Hamoukar survey 2000–2001. *Akkadica*, 123, pp. 57–88.

Urry, J. (2012). *Consuming places*. London: Routledge.

U.S. Census Bureau. (2017). Annual estimates of the resident population: April 1, 2010, to July 1, 2017—Combined Statistical Area; and for Puerto Rico—2017 population estimates. https://factfinder.census.gov/faces/tableservices/jsf/pages/productview.xhtml?src=bkmk. Retrieved 1/11/2019.

Van Auken, P., Rye, J.F. (2011). Amenities, affluence, and ideology: Comparing rural restructuring processes in the U.S. and Norway. *Landscape Research*, 36, 1, pp. 63–84.

Vance, J.D. (2018). *Hillbilly elegy: A memoir of a family and culture in crisis*. New York: Harper.

Vecchione, J. (2011). *Welcome to Fleischmanns*. Vecchione Productions, Documentary.

Vieira, A. (2016). Build it and they will come? The EB-5 immigrant investor program and Vermont's Jay Peak resort. Pp. 131–148 in Thomas, A.R. & Fulkerson, G.M. (eds.), *Reinventing rural: New realities in an urbanizing world*. Lanham, MD: Lexington Books.

Waara, P. (2000). Rural young people in Norrbotten and Va¨sterbotten in the north of Sweden. Pp. 134–140 in Helve, H. (ed.), *Rural young people in changing Europe*. Hakapaino, Helsinki.

Walbert, D. (2002). *Garden spot: Lancaster county, the Old Order Amish, and the selling of rural America*. New York: Oxford University Press.

Wallace, J.L. & Pruitt, L.R. (2012). Judging place: Poverty, rurality and termination of parental rights. *Missouri Law Review*, 77, pp. 95–147.

Wallerstein, I. (1987). *World-system analysis*. Stanford, CA: Stanford University Press.

Webber, M. (1964). The urban place and the non-place urban realm. Pp. 79–153 in Webber, M.M., Dyckman, J.W., Foley, D.L., et al. (eds.), *Explorations in urban structure*. Philadelphia: University of Pennsylvania.

Weber, M. (2002). *The Protestant ethic and the "spirit" of capitalism and other writings*. Translated by Baehr, P.R. & Wells, G.C. Penguin Classics.

Wenzlau, S. (2013). Global food prices continue to rise. *World Watch Institute* (April 11). Retrieved 1/21/2019 from http://www.worldwatch.org/global-food-prices-continue-rise-0.

Weston, K. (1995). Get thee to a big city: Sexual imaginary and the great gay migration. *GLQ*, 2, p. 282.

Wilkinson, K. (1991). *The community in rural America*. Middleton, WI: Social Ecology Press.

Williams, R. (1973). *The country and the city*. New York: Oxford University Press.

Willits, F.K., Theodori, G.L. & Fortunato, M.W.P. (2016). The rural mystique in American society. Pp. 33–56 in Fulkerson, G.M. & Thomas, A.R. (eds.), *Reinventing rural: New realities in an urbanizing world*. Lanham, MD: Lexington Books.

Wimberley, R.C., Morris, L., & Harris, R. (2014). A federal commission for the Black Belt South. *Professional Agricultural Workers Journal*, 2, 1, 6. Retrieved 1/19/19 from https://tuspubs.tuskegee.edu/pawj/vol2/iss1/6.

Winders, W. (2017). *Grains*. Malden, MA: Polity Press.

Winders, W. & Scott, J.C. (2012). *The politics of food supply: U.S. agricultural policy in the world economy* (Yale Agrarian Studies Series). New Haven, CT: Yale University Press.

World Urbanization Prospects, United Nations. (2014 revision). Retrieved 2/12/2018 from https://esa.un.org/unpd/wup/publications/files/wup2014-highlights.pdf.

Wright, W. & Eaton, W.M. (2018). Representing rurality: Cider mills and agritourism. Pp. 65–82 in Slocum, Kline, and Cavaliere (eds.), *Craft Beverages and Tourism*, v. 2. Cham, Switzerland: Palgrave.

Zians, J. (2016). Doggonit people live here: The unmet challenges in rural behavioral health. Pp. 179–214 in Thomas, A.R. & Fulkerson, G.M. (eds.), *Reinventing rural: New realities in an urbanizing world*. Lanham, MD: Lexington Books.

Zipf, G.K. (1949). *Human behavior and the principle of least effort: An introduction to human ecology*. Cambridge, MA: Addison-Wesley.

Index

About the Authors

Gregory M. Fulkerson, PhD, is associate professor of sociology in the Department of Sociology at SUNY Oneonta. Along with Dr. Thomas, he is coeditor of the Urban-Rural Dynamics book series with Lexington Books, and has published coauthored and coedited books including *Reimagining Rural* (2016), *Reinventing Rural* (2016), and *Studies in Urbanormativity* (2014). He has published peer reviewed research on environmental issues, social capital, and rural sociology.

Alexander R. Thomas, PhD, is professor and chair of the Department of Sociology at SUNY Oneonta. He is coeditor, with Gregory Fulkerson, of the Lexington Series on Urban-Rural Dynamics. He has published numerous books and articles on cities and their relationship with the countryside, including *In Gotham's Shadow* (2003), *The Evolution of the Ancient City* (2010), and *Critical Rural Theory* (2011, with Brian Lowe, Gregory Fulkerson, and Polly Smith).